Triathlon – IT HURTS!

Triathlon – IT HURTS!

INSPIRING STORIES ON THE PATH TO BECOMING AN IRONMAN

Edited by
Gary Smith & Justin Roberts

Matador
9 Priory Business Park,
Wistow Road, Kibworth Beauchamp,
Leicestershire. LE8 0RX
Tel: (+44) 116 279 2299
Fax: (+44) 116 279 2277
Email: books@troubador.co.uk
Web: www.troubador.co.uk/matador

ISBN 978 1784623 609

British Library Cataloguing in Publication Data.
A catalogue record for this book is available from the British Library.

Printed and bound in the UK by TJ International, Padstow, Cornwall
Typeset in 12pt Aldine401 BTRoman by Troubador Publishing Ltd, Leicester, UK

Matador is an imprint of Troubador Publishing Ltd

For Simon

1st September 1973 to 6th October 2013

#gonebutneverforgotten

To those who played a role in the research, the race, and the incredible love and support of family and friends, we are forever grateful…

To all those who hold a dream in their hearts, triathlon or otherwise, this is for you… dreams are there to be lived.

To all our co-authors, whose names you will see against every chapter, who selflessly gave up even more of their time, passion and energy to capture their experience in writing, no matter how personal… there simply wouldn't be a book to publish!

Foreword

There are two types of people in society, those that accept the status quo (not the 300-year-old rockers) and go through their lives following their chosen path, and those that for whatever reason question the validity of the path. In the following pages you'll read the accounts of normal folk like you and I that stepped off the path and dared to dream. They took their leap of faith and placed themselves firmly in what they hoped would be the safe hands of a university academic who wanted them to push themselves mentally and physically so far out of their comfort zones that they'd each need a pair of binoculars to see their regular path.

In this day and age of modern living most of society wouldn't even dream of walking 2.4 miles to buy a pint of milk, yet the individuals in the following pages decided to swim that distance in the sea before breakfast. Not content with such a physical challenge they would then jump on a bike and cycle 112 miles, the distance from London to Birmingham. Yes you did indeed read that correctly; think about that the next time you make that same journey on the M6 or by rail. If that doesn't fail to make you think then add in the fact that once they drag their tired bodies off their bikes they then set out to run 26.2 miles, a marathon – a run that is an amazing achievement in itself. So, that is a total of 140.6 miles under their own steam; that is the challenge of an iron-distance triathlon. Oh yeah, did I mention that they had to finish it all in under seventeen hours. Now do you see what I mean about the path through their comfort zone being lost in the mists of athletic and mental competition?

Each of the stories contained in this book is filled with a nervous energy and a sense of achievement that the majority of the world will never have the joy of experiencing. I have been lucky to have completed five of these stupidly long races and reading the stories contained within the following pages brought back so many memories of pain, fear, achievement, purpose, desire, but above all else, fun. To achieve something that seemed impossible and to do it with a smile on your face is simply magical. The stories that follow turn magic into reality, and that is down to the hard work, dedication and sometimes sheer bloody-mindedness of those putting one foot in front of the other nineteen miles into their iron-marathon. However, it is often forgotten that endurance racing is actually a team sport, without the support of their friends, training partners and loved ones they wouldn't have even made it to the start line and that shines through in these tales.

More than being an ironman, I am a father. It is my greatest achievement and not a day goes by where I am not thankful for that blessing. I can only imagine the anguish of watching your child battle with an illness and admire the will and courage of a family that fight to change that by seeking a cure. I have never met Alex Smith but his story is one of true inspiration that every parent on the planet should read.

All of this is a timely reminder that as we go about our daily lives we should keep moving forward and each morning when we look in the mirror, smile and tell the face looking back at you that anything is possible. The men and women in this book are living proof of that.

Andy Holgate
Author and Ironman

Contents

SECTION 3 – A REASON TO SHINE

SECTION 4 – THE WISDOM WITHIN

Prologue

Simply WHY?

It's a question we've been asked time and again, and one probably every endurance *athlete* has been asked at some stage in his or her career.

Athlete is an interesting concept, but in reality it doesn't matter if you're a pro or an amateur, fast or slow, fat or thin, male or female, old or young, a weekend warrior or a full-time parent. It doesn't matter if you're in musical theatre or a bike messenger, a shark or a bean counter (that's a lawyer or an accountant giving them their official titles) – endurance *athletes* are similar, but different, in many ways, with two definitive things in common:

Firstly, they all will have been asked "Simply WHY? WHY do you? WHY would you? WHY voluntarily put yourself through [*insert insane event name here*]?"

Secondly, they will all possess a similarly immense willpower and insatiable appetite for physical suffering, or that's how it at least appears to literally every single non-endurance athlete that we have spoken to.

If you choose to continue reading, which we hope you do, we may answer THE question (or a question you may have), but if we don't... you will at least be closer to understanding what exactly makes a 'normal' endurance athlete tick and what it takes to earn the right to call yourself one. And if we don't, perhaps we may encourage you to smile or even laugh at our endeavours, journeys and tales.

But this book is more than just that...

This book collates messages from a cross section of 'recreationally active' men and women, aged eighteen to fifty years based in the UK who undertook their own "personal adventures" to complete their first iron-distance triathlon.

The stage: the 2013 Challenge Barcelona iron-distance triathlon. An iron-distance triathlon is possibly one of the toughest single-day endurance events in the world, based on a gruelling 3.8km sea swim followed by 180 challenging kilometres cycling, and a tiny little 42km run to finish!

The platform: one of the largest, multi-disciplinary research studies undertaken; a study to investigate how 'recreationally active' men and women cope with the demands of a nine-month ultra-endurance training programme. Led by Dr Justin Roberts and the team at the University of Hertfordshire, this ambitious project aimed to recruit, train, monitor, probe and pursue to the finish line the dreams of eighty-five 'hopefuls' in their attempt to become IRONMEN.

Many people could be forgiven for thinking of each leg as an endurance event in its own right and, after all, a 3.8km swim is certainly considered to be the gateway to long-distance swimming, 180 kilometres is more than a typical CycloSportive distance for cycling enthusiasts, and when was the last time you heard someone say "it's only a marathon"? Can you imagine putting them all together? Can you imagine the commitment, the challenges, the constant discomfort, pain, suffering and the effect on loved ones? That's what makes this a real challenge to us 'normal' folk.

But more than that...

Those words... challenge, pain, discomfort, suffering, effect on loved ones – this is the world also of Duchenne Muscular Dystrophy, a fatal, debilitating muscle-wasting disorder, which robs young children of their muscles, and ultimately their lives. This is the story also of one of our

HURTS cohorts (Hertfordshire University Research Triathlon Study – as we affectionately became known) – Alex Smith, a man who never ceases to smile, who simply inspires those he meets. In 2011, his son Harrison was diagnosed with Duchenne Muscular Dystrophy. The clock has begun, the countdown has started... Faced with the challenge of saving his son's life, "Harrison's Fund" was established – its mission: to fund breakthrough research to 'cure' Duchenne Muscular Dystrophy. His slogan is simple – 'make time'. Time is something we all take for granted, until it's gone.

Our hope is that you will find this book inspiring, perhaps it will encourage you to play out some of your own dreams you've been holding back on. At the very least, we have all 'made time' from our relentless, busy lives to contribute to this book; hoping that by 'making time' you will directly support Harrison's Fund to get one stage closer to their goal.

The clock is ticking...

Gary Smith & Justin Roberts

SECTION 1

The Power of Ironman

CHAPTER 1

"Desire" *by Justin Roberts*

"It's not just a question of whether something is important to you, it's a question of whether it's important enough to you right now"

The Bose speakers in my room blast out as I get ready for another training session: "Lover, I'm on the street, gonna go where the bright lights and the big city meets, with a red guitar on fire… desire. For the love of money, money, money…" (Obviously all sung in my best Bono accent). Actually when you think about it, U2's lyrics emulate perhaps the secrets behind true desire. The key words being ON FIRE. And instead of a red guitar, it's a white bike. And instead of money, it's that magical feeling of achievement – overcoming the seemingly impossible, or overcoming something within (unless you're a pro and winning a ton of money). Put it all together, and you have FIRE.

I can't begin to recall just how many times I've been asked why do I do the things I do. Over the years so many people, some close, some not so close have told me in their own way that taking on some of the challenges I have faced was ludicrous, stupid or "what's the point of that". That could be answered with a "why not?". It could be answered with "because I can" – but, as Neo from *The Matrix* would say – it's because I choose to.

What motivates someone to wake from their dreamland, the comfort of their own warm bed at silly o'clock in the morning to once again push the body, brush off those proverbial cobwebs and **'do'** the stuff of champions. Is it ego? Is it stupidity – perhaps that one could be true – so I've said to myself on many a morning. Or is it because we know that's what it takes to be our own 'best' – a desire, a dedication, and intense motivation to find out what we are made of. Someone once said to me that if it was easy, everyone would do it – but not everyone takes on the enormity of an ironman triathlon. I love that word – **enormity** – no its not meant as a crude double entendre but let's face it – a 2.4 mile open-water swim would finish most people off on its own (well that's the impression I get when people always tell me they would love to do such a challenge, but they can't swim), but to then get on a bike, wet and sometimes cold, and cycle the equivalent of a Tour De France stage and then run the London marathon would strike fear into most mortal's hearts. So by that definition, are we just insane mortals – perhaps – but I think the desire to put in the hours, to push our own limits when the voices inside scream stop, lies with two questions – what am I made of? What reason am I doing this for?

***

I recall back to when I first started thinking about running and triathlons – I wasn't fit at all. In fact I was in a galaxy far far away called fatland. I was never good at sport (I think that came from secondary school beastings on the rugby pitch), and one day I injured myself at a local gym – think I twisted my knee or something, and the physio who saw me had the audacity to tell me I probably wouldn't run again – no testing, no proper diagnosis – just a bullshit opinion. I remember saying to myself "you can't say that, bugger you, I'm gonna run a marathon". I remember going home and thinking ok I can't run at the moment, but which marathon should I do – well I was born in London so it had to be a home advantage – one of the biggest marathon events on the planet. I remember putting in my ballot entry via post thinking "ok it's ten months away and I can't run at the moment – but let's see" – and you know what I got in. That was a funny day – opening the post to read "*congratulations*" – I mean I hadn't even completed the event and someone was already congratulating me. **Awesome**. I was beginning to like this getting-fit lark already.

Then the realisation of running a marathon dawned on me – perhaps the physio was right, perhaps I shouldn't attempt this, perhaps I should just lay down and give up – yeah right – that just isn't me, *and I don't think it's you either*. There is something inherent in all of us to 'try', to 'endeavour', to 'give it a go' – it's our doubts that proverbially get in the way. I remember the very first training session for the London Marathon – a one mile jog/walk around a local field – YEP YOU HEARD ME, one flippin' mile. To say that I nearly went home and coughed up a lung was an understatement – was I that unfit? – Heck yes! I remember lying on my bed that night thinking "if I can't run a mile what hope in hell do I have of running the marathon" – in fact in that single moment I decided I didn't want to be this unfit. That realisation of knowing how bad I was, *was* enough for me to do something about it. Over the years I've worked with many people – average Joe through to Mr Pro, I've worked with Senior Execs and World-Class Olympians. When I've listened to their stories at some level the same message comes across – something got to them, something spurred them to 'make a difference', take a chance and give it go – and so... what have YOU got to lose?

So the next morning, another run beckoned, this time I was

determined to reach two laps – two miles (*stop laughing I know that's pathetic*). As 50 Cent says "*get rich or die tryin'*" in my case it was "get fit or die tryin'". I wanted to know that I hadn't given up on myself, that the real 'me' was there in the background – itching to be realised. This was my chance – over the weeks, the months, two miles became ten, ten miles became fifteen, and then fifteen miles became twenty. A simple gradual progression was the key – nothing fancy – simply listen to the body, rest when it needed, and gradually give it a bit more to deal with. You see the body adapts to stress, and in this case the physical stress of running meant that every time I overloaded the mileage without going overboard my body adapted. More importantly, my fitness increased, my weight dropped – hell I could actually see some muscle. I felt good; some people even said I was glowing. That was the year I ran sub four hours in my first proper London Marathon, a PB, which still stands for me today. I would love to go back to that physio and say "you should change your profession pal!" *(Or words to that effect)*.

★★★

Completing the London Marathon was one thing, but a triathlon (let alone an ironman is another). Somehow I got roped into doing a local sprint triathlon shortly after the 1996 London marathon. How on earth can a triathlon be a sprint? What's all that about? But after my third Guinness one evening, I agreed to give it a go. Once again those pesky demons came to haunt me – "you can't do this, you're not fit enough, you can't even cycle properly". But once again, that mystical sense of 'what if' came to life – what's the worst that could happen – *really.* I remember borrowing everything for that first race – a bike that was too big, a helmet that wouldn't fit (*past the newfound ego)*, a pair of sunglasses to look cool (*isn't that why the pros wear them – or am I mistaken?*) but too small. And most funny of all, a tri top that made me look like a squashed and badly shrink-wrapped sandwich.

I remember standing in a field surrounded by David Hasselhoff wannabees – surely I wasn't one of them. I was nervous for sure. Had I checked my brakes? Had I checked my tyres? Was everything neatly setup next to my bike in transition in an OCD kind of way? All I had to do is cover 400m in a pool, cycle 20km on some unknown suburban Surrey roads, and then leg it 5km to the finish. Before I had reached 200m I was blowing pretty much out of my bum. *This was going to be tough.* I tried so hard to put on a smile for the cameraman on the cycle course perched gingerly at the side of the road; but when the picture came through – OMG! OMG!! I was wrong, not a shrink-wrapped sandwich, shrink-wrapped cookie dough, an athlete in waiting I was not!

But despite the discomfort, the feeling of I don't belong, despite all that – I finished, and little did I know I was only one of about four hundred people who were new to the event that day. Ahhh so I wasn't the only newbie – and more importantly I DID IT! Over the years this led onto bigger and better triathlons and challenges – but the *big 'un* always eluded me – could this unfit kid from South London ever make it round the daddy of all triathlons. My brother – sure – he was the athlete in the family, but not me. I remember reading about the enormity of Ironman somewhere and despite a few attempts to get fit and strive to take on this giant mountain of an event I had somehow never succeeded plucking up the courage to enter one. Maybe I should go back to sticking with sprint events – all I've gotta do is get a new bike and a less skintight-looking vest and it will be fine.

Hmmmm – no no no – that won't do. It was around 2006 when I finally plucked up the courage to enter an Ironman – the desire to give it a go finally won me over – I entered the

2007 Karten Austrian Ironman in Klagenfurt. Why? Well, for the first time in about four years I was feeling healthy and fit without any injuries. But most importantly I was raising money for a local charity supporting children with muscular dystrophy. Having lost a good friend to a muscle wasting condition, what on earth did I have to moan about. I hear so many excuses from other people – I don't have time, I can't do this or I can't do that – get over yourself – you're bloody alive – what more reason do you need? And if you do need a reason, do it for something other than yourself, for those who perhaps don't have the good fortune you or I have. For me, yes I was scared but I recall the words from Timo Cruz in *Coach Carter*:

"Our deepest fear is not that we are inadequate. Our deepest fear is that we are powerful beyond measure. It is our light, not our darkness that most frightens us. Your playing small does not serve the world. There is nothing enlightened about shrinking so that other people won't feel insecure around you. We are all meant to shine, as children do. And, as we let our own light shine, we unconsciously give other people permission to do the same. As we are liberated from our own fear, our presence automatically liberates others."

So true – seriously what did I have to be scared about! If you really want something, no matter how tough, how challenging, then go realise how powerful you are. Now I don't want to start hearing the *Rocky* theme tune come on at this point or hear expressions like "*it don't matter how hard you can hit, it's about how many hits you can take and keep moving forward, that's how winning is done*" – in my worst Sly Stallone accent. I wanted this event, to prove to myself that I could do it – no one else – just me. I wanted to realise my 'light'. So what did I need…

***

It was January 2007 – seven months to the big event and I was halfway round the world in Australia – over one too many flat white coffees I had come up with a genius training programme, the diet was going good (except the flat whites), and I was into my second read of *Triathlete Magazine* that day. Now all I had to do was get out there and train. I remember reading about the infamous ironman logo tattoo, some guy in the editorials was ranting and raving that people shouldn't get the M-Dot tattoo unless they had taken part in the Kona World Championships. Since entering the Austrian Ironman I had thought about getting the M-Dot (perhaps my way of saying I DID IT), and this one article really pissed me off. I remember thinking that day "what a complete prick!" I mean who was this guy from the US telling me (and the rest of the triathlon community) what they should and shouldn't do? For me, if you have the heart, if you have the spirit and if you have the goddam determination to make it to that start line come hell or high water – then you are an IRONMAN, my friend. The only thing that differentiates the title from the feeling, is crossing that all-famous finish line.

It was a Sunday, the alarm went off at 5:45am – normally the sun would be up over the Melbourne skyline, but today it was pouring. My training diary read – 160km long-distance ride in zone two (lower-end heart rates). BUT IT WAS RAINING, NAY POURING! Hmmmm the choice – snooze some more in the comfort of my nice warm bed, or cycle in the rain. Another 5mins! I woke up at 7am – STILL pouring – hmmmm with my eyelids barely open – another 5mins! It was suddenly 8am. THE CHOICE BECKONED... Do you want IRONMAN? What if you don't train today, would it matter? Maybe not – but to me YES. This was one of those big sessions. Ok I'm up out of bed. The rain was battering my flat window. REALLY! Do I have to go out in this – YES I DO! I thought to myself this is Melbourne, it will rain 'til 9am then the sun will come out.

20km into the ride, the only thing left to do from my drenched perched position on my bike was to laugh. Here I was the other side of the world cycling in the pouring rain. THAT'S DESIRE. THAT'S THE SPIRIT. THAT'S IRONMAN. Later on that day, I found myself close to Rye on the South Eastern peninsula of Melbourne some 90km from 'home'. I remember being the only person cycling on an empty highway. I felt alone, I mean if something went wrong I had no phone and nobody would even know who I was. Then a remarkable thing occurred – I found myself literally sandwiched between two fronts – on my left was pitch-perfect sunshine, on my right – that blasted rain. A ray of sun shone down on me as I stopped to get my water bottle. Hand of God? An Angel? Mum? It was as if the universe was sending me a message. Now I wouldn't have got that still lying in my bed, would I? It felt good to be out here, I felt… **alive**.

It's times like these that true desire come into play – again beckoning the questions – what am I made of? IRON. Why am I doing this? BECAUSE IT MAKES ME FEEL ALIVE.

★★★

Some years ago I was fortunate to attend an Anthony Robbins weekend in London – for those who are puzzled – Mr Robbins is one of the world's best motivational speakers. The giant of a man came on stage to a thunderous applause by an audience that probably belonged at a One Direction concert. It was weird. He boomed out on the microphone "by midnight tonight everyone here will have walked over hot burning coals barefoot". I looked up from the course manual – "exsqueeze me" – hot what? As I sat there thinking "what the f**k" – this hand came over my shoulder and an Arnold Schwarzenegger lookalike (with the same accent) – said "you and me do this together ya". I shate myself literally. This was my worst fear being realised right here. I'm not the most confident of people at the best of times and here I was being expected to "prove myself". Perhaps I could just say NO – perhaps I could pretend to go to the loo and leg it. But that strange sense of personal pride crept in.

It was nearing on midnight – the coals were lit, 10,000 people were outside the arena. You could literally feel the heat, and smell the fear. My new friend Arnold was in front of me – I wonder how that happened? When it came to his turn, he looked up and went. Holy shit! No hesitation and now it's my turn. A small petite girl at the front of the fire walk looked at me and said: "When I say 3-2-1 go, YOU GO, OK?". A sheepish "hhhhmmmm ok" came out of me. 3-2-1 GO – and I looked at her and said: "I'm not ready". This pintsize powerhouse of a girl screamed back "well make yourself ready (with a few expletives for good measure)" – partly out of sheer fear and partly a need to get away from this rather scary girl I started to walk over white-hot coals. A strange thing happened – we had been told to think about 'COOL MOSS' as we moved forward and to think of a finish line. However for me, I imagined the three most important men in my life – my granddad, my dad and my brother – where did that come from. They were ushering me to them. Failure was not an option. I had to join them – be a man – and MOVE goddamm it.

20ft later – broken from this trance like state, two more ushers stopped me and asked to spray my feet with water (in case of post-fire-walk incineration). Then they told me "celebrate – you did it" – COME ON I screamed and in that one moment you could have put me in a ring with Mike Tyson – yeah ok I may not have lasted a single punch – but I believed. I believed I could do anything – except fly of course. I was that red guitar, on fire… DESIRE.

Perhaps this is the key to any challenge you face in life – physical or otherwise. You have to see what it is you want clearly in your mind. Make it real, make it clear, and make it mouth-watering. You have to want it. This is just one part that makes the athlete mind-set – believe that the impossible is possible and then make steps (however small) to get to that big goal. Desire infers passion, a desire to dream big, to push the boundaries, to overcome the odds.

We all like the underdog stories don't we. Well one underdog story that sticks in my mind is the film *Cool Runnings*, especially the bit when Deris the bobsled team captain asks COACH – when will he know (he is an Olympian) – and coach's reply was simply "when you cross that line, you will know". I used to have a screensaver on my computer of the Austrian Ironman finish line. I would imagine myself crossing that line, hands high above my head, screaming I DID IT. Was I scared when I arrived in Klagenfurt – of course! I was terrified when I saw the finish line up close and for real. When did I know I was an IRONMAN – when I crossed that same line. And you will too... If you choose to believe YOU CAN.

The Message: The seemingly impossible can become possible if you believe you CAN.

The DESIRE to dream big: Ironman Austria

CHAPTER 2:

"Challenge" *by Kevin Higby*

Cold. Wintery. Frosty. Morning. Do I feel like getting up and swimming in an open-water lake? Not really… But with the ironman date looming I drag myself out of my warm and cosy bed to join a group of other crazy triathletes at 6:30am on a Saturday morning at the lake at Box End, Bedford.

Having started getting into triathlons in 2010; earlier this year I set myself the goal of completing an ironman triathlon – a once in a lifetime achievement and an amazing test of stamina, self-control and inner strength… or that's what I'd been told. I'd always enjoyed running and through joining my local triathlon club, my swim and bike techniques had improved.

To the bane of my girlfriend, for the past nine months, my life has been a mixture of early morning training sessions, turbo training in the spare room and weekend triathlons. With mounds and mounds of lycra training clothes in the wash each week and drinks bottles gathering on the kitchen draining board, training for an ironman has been ten times more intense than I ever expected. I'm surprised she hasn't thrown some of my ten pairs of trainers out by now, however I think she's got used to the constant deliveries from various sporting websites. Have I got all the gear and no idea? Probably!!

It wasn't until I got into triathlons that I became obsessed with having a colour-matched bike, helmet, socks, glasses, visor, cleats, tri suit, socks etc etc… Triathlons are definitely a rich man's game and I can definitely say that I have caught the bug – the big bad triathlon buying kit/gear bug!! New trainers every three months, new bike every twelve months, new helmet to match the new bike, new tri suit to match the new bike, new cleats – of course! New laces to match the new trainers, new visor to match the new tri suit, new wetsuit just because... But they, of course, make me go faster, every second counts!

I'll rewind back to 2010 where it all started, when I decided *"RIGHT! I'm going to do something with my life!"* Instead of spending every weekend out in our local, and playing footie twice a week for a local team, I really wanted to get fit and achieve something before I turned thirty. I remember finishing my first sprint triathlon, greeted by my girlfriend and thinking "f**k! that was hard" – but at least I got a free t-shirt and a medal! Three years down the line, I have well and truly caught the triathlon bug, much to my bag-carrying/spectator/pro-triathlon watcher girlfriends' despair.

So how have I been training for Challenge Barcelona? With... much... difficulty – that's how! It's not until you sign up to an event such as this that you really put your self-motivation to the test. Christmas and New Year came and went, without much thought of the ironman in my mind, I enjoyed the festive season and although I kept fit in the gym and the odd run around the park, I made the most of the cosy evenings and lay-ins at the weekend. When it got too chilly to go out cycling, I invested in a Cyclops trainer – my spare room turned into a Cyclops training fitness room – with my laptop perched on the ironing board and iPod dock powered up, I would sit up there for 2-3hrs at a time. Then springtime came round and finally we could get out and about more, so of course I invested in a new bike. *New season = new bike!*

We booked our summer holiday for late June and of course

my first question was; can I take my bike? I researched various cycle routes and planned to get up at 7am every other day for an early morning sea swim – that was until the first morning I jogged down to the beach all spritely to be greeted with tsunami-type waves – great for surfing, not so great for training in. After 10mins of swimming against the waves and being dragged from side to side, I gave up on the idea. I did, however, enjoy the early morning bike rides and late evening jogs and I was proud that I kept up with my training whilst we were there.

I took part in my first half-ironman in early July – which can only be described with swear words not to be repeated. I... was... exhausted!! Not just worn out – physically and mentally traumatised. Not only was the weekend one of the hottest of the year, I had no spectators to cheer me on and I came home thinking what have I let myself in for?!? The half-ironman requires extreme strength in itself and most importantly positive mental attitude. The days that followed the event left me feeling disgruntled and very very worried about the full-ironman event. But alas; I'm not one to ever get scared off and I turned my negativity into motivation to ensure I was fully set to complete the big event in October. I booked my next half-ironman for early Sept and knew I had A LOT of training to do beforehand to ensure I didn't have a repeat performance.

Now I'm sure all triathletes can relate to the next subject that I'm going to discuss – SORES! PROPER ONES! It wasn't until I started training properly that I realised that you could get sores in all sorts of places, places that I didn't even know existed! Sore feet, sore bum, wetsuit sores, and blisters... Padded shorts do not help you when you're sat on a TT bike for five to six hours. My first long ride that I planned took me on a round trip – five hours around the local country roads. I prepped some snacks to take with me (flapjacks and bananas) and made sure that I was well stocked with water. 4hrs 40mins into the ride – I COULD NOT RIDE ANY MORE!! I was sore, sore, so sore… So I stopped, laid on the grass and yes, I called the girlfriend and got picked up. All I can say is that calamine lotion is now my best friend, along with athlete's foot cream/spray, germaline and chafe cream. I can evidently say that triathlons are not a glamorous sport, what with the sores in all sorts of places, athletes foot from running with wet feet and tan lines in awkward places, my body has definitely suffered this year from all the training.

But there are positives too! The amazing feeling of completing an event that you've trained and trained for, the atmosphere of the crowd when they're cheering you on and the feeling of self-fulfilment at the end of a race. That's why we all do it, right?? I must say that although this year has been filled with a mixture of emotions, the sober weekends and early mornings have all been worth it in the long run. Yes I have missed out on numerous social occasions, I haven't drunk alcohol since June, and I haven't even joined a team for the new footie season. I've argued with my girlfriend about the cost of training kit, woken up at 6am most weekend mornings for the past six months and my house is full of drinks bottles, tri suits, running socks, trainers and bikes – yes bikes do live in the house!

Talking of bikes, over the past year I would have hoped to have picked up some basic bike maintenance skills; but I still spend most Saturday evenings trying to put my bike back together after taking it apart to clean it or fit a new part – wishfully hoping that I've put it back together correctly before my early morning ride on the Sunday.

Another piece of gear which I've now become obsessed with is my Garmin 910XT. Is it a watch? Is it a computer? Who cares?… But it's so clever! Not only can it time my swim, bike and run times, it also measures my heart rate, speed, distance travelled and elevation. It's been a godsend in my training sessions and definitely money well spent. Not only that but there's also a geeks version of a social media site where you can log on and sync your rides/runs/swims – this makes it all so much more competitive when others can see your routes and you can see theirs!

Like the other people writing this book, I've been following a programme set as part of a research study for the past twelve months. After easing us in at the beginning, I've found some of the sessions pretty testing – not just fitting it in around a full-time job, but performing to my best ability at the test days. I wasn't selected to take part in the nutrition group, however through the programme I've tried to watch my diet and, especially towards the end of the programme, I've been ensuring that I'm eating the correct nutrients that my body requires. One day back in the summer we went away for the weekend and the mother-in-law stayed at our house to look after the dog – unfortunately this coincided with the '*poo testing*' part of the programme – she had a bit of a fright finding excrement samples in the kitchen freezer!! – How do I explain that? I'm just glad she didn't mistake them for a nutritious meal...

I've really enjoyed some of the test days, however one of the sessions we attended was to test our immune systems and we had to undertake a maximal exercise (or VO_2) test. This was extremely difficult, exercising with a mask on, feeling like you can't breathe whilst it tests your oxygen and carbon dioxide levels. It will be interesting to find out all the results.

So after nearly twelve months of training, with my entire kit ready and feeling the fittest I've ever felt, we flew out to Barcelona on 3rd Oct 2013. I was very fortunate to have a lot of family and friends come out to support me and we booked up an all-inclusive deal at one of the local hotels. When my parents arrived, all they could describe it as was a 'Butlins Camp' – that made us worry. However, with the ironman day looming, the drunk Brits abroad and standard of the hotel were the least of my worries, however other travellers had described it as *'worse than prison'* on the tripadvisor site!!

After registering and attending a briefing, I felt fully prepared, even though the weather was touch and go and we had been drenched on several occasions. One of my friends from home had recommended salt and vinegar crisps for the bike ride – mainly to give your mouth a different savoury taste after eating so many sweet energy foods/drinks. Could I find a small bag of salt and vinegar crisps anywhere in Calella?! No I couldn't… I think my girlfriend could have throttled me after visiting every supermarket, shop and bar in the town… We eventually found a packet in one of the English bars, two hours later.

Saturday evening came round and after a nice healthy carb meal and racking my bike, we headed back to the room to complete final preparations. Swim bag, Bike bag, Run bag – all prepped, snacks for the ride, drinks for the ride, breakfast for the morning, I was ready!!

6:00am – the alarm went off!! Pitch black outside. Silence in the hotel. The girlfriend arose first. Get up!! My adrenaline was pumping, I was ready!

I gulped down the rice pudding and banana that we'd bought the previous day and ensured I was covered in suntan lotion. We then headed towards the seafront. As soon as we turned the corner, the area was buzzing. Athletes everywhere, music playing, family/friends gathering around and we were soon met by my group. After lots of photos and good lucks, I headed towards the beachfront and before I knew it my wave was off. Crazy swimming, arms, legs everywhere – the first 1500m went by and I felt okay. Then it hit me – seasickness.

I'd experienced this previously in a same distance sea swim in Bournemouth, but I knew I had to swim through it. I lay on my back a few times to try and let it settle and managed to swim through. As soon as I was on dry land my stomach settled and I ran through to the transition area.

The bike leg was enjoyable and the sun was shining for the first loop, I managed to stick to my plan of eating every 20mins or so and I was going steady. Then the heavens opened!! The rain was so heavy that we had to slow down, puddles were coming up to our knees at some points and the roads were becoming dangerous with water. I took my sunglasses off to put them away but dropped them – they were then run over by a fellow rider – ouch!! The rain subsided and I continued on until I got to the last 20km of the route. Then I heard a hissing coming from my tyre – I had a puncture…

Luckily I'd screwed two CO_2 canisters to my bike and as there was only 20km left of the route; I thought I'd just inflate the tyre and coast back to transition. That was until I tried to inflate it and because of the rain, the CO_2 froze the adapter and I snapped it off as I released the canister – not a good move! My only chance was to coast back for the last 10km – I was so happy to see the last roundabout and managed to get back to transition without damaging the rims.

Now the running leg is usually my strongest one and the first two loops I was managing to keep up a steady pace. With family/friends at the sideline, they encouraged me on and really gave me a boost when I came past.

Then it hit me, the wall, the doubt, and the thoughts that I couldn't go any further.

My legs wouldn't move and I felt like I couldn't put in another step. I asked someone to walk with me and luckily my father-in-law with words of encouragement walked me to the next. I'm not sure how I got through the last part but suddenly

I was coming round to the last straight. The atmosphere around the finish line was amazing – cheering, music and the crowd was a great encouragement. The feeling when I came over the finish line was relief. I couldn't believe that I'd finished and I was in a bit of a daze. I came out of the athletes' tent and was showered by champagne from my family/friends, lots of photos being taken and cheering – I was still in a daze.

After lots of "goodbyes" and "well dones", my family/friends left and the heavens decided to open again. We walked, soaking wet, freezing cold to go and collect my bike and bags – a walk that usually took 10mins, took us nearly an hour!! I think I was still in a daze when I got back to the hotel, I knew I couldn't stomach anything. I laid in the bath, feeling slightly feverish and got straight into bed.

I was surprised to feel okay the next day. Other than a bit of joint ache in my legs, I felt spritely and we walked into town. We'd arranged a big meal in the evening with all the family/friends and I thanked them for their support – that little bit of cheering and just being there definitely shouldn't be underestimated. The main person I thanked was my girlfriend, who I asked to be my wife in front of all our family and friends – of course she said yes!!

The past twelve months has been immense, it's been a mixture of emotions, and I've never been so scared and excited about completing an event. When asked the next day whether I'd do it again, my answer was "HELL no!!" When asked this week whether I'd do it again, my answer was "probably in a couple of years (if she'll let me)". Life is a challenge, this has been a *real* challenge… but like L'Oreal: it was worth it.

The Message: Challenges are there to test you. See them as a positive part of achieving your dream.

Kevin Higby: "Ironman"

This is to all of my family and friends who put up with me throughout the training and who gave up their time to come out to Spain to support me: Mum, Dad, Alison, Michael, Mark, Caroline, Michelle, Sam and Becky. Sarah and Greig, David and Melissa and of course my fiancée Naomi. Couldn't have done it without you.

CHAPTER 3

"Why Not?" *By Katherine Caris-Harris*

So – apparently I need to be inspirational. A tricky one. I do not really believe anything I have achieved or have done is inspirational, you may disagree, however, what I can offer is encouragement. It is possible for a very ordinary, middle-aged, full-time mother, such as myself, to have something extra in your life that is just for you, challenging but also highly rewarding at times, which stops the boredom of the everyday routine setting in while still fulfilling everything else that is required of you (bar perhaps ironing all your husband's shirts on time). A fair amount of juggling is required and a lot of desire, will and determination but nothing insurmountable. I would also like to add at this point, as I believe it is an important point to highlight, that it is not necessary to give up alcohol. Red wine (in moderation perhaps) and excessive amounts of training are not mutually exclusive. If they were I would not have got this far.

I was never sporty at school, I would go so far as to say, I was distinctly un-sporty. My parents put little importance on sport with academic success being paramount. I was always active but had never entered a race or run further than perhaps 5km, until my late thirties. I would have described myself more as a "gym bunny". A significant factor in following the road that now leads me to doing Challenge Barcelona is that I stopped working when I had children. Something I never thought I would do. I took my career seriously and worked hard at it. I shall provide a brief career synopsis below, which highlights my restlessness and desire for focus, but I shall not be offended if you skim the next three paragraphs!

I left school with A levels good enough to get me into Medical school but soon realised this was not really the life for me. I think my parents were distinctly unimpressed. I followed the medical route purely because I was doing the right A levels to get in and with a number of medics in my family, knew enough to bullshit my way through my interviews. Then I arrived in London – freedom, and a whole new world to me – fresh from a very closeted, spoon-fed, all-girls boarding school. Needless to say, I attended very few lectures and did not do very well.

A quick change in direction led me to Newcastle University to read Maths and Economics; I soon dropped the Maths to read only Economics, as the men in their socks and sandals were just not for me. Economics offered much greater potential. Off from university to a broking firm to train as a Private Client Investment Manager, in the days when job opportunities were more abundant. In my first firm I passed my professional exams quickly, too quickly according to the MD when they would not pay me what I felt I deserved. So I left. The next firm I met my now-husband. I left there quickly too once we started living together. The third firm my boss was a woman who effectively put a glass ceiling on my head. I moved over to the institutional side briefly to run a fund but this was not really where I wanted to be so – you guessed it, I left.

My last firm was perfect. JPMorgan – it was challenging, well paid and no resting on your laurels. Unfortunately, I did not know how I would feel having had a baby, never having held one before, never mind changed a nappy, and I found it too hard to leave her and return. I was fortunate to have a choice, and it was one I have never regretted – but it did leave a gap in my life as time moved on – a challenge and something to push me.

My son was two and a half and had just started nursery when suddenly I had two whole hours a day to myself. What to do? Of course I could have returned home to get on top of jobs, clean and cook and prepare the house, and myself, for when my husband returned from his hard day in the office. Naturally, this was not the route I gave much thought to, or followed.

Instead, I found a personal trainer at the gym who has had a significant influence on my journey to today. I saw David for four years, stopping only last December as a result of the programme I am now on. If I get through this ironman in one piece and uninjured, David must take some of the credit for it – he taught me the importance of stretching, rolling, a strong core and how to listen to your body and when to stop (*I am not always very good at that*). He introduced me to my first spin class, Pilates, hot yoga, encouraged me to enter my first 10k. There was no going back. I was addicted.

Three years ago another trainer at the gym asked a group of us if we would like to enter a team sprint triathlon at Dorney Lake. My initial reaction was to say no – basically I could not swim, had not cycled since I was fifteen, nor owned a bike. The only thing I could do was run in a moderately ok fashion. I have never enjoyed swimming and never in my life swum front crawl. If I put my head in the water I would hold my nose and close my eyes. However, there was another girl in a similar situation to me, Jen. Jen and I formed a friendship, which made many of the early days great fun. We learnt to swim together – our main mutual aim being not to drown during the event – bought bikes and spent many hours out cycling learning how to negotiate a traffic light, stop on a hill or avoid running over a pedestrian. In fact, I still can't really start again on a hill if I am forced to stop.

Our first foray together into open water was quite an expedition. Our swim coach from the gym came with us, along with a number of the 'elite David Lloyd swim crew' for moral support – secretly I wondered if this was because they all thought we really might drown. We did survive however and, naturally, it was celebrated with a glass of wine to finish off at Box End that evening.

The team sprint tri I completed – just. My team members let me down at 11:30pm the night before. They were still on their way back from Portugal (this flight had been booked and known about for months) and they rang me late at night to say they thought they might be too tired. Fair enough. So I turned up anyway, ready to take someone's place should they be hit by a bout of food poisoning (fingers crossed – after all this build up, expense and stress I was determined to complete the race). I gave my name to the organisers and as chance would have it two random men were short of a teammate so I joined up with them. The first team member was in fact last out of the water, which in a way comforted me as I thought at least I wouldn't be letting the side down too much. Once again, there were the celebratory drinks at the end.

I have done a few more triathlons of varying distances since. I did actually book to do Challenge Henley (an ironman) last year on a whim. I had been out cycling with Jen and we had been planning as we did, and I thought really, I am sure I can do an ironman let's just book it. I went home and booked it. Jen did not. I then put it to the back of mind – my training plan was a couple of big bike rides nearer the time and I will be able to wing it. I had done a 3km swim earlier that year and reckoned I could probably do another 800m so that was the swim sorted (not in the sea like Challenge Barcelona I should add – a whole extra dimension).

Post first ever Open Water (Team) Race (me at the end on the right)

As the summer holidays approached I began to realise that maybe I was a little bit mad – and for once sensibly downgraded my entry to a half-ironman. My longest training session was two months before the event (i.e. before the children broke up) and I did 80km on the bike (broken up with a coffee in the middle) and then a 10km run. That's it I thought, I am sure on the day I will be able to do another 11km afterwards – it will be fine. My bike rides then fell down to 40km with 1 or 2km off the bike if I was lucky. To be honest I was ok – I turned up on my own, my family would be bored waiting, and I like to be anonymous. The swim was not too bad although I was very very cold when I got out of the river but I wasn't last, and the run hurt as I was just not 'bike fit' as they say. I did quite well on the bike until about 60km and I could feel my legs tiring and I just thought I need a coffee! However, I managed it all in six hours and one minute (rather annoyed I was not just two minutes quicker) but I was quite pleased when it was over.

Then I heard towards the end of last year of the opportunity to go for pre-screening at the University of Hertfordshire with the view to getting a place on the Challenge Barcelona Research Project. I would get to do an ironman, with a training programme (something I have never had before),

VO_2 testing, lactate and body-mass levels, personalised heart-rate training zones, bone-density scans to name a few as we went along – why not? There was no good reason – why not. That is why I am doing it.

It is probably worth saying that I really hate races. I love the training, but racing makes me feel sick. Why do I do them you may ask? The answer is simple – it gives you a goal and, if you are like me, you will want to reach it. Everyone has days where they cannot be bothered, too tired, too busy, it is too cold, too hot or you get a better offer of a night out with the girls. However, if you have a goal and a plan you will fit it in and make yourself get out there and just do it. Even if you don't always do it very well. You will always feel better afterwards, however much you hate it at the time. One of my husband's endearing phrases before I go out for a six hour bike ride, interval run session where I want to throw up, jump into a freezing lake at 6:30am or have an agonisingly painful sports massage is "have fun". If only he knew. However, "I will be happy afterwards" I always reply.

There have been some events for fun (all in the last four years) – Mucky Mud races, obstacle races, a cycle from London to Paris for charity, cycling 600km in Northern Vietnam (my Fortieth Birthday present) and a 67MileRun (two-thirds of the official 100MileRun for reasons I shall not bore you with) this August to name a few. I have done one marathon before which was April last year – Paris. I swore afterwards I would never do another. Obviously I changed my mind the next day when I thought maybe I would do London (GFA place in April 14) having heard so much about the atmosphere. I did Paris in 3hours 37mins but, again, me being me, was not happy, as I really wanted sub 3:30. Fingers crossed for London.

I am quite competitive against myself. Bizarrely, I had never really realised this until I started doing local races. My husband

Celebratory drink after the first day cycling ninety miles London to Dover

apparently thinks I am extremely competitive – I think he is wrong and is just trying to wind me up (a hobby of his). I do frequently set myself targets and I achieve a huge satisfaction from achieving them, equally I feel my failures deeply too – somewhere this must come from my childhood, but I haven't delved there yet.

Thus I strive hard to meet my targets and give myself little slack if I don't meet them. What I do think is good, is that my competitiveness is focused on myself and my sport, and not my children. I have no time to be a competitive school mother, thankfully for my children, so long as they are happy and healthy... So far, so good I think. I am also a perfectionist and mildly obsessive – traits I think that need to be channelled in the direction or they are not healthy. In this respect triathlon suits me well.

There are other factors that have affected me as I grew up – my father is a workaholic, teaching me from an early age the importance of working hard. My brother sadly died when I was thirty, this taught me to not take life for granted and sometimes you just have to grab opportunities as who knows what will happen tomorrow. I have suffered from anxiety issues before

Post 8 Miles Mucky Mud Race – Great fun!

in my life and exercise is fantastic at helping you remain calm and keep life in proportion. The ethos of 'living life for today' I do moderate as hopefully the children's future will be long, healthy and prosperous and for that we try to plan – although my husband would argue that if the financial planning was left in my hands we would be penniless quite quickly as I would have booked us all a year's first class trip around the world a few times over (probably to coincide with local ironman races). The children would be very well dressed too as I still do love beautiful non-lycra clothes.

So to the race itself – I arrived on the Friday and the waves in the sea were HUGE. I yo-yoed between finding the thought of swimming 3.8km in such conditions mildly hysterical and complete panic. However, on Sunday morning it was calmer and, as I stood on the edge of the beach waiting to start I felt strangely calm. I knew there was no going back; I just had to get in and do my best.

The swim was hard – the buoys were very hard to see and for most of us it took longer than expected due to the tide I believe. After what was probably about one and a half hours (although I didn't know this at the time) I did begin to wonder if it was ever going to end. Fortunately it did, eventually, and onto the bike. I will not go into too much race detail but for me my major problem was nutrition. I felt horribly sick on the bike and struggled to eat very much. This then impacted my run where I felt very weak and quite a few times really just wanted to lie down at the side of the road. I did realise that these thoughts were not particularly good news so I forced caffeine gels down myself quite early on and managed to keep a plod going – this I believe is where everyone starts talking about mental strength.

Will I want to do more? At the time, NO! NO NO NO! However, forty-eight hours later I was beginning to wonder – mmmm – if got my nutrition right and did the swim in a lake – I am sure I could go under twelve hours… However, I have said no for next year due to the impact the training had on family life so half ironmen for now along with a personalised programme and to get faster is my plan! There is also the impact on your body, "excessive" training does take its toll and I would rather moderate the distance but keep my body going until I am eighty. This will have been helped obviously by my Monday night recovery plan of around six to seven Spanish gin and tonics.

If you have read this because you are tempted to do an ironman or in any strange way you now feel inspired to do one… my advice is *just to get out there and do it*. You can – and you certainly won't know if you don't try. It will be hard but that is half the pleasure. There is no sense of achievement in doing something easy.

Best of luck!

The Message: Go for it, you won't know if you don't try!

CHAPTER 4

"Transition" *By Tony Dawkins*

It's the summer of 2012, as a sports-science student enjoying the annual family holiday on the calm coasts of Cornwall I receive a text from my university lecturer saying "we got the study with Barcelona!" As a footballer by nature and no initial inclination as to what the hell he was talking about, my immediate reaction was that we would somehow be working with Barcelona FC. After kicking up a storm of excitement I was soon flung back to earth when I was told he was referring to some study involving 'recreational' athletes participating in a triathlon…, which wasn't even held in Barcelona.

Little did I know this would be the beginning of an amazing journey meeting characters from all walks of life that I have the utmost respect for; who's Lionel Messi anyway?

Anti-climax: a disappointing end to an exciting or impressive series of events

Third, and final year begins at university and in the first lecture of the year we were presented with the opportunity to be a participant in this 'ironman challenge', which was swiftly laughed off by every student in the room. My response: "you must be joking!". However, the seed was planted and I wasn't the only one. The thought progressed and after much deliberation in November 2012, I decide for final I'm going to do this. I told my mum who knew way before I did that I wouldn't be able to pass up the opportunity. Her pupils dilate and face turns pale; it's as if she's seen a ghost. I can see a million thoughts run through her mind in the space of just a few seconds but, supportive as ever, she switches back to reality and says five words: "I know" and "PLEASE be careful". My Dad has one thought in his mind "what about football?" I think I shattered his heart when I said I was going to have to give football a rest for a year. After coming to every game since I first started playing when I was eight, even to the extent that he would bring his fire engine (with the fire crew still in it) to some games if he couldn't get off work! None the less, with an intense Uni schedule, final exams dawning and obvious training needs, something had to give. This year was going to be a big transition in every sense of the word from footballer to ironman athlete.

When I first told my best friends I was doing an ironman and just exactly what's involved, they thought I must be mistaken since the human body is incapable of such feats. The same friends that I have been closest with since seven years old actually put on a bet that I wouldn't get to the finish line. I'd like to think the only reason they did this was as an incentive for me to prove them wrong, knowing them... definitely not. After announcing this challenge coincidently, my best mates began training more frequently. Every so often they would join me (for part) of my runs, though more often than not this was instigated by me arriving on their doorstep, and receiving a long health and safety lecture from their mums. I'm not sure what they thought I was going to do to them, but they got through.

I create a checklist of everything I need and everything I have already. First things first, I need a bike and my twenty-first birthday is coming up. The rusty red mountain bike with tassels and basket left at the bottom of the garden would probably get me a place on the 'specials' team and I aim on finishing this race. Although, in hindsight the front basket accessory would have been a great help during the race, storing the twenty gels, two water bottles, three energy bars, and pack of nuts. In 2006, when I was fourteen years old, I invested in a twenty-pound body boarding wetsuit while on holiday in Cornwall so that I could brave the treacherous four foot waves and twelve degree water. The same wetsuit held out for seven years, and six months into ironman training in 2013 I still believe this same wetsuit can get me through the big day. After the second open-water swim however, with my shoulder feeling as though it was hanging out the socket, I realise my shoestring budget must take another hit.

Road cycle number one, my dad's mates offer to take me out for a morning's cycle. Unused to the early morning training sessions at this point I'm promptly woken. With ten minutes to spare I jump into my shorts and shove in a slice of dry toast with a pint of water. Next I'm faced with the daunting challenge of fitting the new road bike into my 'spacey' ford KA. Challenge one complete. After an hour of cycling the old boys turn to me, ask if I'm okay and whether the pace is okay for me. In a chirpy manner I reply "yep, feels like a nice leisurely pace for me" and explain how training in zone one is most beneficial. This must have aggravated them somewhat, since I'm certain plans changed from here on and the morning cycle turned into a marathon ride in an attempt to reiterate their dominance. Three hours in and without trying to give away any signs of fatigue I finally ask how much further we're going, "probably half an hour". We reach the destination and due to the fact it wasn't my house it dawns on me, we're only half way round! Seven hours in total to clock up sixty miles, and I return in a zombie state ransacking the cupboards before passing out on the sofa.

With the event nearing, there were no more excuses. No more jokes about how there is plenty of time to get ready. A year of training, all for this. A year of countless 4am starts, several days spent on zero hours' sleep, and dedicating weekends to the all important long sessions. A year of manipulating my diet to a rigid set of meals treating each bite like medication. I knew at the beginning that for me, getting to the start line in one piece would be half the battle. In the last couple of months I even carried out the majority of training in the gym just to avoid any potential hazards on the road that might undo all the hard work I put in.

At last the big day had arrived, not my wedding, but the triathlon. A small group of us depart for the transition tent with an array of mixed emotions including anxiety, excitement, stress and to some extent relief. In addition, to my surprise I soon realised there were no changing facilities and promptly stripped butt naked in front of the thousands of supporters, probably more to their horror than my own. At the start

Transition one in sight after a tough swim

position awaiting the claxon, I spot amongst the huge crowd my two-year-old nephew being waved in the air like a flag. I just about have enough time to run over and grab a good luck kiss before diving into the swarm of yellow hats. I finish my first attempt of sea swimming with a personal best in tough conditions. Challenge 2 complete.

Next I reach the transition area, and with an experienced triathlete's words ringing in my ears I remember, put the jersey on BEFORE putting the gels in the pocket. When I got to the bike one thing and one thing only dawned on me, "someone has pinched my nuts!" My honey-coated peanuts I might add. Nutrition strategy flawed already, "not essential, get on with it" I remind myself. I grab the bike and start running to the start line, calamity strikes on the red carpet in front of several cameras; gels fly everywhere, the rear bottle cage loosens and my sports drink falls to the floor. After a confident and promising start I'm met with overwhelming embarrassment and my personal best swim is becoming more and more negligible as I'm left picking what's left of my nutrition off the floor. Luckily I don't speak much Spanish, but I'm pretty sure I was on the receiving end of a lot of abuse in that moment. One kilometre down the road and the drinks bottle comes off again, this time I'm cutting my losses. I'll stick to the water and gels till the next aid station.

"Stay flexible, stay calm," I remind myself.

Six hours is a long time to spend on the bike, and many people have asked, "What do you think about for all that time". Firstly, do not underestimate a man's ability to think about absolutely nothing and feel content. There are moments of doubt of course, moments when you think you really can't give anything more, and the thought of finishing becomes less and less promising. But those thoughts always seemed to be countered by a moment of motivation: an inspirational sight such as the paraplegic guy ploughing on through the 180km using only his arms, the recollection of all the emotional speeches and words of encouragement from over the previous twelve months. I clung on to those moments for the next nine hours and pretty soon all I could think about was finishing. Challenge 3 complete.

Transition time again, I leap off the bike and unclip my helmet. All of a sudden I'm being screamed at by an overweight Spanish lady with an 'official' top on; I think she must have had some kind of OCD because she really wanted me to put my helmet back on. I assured her I wouldn't be getting back on the bike, but complied in the end and made my way into the tent. As much as I appreciated the help inside the transition tent from the underage volunteers, they might have got more than they bargained for when, for the third time of the day, I'm forced to publicly strip again. Finally, I can start running. Immediately I'm faced with blisters the size of my fist, but each step I take is one foot closer to my ultimate goal I've been training for all year. The pain is overwhelmed by the massive amounts of support, not just from my amazing family and friends, but random Spanish locals who seemed to be treating each athlete with the same crazy enthusiasm for the whole duration. I remember thinking "wow, surely they must be getting tired by now". Every lap there was at least one muppet asking "Is this your last lap?" Never have I had a smile wiped from my face so quickly. Even though finishing in what I regarded as a very impressive time in my opinion, my family obviously had higher expectations after waiting at the finishing line three hours too early!

One hundred metres from completing the biggest challenge of my life, and all that is going through my mind is "thank god that's over!" the next thoughts, "who the hell is that crazy lady steaming towards me!" She gets closer and through my bloodshot and sweaty eyes I realise it's the same girl who's been cheering me on through the whole race and the last intense year… my girlfriend.

"Come on, come on" she yells with the biggest grin on her face. "Come on", I've just finished twelve hours and twelve minutes of this, I'm not running anymore, I'm falling with one foot just about in front of the other. We finish together and I'm greeted at the line by the face of the same man who instigated it all and made it happen, Justin my lecturer. It's only right that he hands over the medal and I join the rank of triathletes. **Challenge completed**.

Five minutes after completing the biggest challenge of my life I'm questioned, "how does it feel to be an Ironman?".

"**It hurts**" I reply in an all too fast response.

I literally used up every last bit of energy in getting to the finish line; you don't consider what's left AFTER you finish. With blistered feet, joints that have taken a hammering and quadriceps that give way on every step, it dawns on me, my bike is 1.5km away (in transition 1) and apparently I'm the only one who can collect it! How sadistic. I hobble along in a kind of penguin dance with my Dad and brother-in-law holding me up either side. A small taste of bittersweet revenge was mine when I took the last opportunity to relieve myself upon the side of the transition tent. At long last, I can eat and drink whatever I want. I later discovered that was a mistake, and spent the next day cuddling the toilet in a tight embrace.

This year has been an amazing experience from so many points of view, watching myself and so many of my newly-found friends develop and change as a person and athlete. Being able to take a step back and realise the enormity of what has been accomplished over the last year brings a massive sense of pride. I started this challenge because I want to be able to say I have made the most of my life because so many others

Tony 'Ironman' Dawkins: Now that's how you finish!

don't get the chance to do the same.

As Dave Scott said at the end of what's quoted as the greatest race in the history of triathlon: "It was kind of painfully enjoyable, and I'm not sure I want to feel that again", "but I will never forget feeling it once!" (*Iron War*, 2012)

Now where did I put that football?

The Message: Ironman: it's more than a fifteen hour experience... It's a life defining journey.

CHAPTER 5

"YES MAN" *By Daniel McCluskey*

YES! Or how I found myself mastering life juggling and became a long-distance triathlete, maybe.

The End, almost.

Its two weeks to go before I take part in the toughest physical activity I've ever been daft enough to enrol for and I find myself tying together all the titbits of writing I've got scattered about. You see here I am writing a book chapter about my journey from general everyday sportsman to iron-distance triathlete. Let me highlight my daftness more clearly, having a full-time job and undertaking the necessary training to complete an iron-distance triathlon I also felt compelled to volunteer to write a chapter for a book. Oh and did I mention my first son Elliott was born almost one calendar year before the triathlon, at the start of the training period? You see, I said I was a bit daft!

Now I'm not sure whether this will be chapter one or chapter twenty (or on the editors' floor for that matter) but I'm sure you've read a number of other people's stories about their own personal motivations and struggles, but ultimately I'm sure you've now read a number of chapters that effectively highlight how 24hrs in a single day is not enough time to satisfy the requirements needed to earn a crust, have a life, and train for an iron-distance triathlon. So perhaps I ought to start at the beginning, the "Why?" so to speak, before I explain the "How and How not".

Who am I? A lot of my general get up and go I attribute to being a cheerful person, for example I 'like' mornings, and I'm willing to get stuck in to most things, but I also have to thank one word, and that word is YES! You see comedian and author Danny Wallace wrote a book called *Yes Man*, a comic "real life" tale of the adventure that engulfed him after he made a bet to say, "yes" to any direct yes/no question. I remember buying that book at Kings Cross station and reading it on the London–Edinburgh east coast train. For some time after reading that book the positivity of *Yes Man* influenced a number of my everyday encounters. I didn't turn into a Yes Man myself, nor did I go on any spiritual journey, but I maintained a more positive outlook on life and I have to say I was genuinely quite happy as a result, and I started some new things in my life.

Summer 2006: Comets Lacrosse

For no obvious reason I can think of I was invited to try out lacrosse by my friend Rich's girlfriend. It turns out I wasn't asked for any special reason but simply because she had spotted a local team training on the university grounds and, as she had played at school, wanted to share the sport with a few others. Having nothing better to do, and having no clue what lacrosse was I humoured her and went along, flatmates in tow. We arrived and twenty minutes later we had been kitted up with gloves, sticks and helmets and got shown the basics. I wasn't a natural, but I seemed to pick up the general gist and was enjoying it. Half-way through that training session we were all informed that the rest of the session would be a training match against the Welsh National team. Talk about being thrown in at the deep end and I was hooked! With no prior experience of the sport I spent the next two months involved in setting up both a mixed and men's lacrosse team at the University of Hertfordshire.

The club was a success and summer 2006 saw us finish our first competitive men's lacrosse season. Aside from the obvious Field of Dreams "build it and they will come" aspect of the endeavour there were three standout points I took away from this year:

If you enjoy a sport then exercise comes naturally, and thus for me, so did my general fitness level;

The whole saying yes thing seems to mostly lead to good things;

And finally,

We didn't come last!

However, after a while the "Yes" became easier and easier to overcome with the old "not enough time" or "not enough money". These were all just excuses really. I knew that, but it's easy to justify with national headline words like, Recession, or Career or any number of other lame excuses. Work got in the way of training and Saturday lie-ins with coffee and cake got in the way of matches, the net result was that my level of fitness declined and I ended up deciding to take a year out from the sport after a few too many injuries.

I enjoyed the more relaxed, comfortable nature of ill-defined weekend plans but deep down I liked getting involved, staying fit, saying yes more. That's what led me to decide that I would make more effort again, set free the positivity I knew was lurking just waiting to pop up and say "Hi". So with masses of support from my partner, Tara, I made a concerted effort and finished my PhD, I got a job, we bought a house, I left my job and got another one – this time right back at the same university I graduated from – you see its still nice when things are comfortable.

Then in quick succession Tara and I decided to start a family and I spotted a tweet from Dr Justin Roberts about a research programme he was running. Generally these two things wouldn't be linked, but this was to be the start of the greatest part of my life so far. On the one hand I would have to be a grown up, I'd be a dad. And on the other I'd be a guinea pig, training day-in day-out to take part in a study, which would culminate in me competing in an iron-distance triathlon (I should add at this point, while I knew triathlons consisted of a swim, bike and run, I didn't even have an idea of which order you did these events in!).

Now I don't expect you to believe that the essence of 'me' can be distilled into the five preceding paragraphs nor that I've indicated each and every one of my motivations and justifications for taking on this triathlon, but I hope I've given you a glimpse of what I was up to before I sent off my application to Dr Roberts, before I got back his reply of *YES!*

So that's how one month before my son Elliott was to be born I found myself explaining to a very pregnant Tara how I would easily be able to fit in the night feeds and the nappy changes and the cooking and the cleaning and the aimless wandering round rocking the baby to sleep and work and the small matter of training for an iron-distance triathlon. Tara had faith in me, she even gave me the opportunity to say "no" and keep my dignity, I opted to go to the September assessment and if I wasn't the right person for the study then so be it. Again Justin and his team said I was in, they gave me a big fat YES! And I was starting to be a little wary of that three-letter word.

Not Elliott's first Christmas

December 2012 was the last month before training really started. We were told, nay instructed, to enjoy ourselves, to not worry too much about the training that would start in January to go wild almost (this part may not actually be true). Christmas 2012 would also be two months since Elliott was born and we had decided that we wouldn't treat it as his first on account of the fact that he'd mostly be sleeping and even if it wasn't going to be *his* first Christmas there could still be a childlike letter to Santa. And so I made my first Christmas list in about twenty years and it focused quite heavily on the one part of the triathlon I was dreading the most, the swim. So while I sat round the Christmas table eating and drinking I looked over at some of my gifts from Tara and it included goggles, fins, paddles and floats and I genuinely thought just owning these tools would turn me into Michael Phelps – this ironman was going to be easy, pass me another mince pie, training doesn't start till January.

On the 2nd January 2013 everything started for real, not only was I on the study, but I was also on the sub-study focusing on nutrition and my first thoughts were that this was going to be great, an extra bonus so to speak. Then the paperwork landed. Psychology and Mental Toughness questionnaires, Nutrition and Sleep diaries, Training Plans and Training Records, Event information, participant instructions, payment forms, Injury Diaries alongside the various tests that would be conducted. Biomechanical and Cardiovascular assessments, Blood and Saliva tests and then the small matter of Functional Screening including lactic uptake and the dreaded VO_{2max} test. Each and every one of these indicated just one thing – Dr Justin Roberts of the University of Hertfordshire, his team and all involved, meant business! I'd said yes, they had said yes and now it was time to *do*!

When the first block of training kicked off I was pleasantly surprised, I could do everything that was asked of me, Tara was still on maternity leave and I found I had the time to juggle everything exactly as I had initially thought – I went for a brisk winter run, jumped on the turbo in the conservatory or popped down to the pool. I dug my free weights out from the back of the garage and cleaned off the rust. I went into a yoga shop and bought resistance bands and a mat. I was killing this training programme and I was enjoying every minute of it, the only downside was that aside from Tara I'd decided not to tell anyone I was doing any of this. So far this was the only part that I was finding hard!

For the first three months I found myself getting up at 5:30am for the early morning gym, swim or run sessions, I wrapped up and trudged through the typical UK winter wind, rain and fog that you might expect between January and March. I recall on one occasion our kettle blew up, and with four inches of snow outside there was no way I was going to drive out to buy a new one, but I found myself strapping on my running shoes, picking up a backpack and setting out for a nice easy zone two steady run that just so happened to pass an electrical shop. The training plan I was following was clear and straightforward and above all *doable*. I didn't think this would be the case, I imagined something out of a Spartan warrior boot camp, but instead I learnt about heart rate zones and maximising muscle memory, about endurance vs. interval training but ultimately even just a short nine months later I can't really remember those first few months' training. I just recall it was fun and manageable. I even managed to take a snowboarding holiday to the Alps, with a four-month-old baby no less. Everything was easy, everything was going brilliantly. Well almost. I had also discovered I couldn't really swim.

I'll repeat that – I'd signed myself up for a triathlon, an event where the first segment is a swim. Not only that but I'd signed up for one of the most gruelling triathlon distances there are, the iron distance and, more to the point, the specific triathlon I'd signed up for, the Barcelona Challenge Full Iron, starts with a 2.4 mile open-water sea swim, and I'd discovered I couldn't really swim. I mean it's not as if I was ignoring the swim when I signed up, I'd even tested myself to make sure that I met the initial criteria (1km or a steady 30mins). It's just that it hadn't really occurred to me that I had never, not once, learnt or even tried to swim freestyle despite growing up in an area of South Africa with swimming pools so easily accessible. I'm also negatively buoyant, if I don't move I sink, and not just a little bit. I sink straight to the pool floor. Those 2.4 miles were starting to look like a tough ask and slowly the swim training was starting to break me. It was looking like it was time to say "NO!".

This was around about the same time that money was starting to get a bit tight. Triathlon training is more expensive than I'd imagined and with Tara on maternity leave the family income had started to drop. But sink or swim it was up to me to sort things out. It was time to get *doing* again and I found myself applying for a second job. Quick as a flash I'd said 'yes' once more and so had they, I got the job. I was now dad, nappy changer, night-time feeder, full-time university researcher and lecturer, head chef of Chez McCluskey, triathlete in training and the new Clerk to the Parish Council of the village of Westoning. I had not said no, I had not given in. And I would soon be adding accomplished swimmer to that list – or so I hoped.

This time help was at hand, as luckily for me I wasn't alone and the Herts team had spotted that the swimming was an issue for a few of us on the study. Fortunately in amongst the other lab rats, as we had come to be known, were a couple of swim coaches and I found myself booking a swimming lesson. The coach took me through some of the basics, questioned why my legs were doing breast stroke while my arms were testing the waters with freestyle. He had mantras such as "swim over a barrel" and "imagine you're hugging a fat man". He told me to breathe, and not to breathe. To slow down in order to speed up. He was as confused as I was to discover that the "Pool Buoy" didn't stop my legs sinking and this made me feel good! It was as if my issue had been validated and that made it ok. Most of all in that one swim lesson I felt that I would be able to do this after all I just needed to work harder at it and to help myself a bit more and the first thing I decided to do to help myself was to tell my friends what I had been up to. At least this way quitting would be one hundred times harder and the thought of saying 'no' would be held at bay just a little bit more.

High days and holidays

As April rolled in it brought with it the first signs of longer days and shorter nights. It was nice to see my old friend *Sol* and I was able to ditch the head torch from my evening runs. With this sunshine more readily present I started to take the bike out on the roads leaving the turbo to be a trip hazard in the conservatory. I also discovered along the way that sunshine doesn't always equal warmth and I promptly bought myself some arm warmers and overshoes. Then just after Easter Tara went back to work, she's a secondary school teacher, and the nicely laid out structure I was working to started to unravel. Training, nursery, work and gym times all started to overlap while motorway rush hour clashed with everything, always and the 80% training volume rule I was working to (as part of the study) was beginning to get scuppered. Fatigue crept in and I got ill thanks in part to an infant's immune system acting as the gateway to my home. By the end of April I started to feel at my lowest so far, I'd missed more than I'd done and I injured myself whenever I did go out, finally through the joys of a stomach bug I successfully managed to lose about 10kg. I also still couldn't swim.

But April goes straight into May and with it came my birthday and a much needed half-term break for both Tara and myself. I also took delivery of a totally unexpected birthday present from my Dad, who only went and bought me a Garmin 310XT! I had said nothing about my desire for such a thing and neither had Tara. This really was a total surprise but a truly welcome gift. My Mum and Gran also got involved in my challenge and bought me a wetsuit, while Tara picked up a few of the things she spotted on my ever increasing Amazon wish list. A set of tri bars, bento box and rear mount bottle holder and a few daft little bits to help along the way, some body glide, a swim hat and a few gels (something I'd never tried before, this may also have been the exact point when 45g of carbohydrate syrup firmly became my "nutrition"). My friend Rich bought me an Ironman t-shirt and NOT the Marvel superhero! I was feeling well supported by all around me and it reminded of one of the things Dr Roberts said in his opening presentation, that the people around you are key to getting through the training and the event itself, to be considerate to them and make time for them. After a few days off to celebrate my birthday over a curry and a beer or two and with thanks to everyone for my gifts and their support, I headed off to Denham lake at 6:30am one Saturday morning for my first open-water swim session. With wetsuit on and Garmin under my swim hat I dipped my toe in the water, eased myself in and after a few breathless moments discovered that finally,

I could swim. Yes!

Now don't be fooled, I've spoken about the general ups and downs of the training and the life juggling and about my trials and tribulations related to swimming but there were three other key sections of training going on at this point. Functional training, cycling and running all formed part of the balanced training plan we were following. I'd already had a couple of hairy moments where I was struggling to complete the 80% required of us. But equally I just didn't have the time to spare and I didn't want to give in. I decided that I had to prioritise and unfortunately the functional training was the first to fall by the wayside. My thinking being that the three core sports were required for the main event, the functional being a way of optimising and improving ability in each of these. Whenever time allowed I would complete the functional work, and I would endeavour to spend some time, no matter how short, on the stretching exercises. I also found myself increasingly following the "Weekend Warrior" approach to training, with the longer sessions accounting for a greater chunk of that illusive 80% minimum. In this way I eeked my way to the end of Phase One of the study and I braced myself for what was to come.

I fell over – I can't say I wasn't warned!

Having completed a number of the longer training sessions on my own I felt I needed to ride with others, both for the experience and to help alleviate the boredom. This has been one of the biggest challenges for me, the boredom. I mean aside

August 2013, Boxend Lake, Bedfordshire – Actually swimming taking place, with witnesses!

from the life juggling and the weather and the lack of motivation to get up two hours after a night feed, after all those things the biggest challenge for me was the boredom, and maybe the weather. So in order to overcome this I turned to our trusty Facebook page to see if a group ride was being arranged for any of the big weekends in Phase Two. Justin had set up the Facebook group early in the study and many of the lab rats used it as a means of sharing highs and lows, tips and tricks, but also as a means of organising group get togethers. In this capacity it might actually be one of the most useful Facebook pages I've come across!

So having scanned through the latest panic-inducing posts (who's booked their flight and are they on the right day? Is your bike making its own way to Calella? Should we be using 23 or 25mm tyres? Why has my Garmin lost all my data etc.?) I found what I was looking for and promptly registered my interest in joining a group heading out to do 180km through deepest darkest Hertfordshire, starting at 6:00am one Saturday morning. A 6am start meant a 4:30am wake up time for me, or approximately 1.5hrs after night feed. Ugh! Still, with gels in hand, I manage to make it to the meeting point, feeling daft I lather on the freezing suntan lotion and set off with the group.

Immediately it becomes apparent that, while I can ride a bike, there are those in the group that can ride just a bit better and we naturally break into a few sub groups segregated by their natural pace. It might be a bit of an over exaggeration but those kilometres flew by when in the company of others and I found myself enjoying the ride and not quite paying attention to what I was doing. That's when it happened. Pulling up to a junction I looked left when I should have looked right, I twisted my right foot out the cleat when it should have been my left and I found myself laughing out loud as I slowly, in true cartoon fashion, tipped over and landed on the road, feet still attached to the cleats, at least on the side I wanted to not be attached. I had always assumed this was a cliché that didn't really happen to cyclists, but I guess I had been warned. Still, while it's nice to ride with others, for the sake of my dignity I happened to be just round the bend and out of anyone's eyeline when I fell. The moral of the story – those clichés exist for a reason, one day you'll find out why and on that day try and have a laugh about it.

Barcelona Looms and Elliott will be one year old

So as I said at the beginning its two weeks to go before I take part in the toughest physical activity I've ever been daft enough to enrol for and I find myself tying together all the titbits of writing I had scattered about. More than that though I've had the opportunity to recount the "why" and "how" of my adventure. I've been able to mentally prepare myself for Barcelona and to put in writing my thanks to all those who have supported me along the way, my partner Tara, my son Elliott (even though he doesn't know it), my family and friends and Justin and his team.

I've already got everything I wanted out of the study, my fitness is back, I feel more invigorated more often. I feel capable of saying yes more and coming through. In less than two weeks I will have the added bonus of competing in the 2013 Barcelona Challenge Iron-distance triathlon and will show myself that I am a triathlete, I can swim! But most of all I am looking forward to the week after Barcelona when Elliott turns one year old because whether I mentioned it or not I did do this for me, but mostly I did it for Elliott.

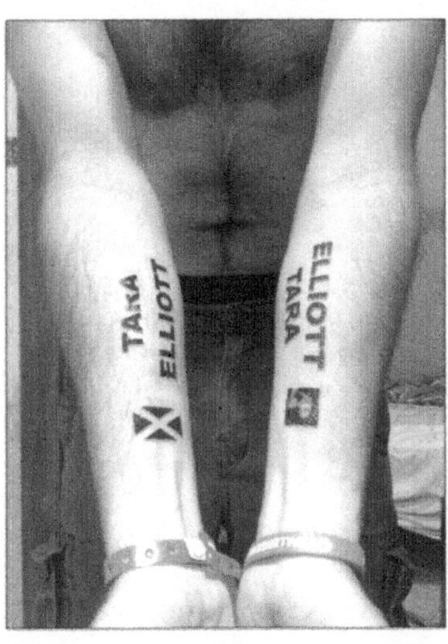

The best motivation is the one that is personal to you. Everytime I dipped my head I was reminded of all the supporters I had cheering me on at home especially my two special people (as you can see Ironman or not, I wasn't going down the waxing route!).

The Message: I did this for many different reasons, but ultimately I did it because life is more fun, more rewarding when you say **YES** instead of No!

CHAPTER 6

"Perseverance"
By Rachel Jodie Lahon

Perseverance must finish its work, so you may be mature and complete, not lacking anything – James 1:4-6

"*Nobody said it was going to be easy.*" So reads my Facebook cover page. When I was young, the leader of my church youth club once said to me that he thought I was the sort of person who would definitely get from A to B, but that I would probably take a detour to M, P and XYZ. At the time I didn't pay much attention, but I remembered it years later when a period of my life saw me trying to navigate a number of disasters, and every time I picked myself up I seemed to get knocked down more forcefully. The worst of these was in 2010 when my dad died.

The month before he died I had undertaken a challenge – the National Three Peaks. I'd organised the event for myself and fourteen colleagues, trained so hard that I did the whole thing at a run and even took my turn at driving the minibus alongside my brother, who was an excellent support crew. It gave me something positive to focus on at a time when I wasn't really happy with my career and I was worrying about my dad's health. All the way through the process he had sent me text messages encouraging me, telling me he was proud of me and that I should "build up my mental and physical strength". He called me an "intrepid adventurer" and always wanted to hear about my exploits, daft as they were sometimes. He was proud of the responsibility I had taken and the physical achievement of completing the challenge.

After losing my dad, who had been so unwaveringly supportive of me, I was utterly bereft. I didn't know what to do with myself. I remember going out for a birthday meal with my family about six weeks later, and being sick with stress and grief. I didn't think I was ever going to feel happy again. I did indeed feel like I had wandered away from A without the slightest clue where B was, let alone how I would get there, and that I had sort of ground to a halt around L for Lost.

Thankfully the wonderful people around me pulled me through this awful dark mess. One very special friend in particular, Rebeca, decided that I needed a new focus, and convinced me to enter the Berlin Marathon with her. So we trained and completed it in 2011. It was an amazing experience and although I choked up at the finish line, I felt really good about my achievement. Although Rebeca had beaten me by five minutes – I am still waiting to get even!

The next year (2012) I was really busy getting married and making big decisions about my career, and I really missed not having a difficult physical challenge like the previous few years. I was looking for a road bike because I wanted to commute to the university campus for the MSc course I was about to embark on in September 2012, and someone on one of the 'bike geek' forums forwarded me the link to the HURTS study advertisement.

I opened the link, read it, and felt a tingle of excitement. Then I switched my computer off and tried to ignore it. I needed to focus on my MSc studies; I would be doing a science course, having never studied science before, at one of the most prestigious universities in the world. Spending twenty plus hours per week training should not have been on my agenda.

But it was, and I kept thinking about my dad who had coincidentally been in charge of one of the engineering departments at the University of Hertfordshire years earlier. I still remembered going to visit him there. It meant something to me. And I couldn't get the idea out of my head. **The pure challenge.** The opportunity to do something that I knew most people wouldn't dream of attempting.

A few days later, I sent an application and from then on, I was determined. I called Justin and pretty much begged him to have me on the study. Having secured a place a few weeks later, I was all set to pour my heart and soul in almost equal measures into my MSc and this challenge, and then... another disaster struck.

The injuries started with a Gangnam Style flash mob. In fact, to be truthful, it wasn't even the flash mob itself that caused me the injury. It was the rehearsal beforehand that left me limping home knowing that I had turned my ankle. But it was only late October and there was still plenty of time to recover. I iced it (a little bit), stopped running for a couple of weeks, and thought nothing of it – after all, I had never really been injured in my life – as a child my family used to joke that I was made of India rubber. I was all set to join the study, and then on December 31st I went for a run locally, to do some hill sprints with my husband.

I don't know what happened, even now, but one minute I was bouncing along happily enjoying the fresh air. The next minute I was writhing on the ground in agony and screaming, "it isn't fair" in my best impression of a three-year-old.

An ambulance ride later, and an X-ray at the hospital confirmed that I hadn't broken anything, but had a sprain that was borderline grade two/three. For the next few weeks all I could do was hop around on crutches and watch in horror (and a degree of gleeful fascination, it has to be said) as my entire lower leg turned a dark shade of purple, and swelled to roughly the size of a baby rhinoceros's leg. I called Justin in a panic and he reassured me that I should still be able to do the ironman, and not to worry, but just rest it and see a physio. So, in an act of defiance I booked my place in the ironman, and also my hotel and flights, ensuring that I would be seriously out of pocket if I didn't recover and do the training.

Three weeks later I started training…

Lightly…

And then a few weeks later I started running again…

And pretty quickly, my OTHER leg said "**no thanks**" and developed tendonitis. Suddenly, every time I even moved my right leg, my Achilles creaked (like you would expect in a ninety-year-old).

Nobody said it was going to be easy.

Thankfully, with the support of my wonderful, encouraging sister and through the study, I found two physios who helped me to get back on my feet and back out training. But at this point I hadn't used my legs much for almost two months, and it was suddenly April. I had spent two entire months lifting weights, practising my pull-ups and swimming with a pull buoy. I felt as if I was dying of boredom. So when I started to cycle again I was ecstatic, but also very anxious: people on the study were posting on FB about their sixty-mile bike rides, and a long ride for me was thirty miles at this point.

However, I persevered, and a few weeks later entered my first ever sportive. 'Sportives' should be renamed 'Supportives' because I went along with a few people from the study and they were amazing – even though I slowed them down enormously, puffing up the hills like a steam train, they waited for me at every junction and encouraged me whenever they saw me struggling. Over the next few months I did more and more rides with these guys and in particular the encouragement I received from Kim Mangelshot, Gary Smith and Jamie Payne was amazing (I could name more!). Cycling with people who were faster than me and knew more about bikes was a steep upwards learning and training curve, but it was brilliant for my confidence and determination, not to mention the logistical support I received from these people in getting to and from ride venues.

The swimming was also a challenge – I went from not understanding how to breathe out underwater in February to a PB of 1:30 in a lake for the full 3.8km distance. I received a lot of help and tips from coaches who gave groups of us tips in open-water swimming. Mastering sighting was the hardest thing. My mum came to visit in June and watched me early one morning in the lake. When I got out, she confirmed the sneaking suspicion in the back of my mind – that I had been zigzagging so much in the lake that I was probably swimming 25% further than I needed to. One unforgettable (forgettable?) weekend in Bournemouth a group of us attempted a full-distance sea swim. Most of us only did two-thirds because of the strong current and tide. I remember swimming solidly away from a buoy for about ten minutes, looking back, and realising that I had barely made any progress. Now I know the meaning of the phrase 'making waves'!

Even the running was a challenge, mostly due to coming back from injuries – even though I had done much more running than swimming or cycling in the past. One memorable weekend, I decided to go for a twelve mile run from my sister's house because there was a nice scenic route nearby. Twelve miles would be a breeze for me a year earlier – I would have classified it as a medium length run – but on this particular day for no apparent reason I had only taken out 8oz of fluid, and having drunk that I proceeded to get lost – and it was an exceedingly hot day. In the end I ran over fifteen miles and, upon return to my sister's house, I projectile vomited into the drain in her garden. She put me to bed in her spare room, I slept for two hours, woke up and projectile vomited again all over the wall. This continued for about ten hours. Thankfully my sister saw the funny side!

Over the next few months, I got stronger and stronger and eventually felt able to start doing long runs again. I had a few personal hurdles to leap over and the MSc course proved extremely challenging in terms of the difficulty level of some of the work and also the time commitment. I also signed up as a volunteer and committee member on an education project, and for three months this also took up large chunks of my time. Finally I had to write a 20,000 word thesis for my course and after the beginning of September my training almost ground to a halt due to long hours in front of a computer, eating pizza and thinking about EU environmental legislation. Not what was recommended on Justin's training plan and certainly not justifiable as a 'long taper'.

Even so, I feel confident that I have worked extremely hard this year. I know there are people coming to cheer me on who really believe in me, and back me up no matter how many times I screw up. So I'll be going to Barcelona like a badass and will persevere with anything that life throws at me. It hasn't been easy so far, it won't be easy in the race or after the race, but I'm going to get on and do it regardless. It will probably be pretty grim to watch, but I'm pretty sure my supporters will enjoy that. So here's to you, Challenge Barcelona and HURTS. I'm an intrepid adventurer and you're on my hit list.

Epilogue

Nobody said it was going to be easy... and it certainly wasn't. The race itself was a tumultuous event, but one that I will never forget. On the morning, I set out with three of my four dedicated supporters – my husband, my sister and my mum – and we walked to the start together. I felt calm until just before the start, and then whilst waiting in the enclosure to go to the start line started to feel incredibly emotional. Once we hit the water, however, I was comfortable. The sea had been extremely choppy over the previous few days, and relatively speaking was not bad. However, it was very tidal and it became apparent halfway through the swim that we were all moving pretty slowly. I came out of the swim in just under two hours and took my time in transition.

The bike started brilliantly – I saw all of my supporters including my friend Rebeca who ran alongside me as I left T1. On the first lap of the bike course, I was flying. The best moment was being lapped by the male elites – as Tom Lowe flew by I screamed my lungs out for him (I hope I didn't put him off!). He eventually came second overall – a fantastic result.

The second lap of the bike saw a huge amount of wind being whipped up. Thunderclouds gathered very quickly, and before I knew it I was in the middle of one of the most intense storms I have ever seen. I have never cycled through a river before, but that is what I found myself doing. At one point, on an exposed part of the course, I was forced to dismount and walk a few steps, as I physically couldn't generate the power needed to move my bike forward without being blown over. Having ridden through that, I was so happy at the end of the second lap to see my family. I checked the time and knew that I would have enough time and about half an hour extra in hand to complete the third, shorter lap before going onto the marathon. I had paced myself very well, with the goal of simply finishing rather than attempting to get a time – and then my final disaster of this ten-month journey struck.

My family had just cheered me down the hill. I was buzzing, feeling incredible, and whipped around the roundabout to go for the third lap. Suddenly I noticed a human chain across the road, made up of official looking marshals. I realised one of my fellow lab rats was there and had dismounted his bike, as had another competitor who I had been racing for the last ninety minutes or so. I stopped and dismounted. I asked what was going on, knowing the answer already in my heart, and being aware that there were at least ten to fifteen people still behind us on the course. We were stragglers, but we were not out of time. The course had been shut by the Spanish police, due to the increased risk and danger caused by flooding.

I was absolutely devastated. Some of the HURTS supporters were there and I openly sobbed into the arms of one of them. My own supporters came running down the hill and were dismayed to find the decision that had been made.

Nobody said it was going to be easy.

Two more HURTS lab rats had joined us by this stage and were equally distraught. But because there were four of us together we managed, somehow, with the help of our utterly amazing supporters, to pull our chins back up. We resolved to get back onto our bikes and finish the race. We cycled back to T2, giving the bad news to two further groups of HURTS supporters on our way. They cheered us and encouraged us to keep going. It would have been hard to do if we hadn't been in a group of four, but we forced ourselves to change in T2 – a slow change, because we were so upset – and start off

Perseverance with a smile: here comes IRONLADY 'Jodie'.

on the marathon. We resolved to stay together, and we ran the first few laps as a group of four and then split into pairs.

Every time I ran past Alex, the CEO of Harrison's Fund, I thought about his words a few days earlier – he said that he kept putting one foot in front of the other because it was easy when he thought of his son, Harrison, suffering from Duchenne Muscular Dystrophy. Every time we ran past our supporters they made an enormous racket and buoyed us up no end. Rebeca took the "Go Jodie" banner that my mum and sister had made and danced alongside us with it, making everybody around us laugh. Eventually, having redefined my own personal understanding of the word *Perseverance*, we crossed the finish line as a group. The first person I saw was Kimberley, who put a medal round my neck and gave me a huge hug. Justin was there as well, looking a little bit like a proud dad. And my wonderful family, who had supported me for fifteen hours solidly, came to collect me and see me back to the hotel.

Perseverance was certainly the word for my day.

The Message: Perseverance is a path of pain. You take it not because it is your preferred choice, but because you want something that is worth all the pain.

CHAPTER 7

"Renaissance" *By Andrew Cox*

ren·ais·sance
A rebirth or revival
A revival of intellectual or artistic achievement and vigour
The period of such a revival.

It's three days before 'the big day' and my legs are so smooth I can't help but stroke them. Nature intended that I should be a hirsute man, and increasingly so with age. For some reason hair is no longer reserved for the areas that my school biology textbooks indicated but instead has begun sprouting from new, illogical locations. There can be no sensible explanation for why the top of my ears suddenly require the addition of special, long hairs or why my eyebrows need to grow to a length where I could plait them.

I can obviously no longer trust nature's decision making about my hair location, length and density so, in the last few weeks, I've taken matters into my own hands. As a result, three days out from my first ironman triathlon, and courtesy of a well-known brand of female razors, my legs are smoother now than at any time since I was first born.

Leg shaving seems to be a rite of passage for male cyclists and triathletes and I figured that if I was going to take part in this ridiculous pursuit I might as well do it properly. I was more than a little self-conscious when I first revealed my new spindly, sparrow legs to the world. Shaving had a definite thinning effect even on my already chopstick-like legs. (*I tried to search for a better description of what they were actually like previously but searching 'thin and hairy' on Google gave me some enlightening, but not entirely relevant results*).

But that's not to say I didn't like them. In fact, I'd go as far as to say that having a (vaguely) legitimate excuse to shave my legs has been one of the unexpected advantages of ironman training. I find the new streamlined look strangely appealing, and simultaneously feel a bit disturbed by the narcissistic tendencies I seem to have developed. This yin and yang of self-love and self-loathing seems to be a healthy attribute in a potential ironman but this isn't really how I'd anticipated it manifesting itself.

More importantly, it's not only to the touch that I feel like a different person to the one I was two years ago. I've barely had time to think about it until the last twenty-four hours but the transformation has been dramatic. The training has given each day more purpose and structure and given me a reason, and the enthusiasm, to get up before our milk has been delivered. It's not been easy but it has been worth it, whatever the outcome on the day. Although I'm still not sure my wife agrees.

The Catalyst

I started on the path towards an ironman at about 10:30 am on a Friday morning in March.

I had expected tears that day, but I hadn't expected them to be mine. And I hadn't expected them to be so completely uncontrollable. A wave of incomprehensible emotion had engulfed me, compressed me and released me, all within a split second. It was like nothing I had felt before. My cheeks had been instantly coated with deep tracks of salty water that had been driven irresistibly upwards from somewhere deep inside of me that I had never before seen or felt. They were visceral and animal, and definitely not manly.

But in an instant the mood of the room had changed. Where had all these people emerged from? A sudden realisation that there could be a problem overtook me. My emotions had spun like a ragdoll in a washing machine. My head felt too heavy for my shoulders and I panicked that perhaps I had misread the situation originally. The tears had stopped flowing and suddenly gripped tight, clinging to my eyelashes and my cheeks awaiting permission to continue their fall. I must have looked like a badly-painted clown.

I steadied myself, regained my balance and pulled my back up straight, as if to attention. Through bloodshot eyes I stared across the room, and through the deep, powerful silence. With my chest still tightening and oxygen still prevented from my lungs I stood upright, at least externally, while all the time praying that things would be fine.

But a muffled noise was all it took. Like a conductor rousing an orchestra the cry lifted the straightjacket from around me and my senses were dramatically restored.

A louder cry this time. And the atmosphere across the whole room lifted.

"Are you going to tell the mother what it is?"

The swaddling, inescapable tightness of breath disappeared as I exhaled loud and long with all the elegance of an elephant hailing the herd. I stared hard at the most beautiful, ugly thing I had ever seen.

"*It's a girl*" I said, almost unable to complete the words. My face was awash with the tears I'd been holding back. I was blubbering like a teenage girl in the middle of her first breakup.

I had a daughter.

The next few hours vividly etched themselves in to my consciousness. Tiredness, relief, joy and love overwhelmed me, and gradually I regained a bit of composure. Despite not having slept for more than thirty hours and having every part of me ache with tiredness, I could feel that a mysterious inner clock had been reset. The flood of emotions and hormones made it feel as if I had been switched off and then back on again. It was as if my batteries had been replaced. It was as if I myself had been reborn and I had another chance.

I cuddled my wife and my first child, and I cried a bit more.

When I went home alone on that March night, in the few minutes before I fell asleep, I realised that a couple of other things had come wrapped up in that little bundle that were to carve their own imprint on me. I discovered that, despite my previous very real concerns, I suddenly knew I could support a family. I could feel inside that things would work out for us. I knew there would be bumps in the road ahead, of course, but I was confident that nothing would be insurmountable. Now we'd taken the first step and we were on our way. I realised that I'd had no need to be afraid.

I also discovered that I had hopes and aspirations for my new daughter. I had dreams for her future and I was sure that anything that she wanted to achieve was within her grasp. I saw all of the opportunities in the world were open to her. Anything was possible for her.

And then the light bulb went on.

If anything's possible for her, why not for me?

The First Step

It had been a dank, grey October day, and the little brightness the sun had managed to provide had now disappeared for the night. From my desk on the fourth floor of an unremarkable office building in a forgettable town I stared at my reflection in the window. The view was not pleasant, but it didn't lie.

My hair was ruffled and my eyes were withdrawn and sad, and it looked like I had jowls. I stared a bit more closely. I definitely had jowls. When did they appear? And was that the emergence of another chin? I moved my head from side to side and flexed my jaw up and down and concluded it was definitely a second chin, and at the wrong angle possibly even a third. I sighed and stopped looking.

I hadn't been physically fit before my daughter's arrival but in the space of eight months I had dramatically metamorphosed in to half-man, half-bean bag. I readjusted my sitting position and tugged my trousers up by the belt. They groaned in their attempts to contain my burgeoning waistline. I felt like my whole body was corroding in front of my eyes. On my floor of the office the cleaners had just finished their evening rounds, the air conditioning had been switched off and I couldn't see anyone else still working. I still had mountains of unfinished work to do but months of sleep deprivation meant that all I wanted to do was sleep.

Since March of that year I had been experiencing the strange contradiction that many new parents feel. The preceding months, weeks, days and minutes had been the most painful and most joyful of my life. This is perhaps one of the most obvious examples to prove that things that are worth doing tend not to be easy. I don't mean this to suggest that things had been unusually tough for us. On the contrary, as far as I could tell we'd been lucky. Our daughter was developing well, was fit and healthy and every day was doing something new. Every minor achievement was a major milestone that felt like celebrating. She was a joy to spend time with… except at night.

But it wasn't just at night I was adjusting to a new world. Outside of work my waking hours were now suddenly consumed with first-world, middle-class concerns that could only make you sound dull to anyone except other new parents. I was boring myself talking about house prices, will writing, the flexibility of IKEA's PAX modular storage system, the cost of children's birthday parties or which brand of nappies suits your child best. I love my family but I had a desperate, screaming, overwhelming desire for more.

As I sat at my desk I rubbed my eyes and, despite my tiredness, resolved to myself that I wouldn't be sitting here in a year's time feeling the same way. I thought back to that day in March and remembered how I'd thought that anything was possible. I recalled thinking that I'd been given another chance to do something special, and then pondered why I'd done so little about it. I thought to myself that all I needed was some focus and to take the first step.

I flicked from my email to the internet and searched for 'marathons'. I had struggled through a marathon ten years previously, and had always thought I could go back and do much better. It wouldn't have been hard to beat my previous effort, and by training a bit more sensibly I could probably do a reasonable time. So a marathon seemed an obvious choice. It wasn't earth shattering or phenomenally novel, but it was both ambitious and achievable. Something I would need to throw myself into, find a way to motivate myself, and as a result drink less and eat better.

I scanned several sites and quickly discovered a large number of local marathons. However, the more I looked the more my enthusiasm seemed to dwindle. I went from immediate excitement to complete trepidation in a couple of minutes. This wasn't the sort of attitude that was going to carry me 26.2 miles. The negative part of my subconscious was screaming at me. "You can't, you won't and you shouldn't! You look like a blancmange, you can't get up in the morning without four cups of coffee and your family need you around more not less!"

As I read about more marathons I came up with more reasons not to do them. Foremost amongst these seemed to be that if I was going to do this I wanted to be part of a big occasion. I tried to convince myself that if I had still been able to get in to the London Marathon I'd definitely have applied, but a local event simply might not be enough of an experience, and certainly not as good a day out for the rest of the family.

I was wavering. I started to think I should just finish for the night and go home. A good night's sleep was probably what I needed. Instead, I discounted marathons and considered triathlons. I naively reasoned that it might be easier doing a bit of three different events rather than a whole lot of one. I liked cycling or perhaps more accurately I liked bikes. Or more accurately still I liked staring at beautiful bicycles. I looked at a few triathlon websites and got the details for several events. They all seemed quite expensive so I knew I wasn't going to sign up for many, already leaving myself some wiggle room and excuses not to actually do anything.

On my trawl I also saw a small advert for a research study in to long-distance triathlons. It caught my attention because it was taking place at the local university, and also because I thought you'd have to be totally insane to sign up to something like that. I looked a bit more at the details and it still seemed a ridiculous thing to do, but there seemed like there would be support and guidance. Whenever I'd done anything in the past I'd pretty much done my own thing and just rolled up, so maybe I was more capable than I realised. And besides what harm could it do to register my interest for the selection process? So that's what I did.

I didn't think I would be selected and a part of me definitely hoped I wouldn't be. But I felt slightly virtuous for even taking the crazy step of applying. And with the glow of having thought about doing something difficult I decided that was enough for one evening. I didn't sign up for any events at all.

I switched off my computer and went home. And for a few days, I didn't really think anything more about it. My grand renaissance was off to a somewhat hesitant and inauspicious beginning.

The Revival

I'm not a great believer in fate or coincidence, but sometimes, when you take the first step, it feels as if the stars and planets align to mysteriously support you. For me, as New Year approached, two things came together to help give me a new start. Firstly, my daughter decided she was no longer nocturnal and started to sleep through the night and secondly, I got selected for the study. Contemplating doing an ironman still seemed foolish but suddenly I felt human again and also had a wider project that I felt I couldn't let down. It seemed strange, that despite embarking on something that is so personal and individual, letting myself down worried me less than letting down others.

I think I have been dealt a good hand in life and feel a little guilty that I've wasted talents and opportunities that a more driven individual could have turned to better use. If I was going to become an Ironman, I needed to stop procrastinating and finding excuses and push myself harder. By joining a programme that was about more than just me it made it infinitely more difficult for me to let myself down.

So I'd got to this point partly by dreaming, partly through

luck, and partly as a result of losing my grip on reality and taking that first small step of registering my interest. From being scared of applying for marathons I'd somehow entered myself into an ironman instead. But I was still at the stage where I'd been thinking of swimming and cycling and running rather than actually doing it. Although I now felt, both physically and mentally, that I was capable of something more actually proving it required me to invest some effort and to commit fully.

More onerously, it also required my family to commit to it too. Even accounting for the fact I didn't really appreciate what I was letting myself in for; I had dramatically underplayed what was involved to my wife, Louisa. As I started to understand precisely what was required of me, I started to panic, more in fear of telling her than in actually putting myself though the training. I hadn't expected to be selected, and thought that if that was the case there was no need to worry her unnecessarily. To me, missing out wouldn't be a problem; I would just have to find another route to pull me out of the physical rut I had been in. I could achieve my renaissance through all sorts of means. Once I found out that I had been invited to join the study, my excitement was tempered completely by the thought of having to explain to Louisa the real scale of what I, or more accurately we, were letting ourselves in for.

In retrospect I probably didn't choose the best time or best way to tell her. Inviting her on 'holiday' to Barcelona at eleven o'clock at night after a stressful day at work, and then revealing my ulterior motive backfired. Her initial reaction to what I was telling her was disbelief. She thought I was joking, and when she discovered I wasn't she looked at me as if I'd just deliberately run over her cat. She was fuming and launched into an attempt to veto it. And that was pretty much her stance for the following week. Her view, quite legitimately, was that when you've got a family you should agree these things together.

I had to work to prove to her that I really wanted to do it and, more importantly, that we'd be able to survive at home and that I wouldn't derelict my duties to my daughter. This was tough, but hardened my resolve. It also left me in no doubt that I was going to have to find a balance that worked for all of us. I knew that I would be walking a tightrope across a deep ravine with people pulling at me from all directions. I was in no doubt that working fifty hours a week, being responsible for a child under two between six and nine every weekday morning, fitting in the training hours and maintaining relationships with friends and family was going to be tough.

Louisa finally acquiesced. "You had better enjoy it," she said with a slightly aggressive undertone.

Her initial reticence, or perhaps more accurately opposition, meant that I had to grab this chance with both hands. I didn't know if I'd ever have the opportunity again, and it looked like I'd already cashed in all brownie points I'd ever earned. I decided I'd enjoy Christmas and then the first of January was going to mark the beginning of a new chapter in my life. The last couple of chapters in my story had been dramatic and thrilling but things very much seemed to happen to me rather than be instigated by me. I was tremendously proud of what had happened but I was very much the supporting actor rather than the lead role. I was determined that the next entry would focus on my own revival.

So with my wife now press-ganged in as the head of my support crew I started to tell other people what I was attempting. At this point, even before I had started training, it all started to become real. January came around and I started running. Not very far and not very quickly, but every step was another step in the right direction. And I started swimming, slowly. And eventually I started cycling, indoors. And, with a plan laid out in front of me, I didn't really think further ahead than what I was doing at that moment.

In the same way that I can't really comprehend the enormity of the universe, I think the scale of the distances involved meant I protected myself from them by largely ignoring them. In the early months of my training the thought of running a half-marathon seemed like an obscene amount of effort and that I'd rather be in bed. By comparison the scale of an ironman was quite literally inconceivable to me. As a result, I stopped thinking about the grand goal and focused instead on surviving the day or perhaps the week ahead. Most of my thinking time was only done late on a Sunday night while I laid out all the clothes I needed for the following week on our spare bed, which now resembled a sportswear jumble sale.

There were initially some significant positives for me from starting from a relatively low base. It was easy to see some dramatic changes month-on-month. The initial impact was a fairly substantial weight loss. I didn't see any real improvement in the times I was achieving but I did feel a lot less like a Teletubby. When days seemed hard I had one particular photo of me that I used to look out. Taken on a visit to the Eden Project the previous year, my stomach was bulging embarrassingly out of a t-shirt, which had once swamped me, making it look like I was the one who was now expecting a baby. This was the shock therapy that reinforced the progress I had made, and it made plodding through the snow in a bitterly cold February infinitely more tolerable.

Other people were also starting to notice the change. In March one of my colleagues kindly informed me, "I remember when you used to look kind of thin and athletic, before you got fat. You're looking a bit more in shape again". Maybe not a full renaissance yet, but I was certainly undergoing a bit of a revival.

Each passing month brought new challenges and successes, and a rollercoaster of ups and downs. The early months were characterised by snow and rain, sore knees and shins, and improving distances. The middle months were memorable for increasingly early starts and what seemed like a continuous cycle of daily diaries, tests or samples that I needed to provide for the University. And somewhere in amongst this, almost imperceptibly, my outlook changed. Steadily, week-by-week my training had changed from something to do, to something I do.

Psychologically, training had become something that I felt compelled to fit in. I hated missing sessions and was doing all I could to shave minutes out of everything else in my life to try and manufacture more time for training. It became normal behaviour to wear my swimming trunks or running kit under my work clothes to try and save myself a couple of minutes when getting changed for a lunchtime session. I was becoming a different person.

I remember a previous boss telling me that if he wanted a task done quickly he allocated it to the busiest person. This seemingly absurd strategy had been working well for a few months. The busier I got the more I achieved. I was getting more done, more quickly at work, training and at home. I was still managing to work ten hours a day, commute and look after my daughter every morning but I had absolutely no contingency built in to this.

Then we discovered my wife was pregnant again and when Louisa succumbed to fairly debilitating morning sickness, and more was required of me at home, inevitably something had to give. In retrospect it was unsurprising it was my health. I was trying to be the perfect employee, husband, father and athlete and I couldn't cope. For several weeks in the middle training blocks of my plan I became too ill to train, or at least to train properly. Every time, my training plan indicated a recovery week I would get horribly ill. There was a particularly bad period of a couple of weeks where the wheels truly came off and my whole body collapsed in protest. I had gastro problems, flu and several huge mouth ulcers. I couldn't eat, sleep or exercise. I felt like a failure, both to myself and to my family. For the first time since I'd started training I thought about the enormity of what I was trying to accomplish and began to worry that I had bitten off more than I could chew. Part of what I'd wanted to experience was pushing myself to the very edge of what I could achieve. I'd reached that limit and kept going. It should have been no surprise I fell off a cliff.

After a few weeks of significantly disrupted training, I was starting to really feel the fear. I tried to keep my game face on, but I couldn't see how I could keep going like this. It was only partly down to me that I pulled through. Again two things really helped me. I was given some advice around my diet that seemed to solve some of my stomach issues and Louisa also got past the fourteen week point in the pregnancy and started to feel better. She had a bit more energy and was able to give me a bit more slack around training. It reinforced what I should have known any way. Although this was a very personal renaissance it simply wasn't going to be possible without the support of others.

I also had to change my own mindset. I was never under the illusion that I was going to win the event but now I was approaching it as though I wasn't even going to compete. My aim was to complete. I wanted to do the best I could but it was more important that I trained well when I could and kept healthy. It was no good to anyone if I broke myself by trying to be everything to everyone. Steadily I recovered from my various ailments and refocused on training with balance.

I totted up sensible predictions for each of the segments, and was confident if I could stay on an even keel that, although I wouldn't pull up any trees, I could comfortably beat the broom wagon. For seasoned athletes this may seem like a very limited ambition but even so, while trying to more successfully balance training with the rest of my life, I still couldn't always keep up. More than once I drove to the swimming pool before turning off the engine and going to sleep in the back of the car rather than going for a swim.

These restorative siestas probably served me well and between early August and October my training continued on an upward path. I was hitting targets again and, for the most part, enjoying myself. Training on my own for sessions of less than two hours has never been a problem, but I struggled without company on the longer sessions. The few sessions throughout all my training that I've genuinely hated were all long ones where I had no company. While this is a selfish pursuit my experience of the long sessions highlighted that it wasn't just at home where I needed the support of others. Getting up before five o'clock in the morning to cycle for eight hours with no company riding a bike with a toothpick for a saddle left me both physically and emotionally scarred. After a particularly harrowing session, I had a bit of a breakdown and threw away an expensive saddle in a fit of frustration. I'm not a violent person but if I'd had a golf club handy I would have wrapped it around a tree.

Although the training, for the most part, was heading in the right direction it must have become more of a chore for Louisa. I'd have understood if she had been upset about me disappearing for most of the day at the weekend, or needing rescuing hours from home when I ran out of spare tubes, or obsessing over the food we ate but that wasn't the case. The support has always been there when I needed it most and I am incredibly grateful. What has left me slightly perplexed is quite how much the smaller things seem to have eaten away at her. Louisa's top gripes seem to be about my wetsuit hanging in our shower like a 'criminal from the gallows', our spare room overtaken by piles of 'spangly-dangly lycra', and my 'ridiculous, lady legs'.

If a renaissance can be characterised as a revival of learning and vigour, by September I had certainly entered in to a period of personal renaissance. I felt fit and healthy and with three events to conquer was voraciously reading anything that looked like it could help shave seconds off any of my times. I was obsessing over equipment, gadgets, techniques, nutrition and psychology. And as the taper in the programme kicked in and I had a bit more time outside of training I started to wonder what I had been doing with my life prior to ironman training. I must have wasted so much time! Already I was thinking about what my next plan should be once this was over. I know I'll have my hands full with the new baby for a bit but maybe I can do a marathon next year…

And here I am three days before the event, still stroking my legs. I'm fixated with what that minor ache in my right knee is, obsessing over what food I should be eating and trying not to waste any energy. I've been avoiding caffeine for a few weeks but this morning I'm shaking like I've been mainlining espresso. I'm nervous about the unknown, but mostly I don't want to let anyone down. My daughter gave me the courage to attempt this, my wife has supported me to train for it, I followed a programme put together by the University and I just had to put the miles in. I'll get the glory and the bragging rights, but they carried me here.

Part of me, a very large part of me, is still saying that this is the most stupid thing I've ever signed myself up for. But the bigger part of me is telling me that I know this is possible. I've

Flying to the finish: Andrew 'Ironman' Cox

taken the opportunity that everyone's given me and already in training I've achieved things I'd have never thought I was capable of. I know there will be bumps in the road ahead, of course, but thanks to the support of others I am confident that nothing will be insurmountable.

The Message: If you think you're capable of something more, don't just dream about it, go out and prove it.

CHAPTER 8

"Iron-Research" *By Craig Suckling, Georgia Peedle & Joe Murphy*

Eight o'clock Sunday mornings are best spent under a duvet or eating a leisurely breakfast, but this Sunday was different. I'm stood on the beach of Calella, a Spanish town 58km Northeast of Barcelona with fellow research testers Joe Murphy and Georgia Peedle. In front of us are some 1300 wetsuit-clad triathletes who are about to start an iron-distance triathlon; ahead of them a 3.8km sea swim, 180km bike ride and a 42.2km run. Somewhere in the mass of black rubber and multi-coloured swim caps are some seventy men and women about to undertake this mammoth challenge for the first time, the air horn sounds... *they are off.*

So why do three research students from the University of Hertfordshire, have such an interest in these iron-distance 'virgins'? The reason is simple. Dr Justin Roberts. Towards the end of our first year Justin told us that he was planning a research project around recreationally-active people training for their first ultra-endurance event. This was going to be a unique study, nothing had been attempted on this scale, or in this area before, and we had the opportunity to be involved. Signing up was the proverbial no brainer, little did we know much that '**yes**' would shape the next year of our lives. So why had we agreed to take part in the study? However you look at the reasons, they are all selfish; what would the study do for us, how we would benefit, and what we would gain from being involved?

The plan was to recruit active men and women who had not completed an iron-distance triathlon, train them over a nine-month period, and study how they adapted over that time. We would look at physiological adaptations, nutrition, biomechanics, functional movement, psychology and immunology. I committed myself to two aspects of the research, physiology and nutrition; Georgia and Joe due to their rugby commitments, the nutrition only. The project was given little thought as first year exams came and went, as did summer holidays. Returning to the second year the research was definitely going ahead, subjects had been recruited from the masses that had responded to the advert asking for volunteers; at this point we had the option of taking on the challenge, an option that was politely declined.

We were involved from the very start, designing the food and training diaries that the subjects so enjoyed completing, questionnaires that awaited every lab visit and taking part in pilot testing so that we knew exactly the procedures we would use. A large part of our degree is our third year research project and this gave us a fantastic insight into how research is set up – and just how much work was involved long before we saw a subject. *I told you we were selfish!* However, by the end of 2012 everything was in place, and testing would start in the New Year.

The testing was split into two parts: Phase One, which ran from January to June, and Phase Two, which ran from July to September. During Phase One the subjects would be tested four times. Testing blocks usually ran for three days at a time from nine till four. During these blocks the subjects undertook a battery of tests: body composition, heart tests, a functional movement assessment, three biomechanical tests including running economy, a lactate profile and VO_{2max} tests. Although the class practicals and coursework had given me the skills to complete these tests, this was the first time I'd tested subjects from outside the student population; this time the results had meaning. The next two months training would be influenced by the data collected, would I sink or swim?

If I am honest I swam, but it was doggy paddle on the first day, I'd taken more body composition measurements and more capillary blood samples in one day than I had in my whole time at the university. Actually all the testing team were in the same boat, in fact the only people in the lab more nervous than the testers were the subjects. It was tiring but rewarding and by the end of the first block of testing my doggy paddle was now the front crawl with tumble turns.

Throughout blocks two and three the interaction between both groups improved and we got to know each other, the loud ones, the quiet ones, the confident ones, the shy ones and those who hid behind a persona. The testing was intense and despite being pushed to the max and having fingers turned to pin cushions during lactate tests; there was one area that caused the greatest interest, worry and disappointment – body composition and body fat percentage.

Any of you who know Justin will know that he likes to throw his students a curveball, here it came and this one had mine, Joe and Georgia's name on: "I want you guys to run the nutrition analysis". So we did. That'll be something to add on the CV! (*another reason why it was good for us to be involved*). We collated the diaries, and we organised the students to help and booked a study suite, let the data entry begin.

The ironmen and women in training had been recording all their food and beverage intake during the training (following specific instructions), all we had to do was input the info into a detailed software press report and 'hey presto', a nutritional breakdown would appear. I'm sure that is a source of great comfort to those involved that the diaries were only identifiable by their research number; it also means there is no need to change the names to protect the guilty!!! It would be fair to say that most of the subjects have handwriting that makes a doctor's look legible. The joker whose entry was '*Curry*', the creatures of habit with their '*Whopper Wednesday*' (*you know who you are*) and the 'athlete' who became an instant cult hero with the following entry:

- Saturday Breakfast: Blank.
- Saturday Mid-morning snack: Blank.
- Saturday Lunch: Blank.
- Saturday Mid-afternoon snack: Blank
- Saturday evening meal: eight pints of lager and a KFC.

The nutrition analysis has to date taken in the region of 400 hours and will support a significant number of scientific papers, and if nothing else if the three of us ever entertain any of the participants in the study we will know exactly what to cook.

Apart from his curve balls, Justin loves to 'raise the bar' and Phase Two did just that. The testing consisted of each participant completing a one-hour time trial, with various measurements being taken at given points. During block one we had tested in teams of three looking after one subject, now we were testing two athletes simultaneously on our own; no pressure then! The pressure was on, could we deliver? Would our skills be good enough and smooth enough so the test ran without a problem? The resounding answer was **YES**, the whole of Phase Two went smoothly – a reflection on how everyone involved had progressed and developed.

Phase Two also included a small study on how training affected food absorption. This required some of the subjects arriving early in the morning with a urine sample, 'donating' two more blood samples and downing a sweet sickly sugar drink. Over the next five hours they were free to do as they pleased with only the minor inconvenience of collecting all their urine, so we sent them on their way with large brown bottles complete with bright yellow lids for the purpose. I'm sure that knowing that we would be measuring the volume and drawing off a sample for analysis influenced the group decision to provide the warmest freshest samples possible!!!

The final testing took place a week before the race; the journey was almost complete and in seven days seventy men and women who for a myriad of different reasons replied to an advert would be on the start line for an iron-distance triathlon. Standing in the performance testing laboratory at the University it was clear that we were desperate for them to achieve their dreams, we had developed huge respect for every single one of them; the selfish reasons that had drawn us to this project had vanished, we were just proud to be associated with such a hardworking, dedicated group.

And herein lies the lure of IRONMAN.

We arrived in Calella on the Friday afternoon after a cheeky Stadium tour of the 'Nou Camp', well – 'all work and no play' as they say! Justin had arranged a cohort briefing at a hotel for 7pm. The apprehension was tangible in the room as Justin spoke, advice, details of timings of registration, racking of bikes etc. Alex, CEO of Harrison's Fund took the floor. He spoke about his son Harrison, and how when he was going to be hurting on Sunday he knew he would finish because all he had to do was put one foot in front of the other and that was easy; something that at some point in the future Harrison would be unable to do. The room broke into spontaneous applause; tears were subtly wiped from eyes. The rallying cry for Sunday was born, "one foot in front of the other". As the meeting broke up messages of luck, words of encouragement and promises of beers at the Oktoberfest were exchanged; we left them with their thoughts and final preparations.

The alarm woke us on Race day, opening the curtains revealed blue sky and pale sunshine, perfect spectating conditions, the weatherman was wrong, T-shirt and shorts were the order of the day, would it be a decision we would live to regret. We ran through our strategy: Start, Breakfast, Transition, Coffee, Bike, Lunch, Bike, Chill out at the hotel, Run, Dinner, and Finish, sorted we were ready. The first three parts of the plan went like clockwork, although we had a warning of what was to unfold as we walked to a café for breakfast, walking parallel to the beach we could see the elite men on their swim, hang on they're swimming faster than we were walking. That's insane! The transition area between the swim and the run was our first chance to lend support and we saw most of 'our guys' through as the number of bikes waiting for their riders like faithful dogs dwindled, it was time for us to move onto the bike course, we were on strategy and feeling great, so far so good.

We set ourselves up near a roundabout where the riders would turn on their loops of the bike course, two for the price of one on vocal encouragement… perfect. The bike leg is arguably the most impressive part of a triathlon from a spectator's point of view. Hi-tech triathlon bikes can be heard before they are seen and make a sound that is best compared to a TIE Fighter from the *Star Wars* films, they are ridden at impressive speeds by their lycra-clad pilots; it has to be said that our athletes did not look out of place on the course either in technique or the quality of their machinery. Our encouragement received smiles, thumbs up, high fives and even an impressive kissing of the guns!!! We interpreted this is as "I'm feeling strong", but it could have been showboating. We were now six hours into our race, the strategy had gone west, leaving was not an option we knew what we had to do and we were going to do it. A quick pit stop for food was required so we retreated to the café for a bikini (*Spanish for cheese and ham toasties before you ask*) and a coffee.

Refuelled, we headed to the marathon course. While the bike may be the greatest spectacle the run is the easiest in terms of supporting. The speeds are less, and identifying people is easier when they are shorn of helmets and sunglasses. We found a good vantage point and began supporting our guys; we would only find out later how much of an influence this would have. The course was a 10.5km loop completed four times, so the runners past us twice on each loop, as they filed past they were all looking strong. Nine months of hard work and commitment were paying off. We couldn't move, transfixed in a heady mix of admiration and pride, but also a fear that if we weren't in that location we would change their perception of how the run was going. It was captivating.

We had now passed the ten-hour mark and we had to take on more sustenance, the restaurants of Calella serve good food but the service would not be described as speedy, there was only one option McDonalds; we were in and out in record time, while learning that a Big Mac meal in Spain is cheaper than a Quarter Pounder meal. It was time to head to the finish, provide those final words of encouragement to those who still had laps to complete and congratulate those who were finishing. It was during these final stages that the "one foot in front of the other" mantra really paid off; it put a spring in the step, an extra determination, and even the odd smile.

As time passed more and more finishers crossed the line all remembered Justin's advice of enjoy that moment; some of the celebrations were spontaneous, some shared with loved ones, but each one truly deserved. During the final push, and we don't know how or when we had started to cross the finishers off a mental list, we knew who was left on the course and how many laps they had left; we waited around the finish area like the parents of teenagers anxiously waiting for them to return from a night out.

The sun had long set, fireworks had illuminated the night sky and faded, and the numbers were down to single figures, we were now milling around on the red carpet that led to the finish line, our race not yet complete. A party atmosphere had taken over at the finish line by the head of the Spanish Triathlon (who is best described as a smaller version of Omid Djalili), who must be sponsored by Oakley that can be the only excuse for wearing sunglasses at midnight! He led the singing and even the full 'greased lightning' dance routine. As the last of the finishers approached the finish they were greeted by a human arch to run through for the last 100m while being cheered long and loud. That was it, the race was done we had seen them home, oblivious to the time we headed towards the hotel that we'd left at 7:15am. It was now 2:15am, we'd been on the course for nineteen hours but we were 'high' on admiration, respect and what is best described as a form of parental pride for every single one of the subjects. We were so tired! Spectating is definitely a hard core iron-level 'sport'!

We spent most of Monday testing some of the subjects as part of the study; it was the evening we waited for; Oktoberfest and time to deliver on the promises of beer made on the Friday night. Three things happened in the beer tent that night which we will remember for a lifetime. An impromptu conga with the oompah band, despite blistered feet and aching legs, was the first. The second was totally humbling as we attempted to make good on Friday night's promise; we were told that we were the ones who were owed a beer. "No way!" flashed through our minds. We haven't trained for nine months, maintained a family life, held down a full-time job; we haven't just swam 3.8km, ridden 180km and run 42km; all we did was stand there shouting and getting rained on.

We definitely weren't expecting such thanks, but to be told "When I thought I couldn't go on and I was just about to quit I hobbled around the corner and you guys were there believing in me, cheering me, telling me I was strong enough, without you I wouldn't have finished". Even writing this now, it is embarrassing to think that we deserve any credit; it was a privilege to help. The third came much later; the bars had all shut, our glasses were but empty. The tent was empty apart from our group – oh and the waiting staff sitting, smoking, and wishing we'd go home. We had shared a journey and we were prolonging that journey as long as we could. We deserved to.

So the race is run and the testing is over, although we have reams of data to analyse and papers to write it is a good time to reflect on the experience. It has been amazing, we have been given a great opportunity, our skills have improved exponentially, and they have been tested and passed the test. We have learned new skills, problem solved; we have worked with athletes who ask questions that students don't. They are not overly concerned what the science is just "what does that mean to me and my training or performance".

We have learned that data is just numbers, unless you question it and use it correctly. We have learned to reflect on everything we do, what has gone well and what we could improve. We are more organised, and concentrate more on detail. We have learned to work in teams with people that we have only just met, to trust their skills and ability. The greatest benefit we will take away from the whole process is an edge;

all things being well we should graduate this summer along with several thousand other sports and exercise students around Britain. All of us will be competing for jobs, but now we have a unique selling point our involvement with this study, which has added value to our degrees.

We entered this study for selfish reasons. Slowly and surely we became immersed, without realising we were drawn in to the world of ultra-endurance; we are now part of the extended family, as we haven't completed an iron-distance event (*although it has been added to three bucket lists*). We are like the second cousins you only see at weddings, but family none the less. And so, we have followed your iron-adventure by taking on our own iron-journey. And along this journey we have come to discover respect and admiration for the people who put themselves on the line for science. We have been blessed with your inspiration. In the words of Vinnie Jones "*it's been emotional*".

Georgia, Joe and Craig: Another day in testing paradise

The Message: Embrace a challenge, test yourself, and never underestimate the influence you have; you can do this, you're better than you realise.

CHAPTER 9

"Discovery" *By Jamie Payne*

An Ironman's journey encompassing Tourette's, toilet paper, Mobility trollies and titanium.

My Race:

"Water" shouted the aide-station worker clearly.

"No banana" I replied, as I passed him at speed.

I focused in on the banana man stretching out my right arm to snatch the half brownish squidgy banana. Sounds appetising, NOT. Trust me at about 160km into the bike leg they taste like nectar.

Bang!!!!!!! The bike twitches under me and I hit the deck hard. **Really hard**. Skidding down the road on my side and hip. Weird when cycling how you always seem to take the fall on your wrists, hips, knees and elbows. The bike doesn't seem to take much impact at all, except the pedal. I feel to the right hand side, the pedal bouncing off the tarmac, and carving a wake trail through the standing water that was now into centimetres of depth on the road surface.

You see I had lost concentration for a moment, and forgotten that the aide-station pattern had been set earlier in the day. Quite predictable in its precision. Three parts to the aid station: – water, gel and banana. As I sped past the water guy, honing in on banana man, gel man stepped right into my path. I swerved to avoid him or her, cannot really recollect. Caught a white line and smashed into the road.

Let me be clear, I am not trying to apportion blame here, just to point out that ironman racing is brutal. One lapse in concentration and it will bite you. And I had just got bitten big time. I lay swearing and screaming in the road for what seemed an eternity. As other bikes swept past. Rather ungraciously spraying me with the rain that flew off their rear wheels. It must have looked a bit like a CSI investigation site. Man lying prone on the floor. Bike a few yards further on. One shoe still on the pedal, one half off the foot. Always a sorry sight at a road accident to see the solitary shoe in the road I feel! Race belt and cycle jersey up over my shoulders and gels all across the road a bit like a game of gel chopsticks. I look at them, count them and bizarrely wonder if I am on or off my nutrition strategy.

A policeman comes over and sits me up with another aide-station worker. I am now in less pain, sat by the roadside 10-20km from Calella just north of Barcelona perched up against an Armco crash barrier. Contemplating a year of training, a year of sacrifice for the family more than me and the prospect of a DNF. Not sure I want to have to tell Julie and the kids I have put them through hell this year and I have not come away with my bit of iron. My ironman medal.

"F#ck that" I think, I am going to get this finished. I try to get up but the policeman says no. He says "just seeett for ten minutes, calm down". His English was excellent and his compassion and common sense obvious and, if I am honest in that emotional state, a bit overwhelming. Didn't even catch his name, but whoever you are fella, thank you. So I oblige. At this stage unaware of any damage that had been done. Adrenalin is a pretty cool thing. Sure my elbow was bleeding, my hip was really badly gashed up and my bike shorts looked like they had spent the night being gnawed on by a guard dog. And I was sat in a 3cm puddle. But somehow my attention was turning to my bike.

Some spectator had gathered it up and wheeled it over to me. I managed to stand. Try to get on and the front crank just spins. Chain is off and I only have one shoe on. "Come on Jamie, get your act together, let's try this again." I tell myself. I get my shoes on properly. I get the chain relocated. Pretty p#ssed off at the scuffed up rear derailleur. And the front bar shifter and brake are banged up. I am lucky enough to have a lovely bike with Di2 shifters. So in my head I am going, '*oh crap, that's a fair few hundred quid's worth of damage*'. In context nothing compared to the cost and damage I will later realise I have done to myself. The frame and wheels are ok, so good to go I think!

My sense of urgency heightening, as I feel time is slipping away. I was heading for T2 in an unexpected 7hr 30 elapsed time. Knowing I can run off the bike a sub four-hour marathon, I was having up until then a great day. An unexpected day really. I obviously am aiming for a finish, it being my first ironman. My target time was to go sub thirteen hours. But reality was, I was nudging 11hrs 30 mins.

We had been watching the Barcelona weather all week. Getting to the stage where it was ridiculous, we all knew at some point in the race it was going to rain. In the days running up to the race, the sea had been really choppy. I remember a warm-up swim where I was with a colleague and I looked up to sight, and the swell had taken her vertically above me. It was like she was standing vertically in front of me. By the morning of the race the sea was reasonably calm and amongst our group there was a palpable difference. A sense of joy and relief. As we got to the beach with sunny weather and a mild sea.

The swim went great. Not my fastest but great in terms of efficiency. I started at the back of the pinkies wave (pink hats for the older gentlemen! I am forty-eight.) Coming from a swim background I gently get in at the back and begin working my way through the pack. Managing my heart rate and breathing. I get caught up behind a few folks from time to time. But tell myself it isn't worth swimming through them. Back off, wait for a gap. It's a bit uneven pace wise for the first 1500m due to traffic. Suddenly I am in clearer water and can begin to just stretch out. Mild sense of euphoria hits me as I exit the water onto the beach. See Julie and the kids, get a quick rinse under the shower. Feeling good into T1. Swim time 1hr 10.

T1 is slow. 18 mins! Bit overwhelmed. No room to move. Tip bag out onto floor. Weather still ok but closing in, so trying to decide what rain gear to take. Take a glug of a small can of coke to wash away salt-water taste, and try and get head around this. Ok full change is the plan. Got a bit of salt chafing from wetsuit. So think change for comfort. Don't want any discomfort around the nether regions on the bike. It's a bit cooler now. So go with tri shorts and vest under cycle jersey and bib shorts. So if race is going well I will just bin cycle shirt and bibs in T2 and get out onto the run. But have a lot of nutrition pre stored in back of cycle jersey. Compression socks on, pick up salt sticks, **go!!!!!!**

Out onto the road, still nice weather, feeling good. Focusing on keeping calm. Getting some gel in and some salt. Check the watch; get nutrition timings glued in your head! Heading out of town, crowd support is awesome, get out of the saddle and start digging into the first hill. Heart rate hits 157. "Calm down you idiot" I tell myself. I sit back down and vow not to let heart rate get over 145 for first lap. It's a two lap 80km course with a shorter out and back final lap.

My friend Katherine catches me on the bike. We chat for a bit and then she pulls away. This is the first test of my resolve. We are quite evenly matched. I am a stronger swimmer, a little stronger on the bike, but she is some awesome runner. I can't stay with her. Big lesson learned, race your pace. Big Neo cruises up too, no point me trying to race him either. We have a good chat about heart rate zones and staying focused and he moves through. Big thanks Neo, your advice pays dividends as I just sit in and tap it out. I know what I can do 85-95 cadence, really trying to stay in my zone. Heart rate 137-145 as I hit the turnaround for lap one. Weather holding. Reasons to believe. Nutrition working well, saltstick every thirty minutes. Energy drink sipping regularly, plenty of water, and taking a banana from the aid stations. I have previously had gut issues, so balancing intake with energy consumption was going to be a race limiter if I get it wrong.

Staying in heart rate zones reach lap one turnaround. This is going ok. Getting deep into lap two and my eye is now on the weather. Rain is imminent, and when it rains we know it's going to REALLY rain! Previous nights it has been a deluge. Feet getting really sore under cleats, feet feel like they are on fire. So when the heavens finally open it's a blessed relief. The cold rain and standing water freeze my feet quickly. I can't feel any pain at all. So we press on. Was hoping to get lap two done before the rain, but sadly not quite.

It becomes comical. The rain is so hard it is bouncing off you. It hurts like hail stones. Going through the towns the standing water is half way up my compression guards on my calves when my leg is extended. All the time praying please God, keep me off the white lines and no punctures. Going through the roundabouts lots of folks are crashing down. Luckily low impact slides though.

One bit of joy is a bunch of pro men go blasting past all on disc wheels. Like a pro peloton. Now it is torrential the marshals have become less visible and there is clearly drafting. They go past as a peloton each rotating off the front. But they hit a hill and slow up, so I get momentary glory as I manage to spin my way back onto them. Down the hill they are gone again.

I finish lap two head out for the last shorter lap. Reach the turnaround. Inside trying to hold concentration, still chasing my T2 target time of 7hr30 elapsed. But inside elated. "I've got this done," I say to myself, "bike leg nailed only 20km to go." If I get in my target time, I can walk the marathon in six hours. I will finish. I will be an ironman. If all keeps going to plan, and I can run well I will be amazing myself.

Beginning to think coach's prophetic target for me was not so unreasonable. At dinner a couple of nights before I had gotten myself in a right state of anxiety. As coach Justin who had tested us to beyond diligence, with a bespoke training programme, VO_2 testing, blood tests, cardio tests, diet assessments, had said I was capable of 11hr 15. As a competitive person, mainly with myself this was playing havoc with my race strategy of just finish, and a good day would be sub thirteen, a brilliant day sub twelve. But thinking in dreamland 11hr 59 etc. Just to nudge under that twelve would just be awesome expression of how far I had come. And now I was working my way towards having strategic options. I had time in hand, so if the wheels came off I could walk in. If it stayed good I could do great. Legs felt fine, nutrition great. Beginning to think T2, let's go for it. No need to change, get cycle gear off, tri gear is underneath. Running shoes on and go. Just remember new pack of salt sticks, race belt pre-loaded with gel. We can do this.

Bang the wheels came off!

So there I was back in the gutter with my policeman friend. 10-15km from T2. I couldn't get my leg over the top tube. But assumed this was just stiffness due to bruising. Policeman offered to call an ambulance. But I said no; just get me on this bike. He and a few helpers practically laid the bike in the road and I clipped in and they lifted me upright, game on. Really was pushing hard now into T2. Wanted to make up time. Trying to concentrate, get another gel in get ready and psyched for run again.

Buzzing again through Calella town, spectators awesome. Slowing now for T2 dismount line. Thinking still going to be in less than eight hours elapsed. Bit sore so run might not be optimal but hey we can still finish. Brake, unclip left, unclip right, OMG pain like you wouldn't believe, come crashing down into a ditch again. Thank God, low speed this time and more of a clumsy tip over type fall. Get helped up and start hobbling to timer chip line. Still hoping to run. But beginning to realise something is wrong. Using bike as a crutch realising leg won't now take weight.

Family and friends arrive and I am still trying to get into transition but it isn't happening. Medics arrive and Ambulance lady says "your hip". I go "yes, badly bruised maybe a tear, just

Jamie 'TITANIUMAN' Payne en route to hospital

badly bruised and swollen." "No" she says, "your hip is broken, the femur should be here, it is now here!" pointing alarmingly close to my leg level with my waistline.

My partner Julie and the kids arrive, around the corner. Due to the adrenalin I appear overly calm and not in too much distress. But as soon as I have to tell her "baby I am so sorry." It's game over, I knew it was done.

They call an ambulance and as I am lying in theatre that evening we hear the fireworks going off to signal the end of the race. Dr Faustino says, "Ah, that is the end of the ironman," I realise it has already ended for me. "Don't worry", he says," I am closing your leg up and **you are a titanium man now**."

Where am I now?

These pages were supposed to be written before the event. But sadly events got past me and since the race, recovery has taken precedence. But now I will start as I originally intended!

As I was sitting in my hotel room about to write these notes, a day before the race, like everyone else here, I thought, what the heck can I tell you, teach you or impart to you about ironman that you have not read already? My kit was spread out on the bed, laid out ready to stuff into the transition bags. I was rehearsing it all in my head. I was then trying to figure out my nutrition strategy and lay all that out too. Sh#t, all that won't fit on the bike. Having been constantly watching the weather and hearing the deluge outside. Having swum in what seemed like twelve foot waves in the afternoon, I was getting into meltdown.

The phone rang, and pizza just over the road with Scott, Camilla his wife, Katherine, Charlie and some of the others seemed like a better option. Avoidance was the strategy and they had given me the perfect get out. Great idea, I needed to eat.

Towards the end of the training and in the run up you may get mixed emotions. A combination of excitement and then massive doubt. Completely overwhelmed, as you try and walk through your strategy and your kit. Especially if variable weather brings you more to think about. It becomes totally consuming. To the point where you begin to lose the joy of it.

This moment will come, when it does step back go out, do something different. But re-connect with the joy. I was going to be going into thirteen hours plus of racing with a mindset of suffering, and overwhelmingness. Not a useful state to be in. At dinner everyone else was feeling the same. They all just wanted to get it over and done with. I knew it was going to hurt, boy with hindsight what an understatement. But I didn't want to just get through it. I had to find joy in it again.

And that for me is part of the enigma of ironman. Reconciling those dualities. Thinking I haven't trained enough, but actually you probably have. And in any rate, you can't control that now. You have trained as much as you have. Some folks didn't even get to the start line.

Whatever you have done isn't enough, but actually it probably is. Because it's what you have done. For sure, I am not saying don't train etc. But realise if you got to the start line, you have achieved a lot already. And nothing more can be done except get your race head on. Whatever that is for you. To race, to finish, but to enjoy!

It will be painful, and it will hurt, but you need to find joy in the moments. And it is humbling. Ironically humility does not seem the natural bedfellow of competitive endurance sport. But it is truly humbling.

My journey

Why did I choose to do an ironman? Honestly I would love to come up with some lovely high-value story about digging deep into my psyche. About understanding who I am. Some kind of self-discovery, demons in my past to reconcile. People have talked about knowing what you are made of or some other highbrow tosh. Sorry, for me none of the above, well not at the start at least. It was really simple. I liked sport and triathlons were a good way of trying to stay fit. I am chasing fifty and felt it was part of my bucket list. Do an ironman before my fiftieth. And honestly I just thought it would be cool to get an M dot tattoo. Nothing more than a bit of bragging rights at the local gym. I have never been the most muscular guy. So an M dot tattoo would at least give me some stock with the body-builder types who look across aghast whilst pumping iron to me sat on the spin bike in the girl's class. Maybe not manly, but potentially ironmanly. BTW, the girls that do cardio at our gym kick ass. They are super-fit athletes.

So all I can impart now are some stories about my journey to ironman Barcelona. Technically, Challenge Barcelona Iron-distance triathlon. So in true triathlon style I will do a swim, bike and run story.

Swim story

My swim story emphasises one central theme. You don't know what you don't know. So be open to learning on your journey. One of my best mates Adrian was doing his first Olympic-distance triathlon. At this time point I had dabbled in a couple of sprints and done very well. As a natural swimmer, I could do a fast swim, bike pretty well and go backwards in the run.

But taking all three disciplines collectively could get quite a good result if things hung together well. On one transition neutral event, I even came second in my age group. So triathlon was catching my attention, as something I could enjoy. I love swimming, like biking, running is a bit boring, but multisport is a great fun way to keep training interesting. So I had read a lot about triathlon, dabbled but not stepped up to anything more major.

As he tends to do, Adrian had stepped things up a level by entering an Olympic at Dorney Lake in Eton. We knew he was like me, good swimmer, ok biker, and going to go backwards on the run. Having a dodgy knee from an old motorcycle accident, and being a chef meant – sorry mate – there was a bit of poundage carriage still going on. So we decided it was go for broke on the swim, lets at least get bragging rights for him smashing the swim, and see what happened after that.

So sure enough after the usual washing machine swim start, the swim pattern emerged. And sure enough at the turn buoy Adrian hit the front. Now what you need to know here is I love Adrian he is one of my best mates. Heart of gold and really decent bloke. But he has had his own challenges in life to overcome, having lost his beloved Hazel to cancer. So his focus on doing this event was fierce as was his resolve. Being a chef, well you know there is also a fiery temper in there.

So he hits the front and begins to kick away. No offence triathletes, but none of that ugly triathlete, upper body muscling and lifting out of the water stuff. Just smooth power. Long stroke fast turnover, great catch and he began to go to his legs. Eight beat leg kick he began to power away. Dropped the pack by 50m. Pool swimmer in a still lake super efficient power delivery. Body roll, the whole bit. Over the commentary team are extolling the virtues of this great swim unfolding. From behind the crash barriers as spectators, we hear them pass over to Richard Stannard on the pontoon who is moved to do a Coleman and say "quite remarkable!"

Adrian hits the pontoon and sets his steely eye on a rapid transition. Goggles and hat disappearing up his fast removing wetsuit sleeve. Richard Stannard moves in with the mic, just to try and say great swim. Acknowledge the performance with an unobtrusive pat on the back. Adrian just drops into him like a front row forward knocks him out of the way powering into transition. I am sure expletives were exchanged that were industrial enough not to be out of place in Adrian's kitchen.

So the race unfolded and an emotional Adrian finished his event, throwing down the gauntlet for me to step up in distance. Later he asked, "Who was that idiot blocking my way into transition, cannot believe they would put such an amateur on the pontoon. Surely they could pick someone with some triathlon experience. It's disgraceful!"

Errrr, Adrian that would be Richard Stannard, 7x multisport world champion and GB representative in triathlon!

Bike story

This story is really about the notion that humility and competitive sports are not natural bedfellows. But no matter who you are, what you do, how good your bike is, someone, somewhere will be better. Knowing that is actually quite uplifting, it means you can turn your attention to you and your race.

I was racing Loch Ness Monster with some work mates. A fantastic event sadly due to the economic climate that no longer runs. A four-person relay race around Loch Ness. A sort of duathlon where each team member does a run and bike leg. This story is about my bike leg.

Having completed the run, you get shipped across the loch to transition for your bike start. Where you can eat and prepare whilst your colleagues are finishing their final run leg and bike leg one. So I was bike leg two.

A long steep climb for about 5km that then flattens out into a fast undulating ride parallel to the Loch. Beautifully scenic. I had the ideal set up. Road bike, with deep wheels and tri bars. So could spin up the hill and then get nice and aero. Well that was the plan anyway.

So despite my lungs bursting and my legs screaming, and after about halfway up the climb thinking I need more gears, I hit the summit of the climb. This was my sort of biking now. Undulating TT style on the drops. Time to get settled into the office (tri bars and tuck) and get this 30km knocked out like a time trial. No one was going to get past me today. A fair assumption as a lot of folk were on varied bikes, hybrids, mountain and roadie. Hadn't seen one TT bike or another roadie with deep section wheels.

So we settled in. Swept past loads of folks thinking we are smashing it today, the guys are going to be pleased with me. As a bunch of old boys, we had targeted a top twenty team position out of 300. So pretty aspirational. We were standing at about thirtieth when I set off and I was passing folk, so the numbers were going in the right direction, with a couple of bike legs to go. But as one of the two stronger cyclists on the team I felt a big obligation to put us in a good position.

Halfway up one of the inclines I could hear a slight clunk, clunk from behind. Looked back, wheels seemed ok, brakes not rubbing, gears shifting smoothly. It wasn't me! I looked back further down the road to see in the distance a billowing yellow poncho on the horizon. Thinking, "sod that you ain't even aero mate, you're not catching me". Back into the tuck, click down a cog and get some power down.

The clunk, clunk kept getting imperceptibly louder. Poncho man was closing. I tried to drop him again, but every incline he took a bit more out of me. Clunk, clunk, clunk, he was hunting me down. Eventually he pulled alongside. By now I was sucking air in through every orifice; I was maxing it and could hardly raise a breath to create a word. My nose had classic bike riders dribble; my face was gaunt and hollow. Legs screaming and streams of saliva like a spider's web trailing between chapped blue lips.

I reluctantly glanced across to acknowledge my nemesis. Moving only my head. I didn't get out of aero. Probably because I couldn't, too exhausted.

"You're part of the race", a highland drool, peaty and rich like their finest whiskey, but sharp too, cut through the air.

"Yep", I said, crushed further as I noted his heavy old steel bike. Racing green with a three-speed sturmey archer shifter perched atop of the standard handlebars. It wasn't even a road bike. It was a shopping style bike. There were even panniers on the back and a basket on the front. His poncho still billowing like an unattended sail in the wind. Work boots on and blue workwear jacket and trousers adorned his tall but angular frame.

Totally crushed the only other words I could muster were the pathetic.

"Do you come here often?"

"Aye" was the reply. "I am the postie, about twice a day. I'd love to chat. Good luck with your race. But I have to go, Mrs McGregor gets a little anxious if I don't get to her before three."

With that, poncho man dropped down one of his sturmey archer three gears and left me for dead, within about 100m he was over the foreseeable horizon!

Run stories

My run story comes much closer to the event in Barcelona and is really about reasons to believe. If you do the training I really believe most folks can get fit enough to do an ironman. It's not really aerobically constrained its energy constrained.

What this process has taught me is that you can get fit enough. But your body's ability to utilise energy more accurately, uptake the nutrition you take and convert it into useable energy is vital. A great nutritional strategy and understanding how your gut works is incredibly important. A good nutritionist will be more accurate with the figures here. But my understanding is you can start a race with about 3000KJ of available energy in your system. In the race you can go into using about 6000-9000KJ. Meaning you go into massive deficit. So no matter how fit you are, if you cannot take on board fuel and use it you are in trouble.

This meant that a huge part of our study was trying to practice race nutritional strategies over long brick sessions. In addition, having to send stool and urine samples to various laboratories for testing, hmmmm. To do this we received lab kits, which the coach estimated to be worth, well a lot. Suffice to say in these budget-driven times like all things, the cutbacks become visibly obvious in certain circumstances. Lots of test tubes, lots of sanitary gloves, lots of pots to pee into. Overwhelmed with receptacles to capture your various poo and wee in. However when you had to collect said poo before distributing it into said pots. The distribution is another story! But the poo collection tray was not fit for purpose at all.

When you are taking loads of supplements and trying to manage your diet, your poo seems to polarize between two places. Either rock solid constipated or runny in a way that resembles a Mr Whippy ice cream dispensed cone. The former being when you are not training, the other being uncontrollably so when you and your body are on the limit. Meaning Mr Whippy creating many caught short experiences when you are a long way from home on a run.

Given that a collection tray four inches by three made of Teflon-coated cardboard is not going to do it. When in constipated mode, said poo just bounces off the tray like a Barnes Wallis dambuster bouncing bomb, splashing into the toilet. To screams of… "No that's all I've got, I can't force another one out". And you are supposed to collect that and spread it between three different collection pots with a wooden spatula. And your sample that you agonisingly pushed out has just gone at speed around the u bend and is heading for the Thames estuary.

In scenario two, coming back from a long run with a gut under pressure that wants to let go, again said small tray is totally inadequate. Mr Whippy let his cup runneth over with biblical proportions. A deluge just slides off the Teflon tray.

Anyhow back to running of another kind. About eight weeks out we were into one of our last long bike run bricks as a group. 160km completed on the bike. Bit eventful, got lost a few times around Windsor. Got caught up in a bike race not realising they weren't our group. Thinking jeez they are going fast for ironman pace. Definitely realising that endurance biking is Tourette's inducing. Every blinking pot hole that you go over, every car that cuts you up produces involuntary swearing and cursing of levels of profanity I didn't know I was capable of.

Anyhow, bike done, into dummy transition and into Windsor Great Park with the coach's goal of running for two hours ahead of me. Deciding I am exhausted and on the limit and navigation never being a strong point I decide to run straight for an hour. Then return and try and negative split, oh the delusions of grandeur.

An hour of shuffling later and a quick pit stop in the cricket pavilion. Oh, those gut issues again. Thanks to whatever cricket club for letting me use your loo. You may have to take an IOU for about 100m of loo roll. I arrive at a Londis seven – eleven type store. Having shuffled through and out the other side of Windsor Great Park, all I can think of is Coca Cola and Snickers, which I purchase and sit by the side of the road exhausted.

Whilst sat down an old lady comes up on her mobility scooter. Gets off and goes inside the store using one of those fold down walking sticks. God's truth, I swear for the first time, and as you now know not the last time, I had disability scooter envy. Oh the irony! As I bounce off the walls at home and fall off my crutches, I am having that moment again. Anyhow, I digress. The old lady seems to be taking an age to come out of the store. I am beginning to think… if she doesn't come out soon I am having that scooter! She's in there walking about with her stick, can't be so bad, and reckon at this moment my need is greater than hers. Shameful, I know. Can imagine the police report; man in Lycra seen racing through Windsor on stolen mobility scooter.

Resisting the desire for grand theft mobility scooter, I get to my feet and begin heading back to the car park and home. Miraculously I get from a shuffle to a run, as my legs begin to come back to me. 160km bike done, 20km run done, legs coming back. Reasons to believe! Knackered, stripped of dignity, but beginning to feel, yes I can.

A month or so later on holiday with the family at Playitas in Fuerteventura. I decide to go for one of my last long runs before beginning my taper. They have a 20km run out to the lighthouse and back from the resort. Rasmus Henning holds the out run record at something ridiculous like 33mins.

So I set off on this bleak run. The island is barren and

volcanic with a wind like walking into a Sir Alex "Fergie" Ferguson half-time speech. Hot as a hairdryer and straight into your face. My pace is plodding, but steady. Well aware of my weak stomach and complete lack of cover if needing to take a poo pit stop! And it, like my mind and body, are working against each other. When the mind is willing, the body is not. And when the body and significantly legs get moving and tummy isn't in distress, the mind is talking them out of it. Several times this inner conflict seems set to derail me.

I keep going one step in front of the other; I suddenly reach the steep ramp up to the lighthouse. I am not going to walk this. I tell myself I can have a five-minute break at the top. For reasons not known to me, I put in a little dig up the hill. As it zigzags up the mountainside, the words altogether better come to the forefront of my mind. As if pushing up from the depths of my collective unconscious. Altogether better, altogether better. It becomes a mantra as I tap out a fast rhythm up the mountain. Not Rasmus Henning pace, but some speed for a steep 20% incline. Altogether better, altogether better, there it is again, like the mantra for an unbreakable spirit.

As I draw breath at the summit peering over the precarious precipice of cliff to the beautiful ocean below, it hits me the message of this mantra. Altogether better, body mind and spirit aligned and working together to the same objective or goal. Not the mind willing, but the body struggling. Or the body coping but the mind talking it out of it. Or the spirit strong but body and mind not having the resource capability to deliver on the will. But all in one sweet moment aligned. Altogether in a flow with one single unifying performance goal. And the bi product of that flow was just joy.

I ran back in 45 mins, my fastest ever 10km light on my feet; just joyous I knew I was ready for ironman. I could find that moment of altogether better, that flow that just made everything joyful. And I had managed to learn how to extend that moment into many moments. Well forty-five minutes to be precise. But I knew I had that capability banked!

What have I discovered on my ironman journey?

It's bloody hard and one lapse in concentration will bite you big time. It's probably better to run into an aide worker (sorry!) than to swerve on a wet road. We'd probably both have ended up a bit bruised but he would have certainly softened my fall.

Ok, I DNF'd but I can tell you what is different since undertaking this journey. Next year I am looking forward to not having to get so acquainted with my stools. I won't have to worry about their consistency, or the colour of my wee and what that means for my nutritional intake.

Ironman is a paradox full of dualities. Have you trained enough or too much? Are you prepared enough or not? It's bloody hard and painful, but you can find joy in it! Savour the moments along the way because getting even to the start line is a massive achievement.

There will always be someone better, faster, stronger or better equipped, but it isn't about them, it is about you. Your race, your strategy, your pace and of course, your nutrition.

You will somewhere along the way get stripped of your dignity. It's inevitable with the duress and adaption to change your body has to go through. It will test you physically but more so your mental fortitude.

Since my accident many folk have sent well wishes and commented on my ironman spirit. Or true iron man spirit because I cycled through the pain and am thinking of doing it again. Which is totally humbling and kind. But I have a slightly different take on it. Having seen so many folks achieve their ironman goals in Barcelona and others who DNF for numerous reasons, it seems to me that we attribute so much to ironman as a nominalisation. A badge of honour, in that achieving that elite status. It shows us what we are made of, who we are and in earning that award we become something new and special.

I disagree; it is not the race that elevates us, *it is that we elevate it.* It is not that we get ironman character from the race. It is that our iron will to succeed gives the race its very character. I did not finish. I am not an ironman. But I honoured the race; I raced as hard as I could.

3.8km swim done. 180km bike done. 42.2km run, unfinished business. I will be back. **I am Titanium man**.

A wise man once told me. Perceive in troubled times that *"It is not happening to you, it is happening for you!"*

I entered because I wanted a permanent tattoo. I got a permanent six-inch scar down my right leg! But I have been enriched by the **discovery** on my ironman journey. And I know what I am made of, very fragile flesh and bones.

Underpinned, however by an unbreakable spirit.

The Message: The journey for any challenge – it's not happening to you, it is happening *for* you.

Editors' Message: It takes great courage to become an Ironman. It takes 'heart and soul' to be a Titaniuman. Jamie, you epitomise the meaning of both – **we salute you**.

SECTION 2

The Challenge Within

CHAPTER 10

"Disturbia" *By Jamie Kellett*

Disturbia:

The moment when you realise the full consequences of an action/decision.

To entertain the idea of or to complete something that others find hard to understand or disturbing.

OR

Disturbia: that feeling when…

*… you wonder "**why?**"*

I'm not really sure why I have entered Challenge Barcelona. It's a long-distance triathlon, mostly on roads and I don't even like cycling. My preference is to enter events that take you well away from tarmac. To places where the best form of transport are your legs and where any other vehicle would struggle. I did the Paris marathon once, it was rubbish. Good to tick off the list, but it reassured me that urban events are not fulfilling – note to self: no more road marathons.

If out in the wilderness somewhere, even when completely worn out with no energy in my legs at all, I still get that smug feeling of… "Not many people get to see this" and "I'm the only thing that could get here". That's my way of dealing with Disturbia.

Disturbia = that feeling when your mind says to you "Oh shit. What have we done now?!"

Another angle on why I have entered this would be that it made sense. It's a tough challenge. You are always hearing about these so called ironmen and whenever someone asks me about the challenges I have completed their trump card always seems to be, "yes, but have you done an ironman?" (It is worth noting here that the people who have the cheek to say this to me have not done more than the Reading half-marathon, and no, I do not consider that worthy of sponsorship. Eat fewer cakes the rest of the year and you won't need the incentive to lose your gut while pretending it's for a good cause). This niggles away at me.

Anyway, I diverge. In front of me I have a training plan spelt out (at this point I am assuming you are fully aware of HURTS – Hertfordshire University Research Triathlon Study). I also get to be a lab rat. Lots and lots of tests over the course of the training programme to tell me how I am coping. I find this fascinating. All of my previous training was pretty old school, just keep going. The three main mantras being:

Slow and steady will get you through.

Time on your feet cannot be beaten.

Unless your leg falls off, it will still work.

Don't get me wrong. Having these instilled in me by my Dad has been good. I have never **not** completed an event. However, these have been applied to ultra-running events. I was never confident that these could be applied across three disciplines, each of which is abnormally long.

Now I have a training plan; a doctor who monitors everything; a group of fellow HURTS participants for moral support; successful ironmen around to answer questions; a bike mechanic; a swim coach. In fact, looking at it… this should be relatively easy.

Now all I need to do is add in real life… and then the various Disturbia moments hit.

Disturbia: that feeling when… you first start cycling.

January was a cold month. Possibly not the best time to get your first road bike and head out on it. You are going to need cleats. There is no way around this fact. As with all situations where you do not have a choice it is better to just get on with it. You will fall off, it won't hurt, and car drivers will laugh at you. My best effort yet was approaching a roundabout on a busy road: The traffic slowed on all three approaches and I am barely moving. I look right and see a big enough gap for the car in front and I to get out. The car driver doesn't. I hit the brakes; try to get my right foot out while falling to my left. It's too late. I am down and the entire roundabout has witnessed it. The speed at which you will then unclip both feet, pick up the bike and get moving again would put Bolt to shame.

Other biking points to accept: Your hands and feet can only get so cold. Frozen is frozen at which point your feet will be numb. The good side to numb feet is that they cannot feel the wet. Your undercarriage will hurt. As will your shoulders and back. Your thighs will burn and you will be the proud owner of the tightest calves in the world. Keep training, don't look for shortcuts and stretch out every night.

You do always need cycling glasses. My attempts to save money by using sunglasses in all conditions did not work.

Equally, rain in the eye hurts just as much as sweat or bugs in the eye. Both of which you will regularly encounter. However, dry eyes hurt more than all of these so wear glasses.

Before every ride pump your tyres up to between 110–120psi using a foot pump (yes, more money). This will stop nearly all punctures assuming you avoid broken glass. While on punctures, get folding tyres on your bike and carry tyre levers as well as a small pump. The more times you change an inner tube the quicker you get and the more know-how you pick up. Two worthy pieces of advice passed onto me were:

When looking for the source of a puncture, leave the valve part of the inner tube inside the tyre. This way once you have found the hole in your tube, you can map back to where the sharp object will be lodged in your tyre wall.

Slightly inflate your new inner tube to stop it getting caught between the rim and tyre and between the tyre lever and the rim. No matter what the bike people say, you'll need the tyre levers to get the tyres off and on.

Finally, 'proper' cyclists are obnoxious idiots who will chase you down and overtake you while frowning at your aero bars, various bottle holders, numerous bags for gels/food and your lack of expensive bike computer. Relax; most of these people have never ridden for more than two hours, let alone 112 miles between swimming and running. Imagine them hitting the back of a lorry and be content.

Disturbia: that feeling when… you can't breathe.

During your new swimming career you will have quite a few experiences of not being able to breathe. Unless of course you are one of those people who swam well at school and mastered it first time round. I am not one of those people. One of the reasons for signing up to a long-distance triathlon was that it would give me no choice but to learn how to swim properly. Year after year I've told myself that I'll get into swimming, but each year it looks like too much hard work.

Fast forward to standing at the end of a 25m pool having gone up and down once and now bent double trying to breathe. You can't help but think everyone is looking at you thinking to themselves "who is this plum?". This situation will subside as you persevere and the breathing issue will transfer itself to after about ten lengths of every practice session. Again, push through this and get into your rhythm and you will be fine. The two remaining occasions where breathing will be a problem is when you cough underwater and when you are doing speed drills.

The feeling of being looked at like you are a plum is something that you are confronted with time and again during your training for triathlon. Lugging pool buoys, flippers (sorry training fins), hand paddles, floats, water bottles and a bit of paper on the poolside so that you can remember the drills, is one of these moments. It is quickly followed by another moment as you attempt a kicking drill and go nowhere!

Find some swimming buddies, grow your confidence with breathing drills and remember that no matter where you are or how tired you might be feeling, you only have to lift your head up to breathe.

Disturbia: that feeling when… your running goes backwards.

If your background is running then triathlon will be a shock to your system. You will be used to interval training and going out for longer, but faster runs, seeing how far you can push yourself. This approach does not work for triathlon. The run will be at the bottom of the priority list for beginners. If you are training in heart rate zones then the long slow runs are usually zone two. To an experienced runner this will kill you, as you will feel like you are not running at all. Be patient, the long extra slow runs will work, and you are simply going the long way round to your marathon goal. It is also worth noting that all other endurance athletes rarely go past zone three during their race events (excluding the sprint finish or the odd mountain climb). They have spent years pushing their bodies to be super efficient at what they do.

Disturbia: that feeling when… you become boring.

This is a fact. As I found out it is impossible to hold down a full-time job, train six days a week, sometimes with double sessions, eat, sleep, see the other half, play football and socialise with work colleagues and friends.

I work in the City and this requires me to be at my desk for 9am. There is no chance of leaving until 6pm on a good day and I have an hour's journey each way. To fit in a gym session or swim I have to be up at 5am in order to eat, pack my gear for the day, get to the gym, train, shower and catch the 8am train. I am now that person who carries a huge rucksack full of wet gear, food and am constantly sipping from a water bottle and drinking a protein shake. I find sanctuary in not being the only sweaty numpty on the train. As any commuter will testify, there are always those people in tight lycra, which is strained over parts of the body I don't want to see that has a folding bike and yet insists on taking up the space of two people on the train by clogging up the aisle with their bike and a seat with their oversized arse.

During your workday you will eat as much as possible while every answer you give to any non-work question will be 'training'. Examples…

Question: What did you do at the weekend/last night?
Answer: Went training.

Question: Any plans for the weekend?
Answer: Training.

Question: What are you getting the missus for her birthday?
Answer: Can't think about that; will be training.

Question: Are you coming for a few beers to watch the football?
Answer: Can't; will be training.

You then hope that no last-minute queries come in at the end of the day and that you can rearrange that client dinner so that you can leave work on time, train, and sit down for dinner (which has been made by your loving, but not really sure why, girlfriend) at 9:30pm, and be in bed for 10pm.

10pm – The new magic time in your day. This is because you are now solely focused on **RECOVERY**. How much dinner and protein shake can you force down before you get to bed as early as possible so that your body has the most amount of time for recovery in the hope that you are able to get up and do it all again tomorrow.

Disturbia: that feeling when… you don't want to do another training session.

The alarm goes off. It's 6am on a Saturday. Your brain immediately thinks… "surely this isn't worth it". At the same time you roll out of bed and rush to the loo to get rid of the two litres of water you drank before bed. It is here while stood over the toilet looking at the cornflake man in the mirror that your legs start to ache, "for f**k's sake, this ironman now means I have to pee like a lady!"

This is England and so even in the summer you will probably have a head wind and some drizzle to deal with as your long bike sessions rack up past three hours to six or seven hours. By now you will be getting bored of the same old bike routes and yet planning new routes is just too much effort. The final nail in your cycling enjoyment will be that your so-called cyclist friends will be too slow and not committed enough to keep you company. You are on your own. Make the most of this, it is character building and reinforces the mantra of "it doesn't matter what happens on race day, I have done this on my own before, and I can handle it".

Another tip for when the swimming, cycling and running sessions are becoming more boring and tedious than anything is to leave your heart rate monitor and GPS watch at home for one of each session. Just go out and perform to whatever level you feel like. Run fast, run slow, stop and stroke the animals, do whatever you feel like. I can guarantee that you won't go so hard that you get injured; you'll be too busy wondering when was the last time you enjoyed exercising so much. One set of sessions every couple of months not sticking to the training is not going to set you back, in fact it is likely to put you in a better place mentally. Just relax and listen to your body. If you can truly listen to your body, you will never fail to complete an event.

Disturbia: that feeling of… I haven't done enough.

Fun event fact: You will never feel like you have done enough. I lied; this is not a fun fact. It is the final feeling of "oh shit". Don't let this apprehension defeat you. Some people have trained more than enough, but they let doubt creep into their mind and then as soon as there is the chance to end the worry and the pain during the race they pull out, making excuses to hide their disappointment. You can't let this happen to you. The simplest way to avoid this is to make a simple deal with yourself… "You'll be taken away in an ambulance before you have to face people at home telling them you didn't finish."

If you think this is a bit severe you can turn it around and think about it like this: If during every training session that you have wanted to skip but completed, struggled at, but completed or just outright hated, but still completed, you have got a little tougher. Each time you are in the middle of a shocker just think, if I get through this now, the race will be easy. Bit by bit, you'll have the race nailed before you even start.

… I've realised "why?"

As I run down the final few kilometres of the fourth and final lap of the road marathon, which I must note was still boring, it clicks and I've worked out why I continually put

Jamie smashing the run

myself through Disturbia. It's simple, *I like going on adventures!*

They are even better when you successfully complete them. Throughout these nine months of HURTS training I have been bled, cycled and run to exhaustion, spent hours out on numerous bike rides with no idea where I am going, or how I am going to get my feet out of the pedals. I have jumped into a freezing lake, jumped into a rough sea and raced horses over the Welsh hills, all without any idea of what I was really doing. How can that not be fun?!

If you were to summarise it all in a tweet it would read:
"I did it. I don't need to tell anyone. I just know. Unless you have done it, I'm not going to value your opinion – on anything #fact #HURTS"

I should caveat this with… this is what I am thinking when someone tells me all the things they have done that don't involve seeing what they are properly capable of, or all the

A well-earned beer… er… medal!

reasons why they haven't done something. They are clearly a wimp when it comes to Disturbia. Time for a beer…

The Message: Go on your own adventure – this is about you.

CHAPTER 11

"Solitude" *By Peter Benson*

Aka "The Glory of Being Alone"

"Solitude"

1. The state or quality of being alone or remote from others.
2. A lonely or secluded place.

I'm not quite sure why I bother. When doing an iron-distance triathlon you're often asked "*why?*" My retort is to usually shrug and say "*why not*?" It's an easy answer.

For me, it's not a simple question and my easy answer hides the acute knowledge that I'm not really sure why I do it. I'm not sure I could ever answer it satisfactorily. I often wonder when sitting there spinning on the turbo trainer – what's the point, is it really worth it? I usually follow those questions up with a no. But yet I still sit there, the monotonous sounds of pedals ticking over, the whirl of the turbo trainer and the slight burn in my quads... Why, if I answer "no" do I not stop?

The question of why I persist with this madness often plagues me. I look at my training plan with lacklustre antipathy. Yet, I find myself up at 5:30am driving to a lake – miserable all the way, tired, worn out and distracted. The water is eleven degrees Celsius. I swim for an hour and half. I'm happy. Strange isn't it?

The real answer to this question is somewhat more complex, inextricably linked to how I feel at that particular moment in time and mixed somewhere in the constant fatigue. I think for me, the Iron-Distance Triathlon was attractive because it is a test, a real test of mental toughness, physical strength and an enduring desire to drive forward. It's also a deep-routed quest for self-recognition. I've participated in sport more or less since the day I could walk. When I had my first swimming sessions, I was still in a nappy. I have competed in rugby, football, athletics (both track and field), horse riding, gymnastics, tennis, golf, extreme Frisbee, weightlifting – the list goes on. I've no doubt I'm lost without sport – it makes me happy. I think this is a pretty reasonable feeling to have given my relationship with physical activity, but why did I have this burning desire to go Iron…

The iron-distance triathlon is no doubt attractive because it's a test, but I think the real driver for me is the *fear I might fail.* I might not even make it to the start line. You can't hide in triathlon; it's all about you, no matter how expensive your bike is.

Miss a training session at your peril; drink that beer if you dare.

It's scary – this was and is a real unknown for me. What I did learn quite quickly though was this: *I was duped.*

I naively thought it was glamorous. I was suckered into watching the YouTube videos of Australian athletes venturing to open air pools in blazing sunshine, cyclists rolling over mountain passes in Boulder, Colorado or long trail runs at the base of the Alps. "This is amazing, that's going to be my training". Sadly not. The local leisure centre doesn't quite live up to expectations, sidestepping the flooded urinals and trying to find a locker that doesn't show signs of being ripped open. Cycling over speed bumps and avoiding traffic in the city centre and running on pot holed concrete and loose paving slabs. Don't even dare to mention the British weather.

Training facilities aside, the videos also let on to a triathlete fraternity, even better, an iron-distance fraternity. Unfortunately, as a mere mortal I like many others have a number of other commitments – work, family, chores and friends. Maintaining balance between these elements is multi-tasking to the extreme, adding in training, diet and recovery only makes things more challenging. Committing time to these fraternities is difficult. Scheduling in a six-hour ride on a Sunday is difficult enough let alone adding in travel time to meets, puncture stops, loo stops, coffee stops and general other pointless stops. Your control dwindles, six hours turns to eight. Day gone. To limit the effect on 'my life' I turn to the hours less used – like most triathletes – those of the early morning – 5am bike starts, 6am swims. Sliding back in bed by 9am after a three hour run like I'd never been away. That way the impact is limited. Training at these times is a funny thing for me – I find it so difficult and just can't get used to it.

I have a Jekyll and Hyde relationship with my training. The night before a long day is exciting, I'm revelling in the expectation of the challenge, the performance, excited about testing myself and seeing improvement. However, when I wake at 5am my emotions are the polar opposite. Another hour in bed, the weather is miserable, it's too cold, my legs ache. Sometimes I win, sometimes I don't. The negativity is what bothers me more compared with missing the training session. Why does my mind let me down before I've even started? What's the difference, why are my emotions poles apart?

It's the exact same reason I'm excited. It's the challenge. But the difference is at 5am the challenge becomes real and the fear kicks in. You're doing it alone. Can you cope with six hours on your own? What if you have a bad day in the saddle, you're in that 'dark place' all alone with your demons. Can I handle it – the fear of trying and failing? For me coming through those dark days, finding out a little bit more about myself physically and mentally are some of the most satisfying moments on the journey. There is a William James quote that means more to me after each long weekend on my road to *'that Sunday'*:

> *"Beyond the very extreme of fatigue and distress, we may find amounts of ease and power we never dreamed ourselves to own; sources of strength never taxed at all because we never push through the obstruction"*.

Now this is where the beauty comes in. *This is the addiction.* Conquering those dark days, spinning on the turbo, running with the burning Achilles, climbing that last hill with your quads in piercing pain – with your mind saying "stop". Overcoming the battle with yourself is the biggest and hardest challenge. Many a misconception would say the biggest hurdle is the distance, the ascent, and the marathon after 112 miles cycling or the clock. **Wrong, it's one's own mind**. There is no doubt an obvious need to condition the body, but delivery and execution is all in the mind and this for me is the joy of long-distance triathlon. That solitude, that challenge with yourself, your toughest opponent.

Solitude provides the perfect battleground.

As I look back over the journey I've taken, travelling over the highs and lows the training plan set out before us all, it fills me with great pride. It fills me with happiness. I'm happy when I look at the progress I've made. I've lost four inches from my waist, lost body fat, gained muscle mass, can ride one hundred miles comfortably, knock out a half-marathon easily and splash about for four kilometres. This progress is the real joy, especially for the 'average Joe', for me. Seeing what your body can do, jumping in at the deep end, fighting that lingering fear of failure and inability and overcoming it. The struggle.

Taking on that struggle alone, in solitude, just you, your body and your mind. Whilst I'm both excited and dreading the 'big' sessions, they provide the battlefield between your body and mind. That outer body experience where your mind tells your body to pull itself together and stop whining, you don't hurt that much. I enjoy the ride down into those dark places, just so you can achieve the relief of feeling strong again. The polar opposites in emotion, from wanting to quit and wanting to pick up the pace, all within ten minutes is amazing. A real test of character, desire, tenacity and your willingness to endure.

You can only experience these things in blissful solitude. Riding and running in a group or swimming at a club provides distraction, external motivations and encouragement. The real test is when you're on your own, when you can shirk off and call it a day, when you can hide. I love the test this provides – me, myself and I, all battling each other to carry on. The euphoria when you complete your peak sessions, joy when you achieve a PB or hit a target otherwise elusive, or when you simply nail a training session.

Solitude also raises its head in a number of other ways. In ways that I had not considered when taking on this challenge, well, not that seriously. As the training volume ramps up, so does your 'social solitude'. Being divorced from your loved ones, family and friends. This aspect of long-distance triathlon training isn't really spoken about in the books, magazines or blogs and if it is, it's in a very blasé manner – make sure you talk to your loved ones. You do this at the beginning, you tell them that there will be a lot of training, some big weekends, but if you've never trained for something this big, neither of you know what is to come. It's like predicting the weather accurately.

Partners support you, they do the right thing – it's an epic challenge and as a side bonus you might raise some money for charity, get 'Iron Fit' and maybe earn yourself a six-pack! What we/I didn't understand were the early days, coming back blue, cold and with headaches from dehydration (*get nutrition sorted early on*), lying in bed all day, too tired to move. Cancelling nights out and being chronically tired, maybe even letting things slip at work. Your life changes from a tri-partite relationship of work, loved ones and socialising to work, loved ones and training. Social life is impacted immensely but with some clever planning and organisation you can mitigate this impact, but rest assured, you become far more selective over the 'parties' attended. This new tri-partite relationship is slightly different to the former in that the three are not evenly weighted and the sums add up to more than the whole. If you give full dedication to one, one or both of the others must suffer.

Interestingly, during some of the long sessions my biggest overriding feeling is guilt. I have the most amazing partner in Roxanne and she supports me 100%, never questions my training, arranges plans around me and has food ready for me on the table when I come in. But this makes it worse. I sometime wish she would get the hump as that way I may be more inclined to ignore the guilt. Nope, never. I feel guilty about the stress I put her through, the plans I'm putting on hold, the things she's missing to account for *my* training. I feel guilty about the lack of time I can invest in my friends. Sometimes training is so all consuming you forget to even send a text. Social solitude is an unexpected event on the iron-distance journey.

Being alone amongst friends, colleagues and family is an unusual feeling – the inability for others to understand what you go through, what it means and what it takes out of you. People ask questions but don't understand, "*how far is it again?*", "*what order do you do it in?*" – they just 'gulp' at the distances. It's funny, but to some extent, that's the easy part, the difficult part is the hours of training, early mornings, late nights, sacrifices, not stopping until 11pm and straight in bed ready to start all over again in the morning.

Although the social solitude for me has been very real, I sometimes wonder if it's mainly in my head. Of course you have those who are close to you, that support you (albeit, you might not see them as much and most conversations focus on training, splits and nutrition) throughout, which goes without saying. As the training volume increases to a point where even your 'fitter' friends faint at the thought of attempting those feats, the respect grows. It's not a distant event somewhere in the future that seems like a crazy idea. It's so very soon and they've seen the changes that have taken place. Weight loss, muscle gain, dedication, drive and ambition all come to the fore and others like it. It becomes attractive and people start to wonder, *"can I do it*?" Maybe it was those thoughts that attracted me to attempt it. When I look back I believe it is, I wanted a bit of that life – strong, both in mind and body, and now I'm nearly there.

Even on rest days you feel you should be doing something. You can't even glean a moment of solitude ***from*** the event itself. When you're alone, all you do is think about it, it lingers there over your head, waiting for you to slip up, drink that beer, eat that chocolate bar… The one place I wish solitude would raise its head, however, is between my bank balance and me. Triathlon is expensive. It can be exceptionally expensive.

I think the closer I come to race day, the closer I come to knowing why I bother. I can't explain the detail on paper or in words – maybe I will be able to after the race itself – but at the minute it stands as a mixture of feelings, which bubble around ever changing.

Training for an iron-distance event provides a number of other benefits outside the mental. There's also the physical. This has been one of my most encouraging aspects throughout the study. My biggest and proudest achievement is the four inches lost around my waist. Now I look back, I can't believe how much weight I was carrying, and what was even worse was that I thought I was reasonably fit! Not so sir. The battery of tests we go through as part of the study are amazing. Seeing your VO_{2max} increase, lung volume creeping up and resting heart rate going down. Knowing your bone mineral density – something I'd never considered before. So cool. My only concern now is watching all this hard work unravel once Challenge Barcelona is complete. Do I do another? *Ssssh, don't tell my girlfriend.*

One of my most interesting discoveries has been my diet. How my food cravings have changed over time, how I'm far more prepared, taking in lunches to work and the fact I would rather go hungry than make a bad food choice. Of course, I still fall off the rails. A chocolate bar here and there is my treat, a beer or two at the weekend to relax. Most of my current research into supporting my performance over the backend of the study has been on nutrition; I've brought vegetarian cookbooks, even a vegan one to expand my repertoire of food choices and meals available to me. The spark that kicked this interest off was recovery. The length of time it was taking me to recover from the harder sessions was really getting me down, why would it take me three days to feel normal again after the weekend sessions? Surely I was doing something wrong. I splashed out on some supplements to make my own recovery shakes which seemed to help and this led me to wondering, maybe adjusting my food intake can help speed recovery up further…

So my exploration with food began. This didn't just relate to post workouts it found its way into my training sessions. The revelation was amazing. Getting my nutrition right in training itself helped improve my performance almost immediately, those dark patches didn't last as long and when they did raise their ugly head a strategically consumed gel or energy bar can help put it back in its cage. Post exercise, a nice recovery shake whilst sitting in an ice bath (really just a cold bath, no ice), shower, stretch and a balanced meal. Focusing on rehydrating and making sure my following meals contained lots of mixed vegetables and legumes seems to help wonders. Thanks to this little routine I can be ready to go again a day later. The power of food has amazed me. My usual beans on toast, coffee and Danish pastry just doesn't quite cut it now, nor does the two dairy milk chocolate bars on my long bike rides either… Looking back this makes me smile – *such an amateur.*

I've also started to consider my plans for what I do after the race. Nothing quite yet has materialised, but keeping up the training (maybe not to the same volume) is a key component. I think I'll look to improve my general strength, especially focusing on the upper body. It's a shame that when I had to let a training session slip it was generally the Functional Strength sessions. That was a bit of a silly move looking back now, I believe I underestimated their importance in providing a solid base to build upon, but this is all part of the learning curve. Maybe I will keep up triathlon, doing some 70.3 distance races.

Peter 'Ironman' Benson at the finish

I've grown quite accustomed to the solitude training provides me; I think somehow I will miss it.

The Message: This is more than being alone, this is a choice, this is self-inflicted solitude – *the glory of being alone.*

CHAPTER 12

"Adversity" *By Warren Potts*

As I waited in the back of the ambulance I remembered the words of my work colleague: "wouldn't it just be easier to buy a sports car and a Hawaiian shirt?" This was the response when I mentioned my male menopausal desire to do an ironman type event. At this particular moment driving around in a colourful shirt seemed really quite appealing even if I do not quite fit the *Magnum PI* persona.

I was six months into a nine month ironman training programme. I was equalling run times from my teens, set thirty years earlier. Swimming was going well, but still pool based as summer started late. Cycling distances were increasing despite saddle manufacturers otherwise efforts. All training had been on my own and it was time to take me out of my comfort zone and enter some sportive events.

On my first event, after three hours the narrow single track lane turned steeply downhill and the cyclist in front had what can only be described as a single vehicle accident. I have never seen anyone just crash in the middle of an open road for no reason. In what appeared to be slow motion I could see his front wheel start to wobble, the whole bike beginning to ripple with larger frequencies until he could control it no further and the front wheel washed out throwing the rider into the road. This left the rider and his bike prostrate across the road creating a perfect roadblock. Normal course of action would be to pull over and assist the poor stricken fellow. Unfortunately I was not going to make his day any better.

At 25mph I think I had around a second before impact, but just like in the movies, time was standing still. My brain knew it was going to crash, but was trying to weigh up the options. I managed to reject trying to bunny hop over as I would not gain enough height and this would probably cause me to flip over upon impact, the fact that I cannot bunny hop strangely wasn't the primary rejection reason. That left the option of riding into the fallen bike or rider, brain said rider; I suppose on the basis it would be a softer impact.

I have now learnt by experience that riding into someone (or, I guess, anything else) at high speed does not lead to a soft impact. The front wheel stops instantly and the momentum that is transferred as you take flight would have made the Wright brothers proud. The rear wheel followed as I performed a Tom Daley-esque pike with half somersault (with extra difficulty points for completing the dive with bike attached). The landing would not have scored highly as I came down on my back but at least it was not headfirst. It was only upon impact that the bike lost faith with my riding ability and the cleats gave way, taking the skin evenly off both shins in a remarkable even format which still shows its mark and impresses me today.

Once I stopped I just lay there corpse-like with my eyes shut tight until it occurred to me that I was now also lying across the road waiting for the next rider to make a bunny hop or not decision. Brain re-engaged, it was time to move, as I tried to sit up I felt my left collar bone separate and move in two different directions. Disappointment meant that I resumed my corpse pose.

By now following riders had stopped and were directing others around us.

I kept being asked, "Are you alright? Do you need an ambulance?"

Whilst I wanted to scream "of course I'm not f**king alright I've just crashed, I hurt and I am really pissed off", with typical British reservation I mumble "I'll be alright just need to get my breath back". However, they managed to get us off the road and called for assistance.

The resultant ambulance had two passengers, myself strapped to one bed and my bike looking smug with itself for creating such an event strapped to the other (for interest the original fallen rider lost a lot of skin but once patched up by the medics made his own way home). Whilst Accident and Emergency is equipped for the human interest story they were less than happy to accept my bike. When you are struggling to move around and only have use of one arm this is a hassle you don't need. However, hats off to the Ambulance Service who offered to store the bike at the local station until I could get someone to pick it up.

The hospital consultant confirmed that I had not broken my back (which I knew) and from my x-rays stated that I had not broken my collarbone but might have ligament damage (which I didn't know). The diagnosis was surprising as I could feel the end of the bone sticking up through my skin, however, was not really up to the argument at the time. I was sent home in a dodgy sling and told that orthopaedics would call me.

Once home, although in pain, the calling was still to upload my route data as any dedicated ironman trainee would do, the website showed I had covered 99.9km, not 100km but 99.9km. I was disproportionately disappointed, the day was getting worse – I could have made up the distance by just rolling further upon landing.

It started to hit me – what had I done!

What was I going to tell people!

When you are training for an ironman, you tell people you are training for an ironman, you tell a lot of people. I don't know what causes this; maybe it is the enormity of the target that requires self-recognition or the single-mindedness that you must apply to reach the goal. Typical conversations might go:

"My Aunt Betty had a hernia operation last Thursday" which might promote the associated reply "last Thursday I was running Zone Two Hill reps – did I tell you I was doing an ironman" or

"Can you help me with this report" – "funny you mention reports, my Garmin stats are all over the place – did I tell you I was doing an ironman".

Again what was I going do, what do I tell people!

It would have been easy to give up, I could have eked out compassion for a few weeks, claimed it would have been too difficult to catch up, claimed it might put my future well-being in jeopardy and other lame excuses that friends and family nod sympathetically to because they don't want to upset you (but know inside that you have given up).

I sat down (mainly because I couldn't get out of the chair) and took stock of what I had achieved so far and what I was aiming for. I was entering an ironman, I was not contractually obliged to win it, I was entering to finish, to be a "finisher", to prove I could do it. Yes it might be difficult, yes it might be painful, yes it might be slow, but I believed I could still start and finish.

Orthopaedics did not ring the next day, or the next. Fed up, I arranged for a private consultation. The cheery Egyptian consultant laughed when I talked about my "potential" ligament damage and showed me the x-ray clearly showing the break with the end of the bone tenting my skin.

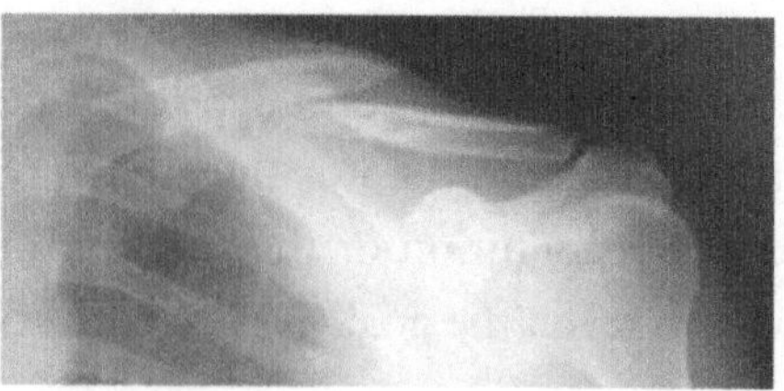

"Ouch!!"

The fall had separated the collarbone into three pieces and the larger pieces did not break evenly across but as long splinters. To facilitate a better fix and a faster recovery it was recommended that the bone be screwed and plated. Four days later and after an overnight stay I was the proud owner of some internal scaffolding. (Titanium alloy plate and ten screws – and no it does not set off the airport scanners before anyone asks). I could now use my left arm although movement was severely restricted by the stitches and subsequent stiffness at the extremes. A lot of the muscle has to be moved around to accommodate the plate and I now knew it.

Unfortunately, the distraction of the collarbone fracture had masked the injuries to my ribs. I could not believe how much discomfort they could cause, you cannot breathe deeply, cannot lie down, cannot lift, cannot twist and cannot do anything to assist. It took me five weeks of sleeping in a reclining garden chair before I was able to support my own weight in bed and two months before I could take a full deep breath without discomfort.

Timing of my accident could not have been more awkward, my wife Sharon had abdominal surgery two days before my accident and was signed off work for five weeks. Simply my job was to look after her during her recovery and to tend to her every need, entering the sportive was a bit of a pre thank you for the care I was to offer. We were left in a situation where

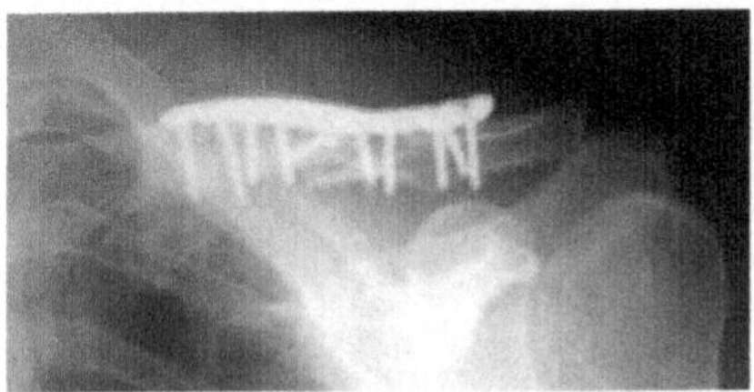

"Double ouch!"

neither of us could drive, lift, bend or undertake any domestic chore. I think the highlight was the effort to make a cheese sandwich, Sharon held the cheese whilst I operated the grater; a window on a future geriatric life was opened.

To assist recovery the physiotherapy team advised that I should not perform gymnastic routines – as a forty-six-year-old who has never been able to touch his toes, it was unlikely I would suddenly get the urge or skill to perform handsprings down the garden. I took the hint and decided not to abuse my potential lack of upper body strength, having just acquired a 6" post op scar I did not fancy a second for remedial work – swimming was going to be a problem.

My shoulder felt "pinged out" as if I was permanently wearing a coat hanger and movement was restricted as if I had a lump of stiff metal holding me in place, which was due to the lump of stiff metal holding me in place. Three weeks had passed and I was worried about the amount of training time I was losing and if the base fitness I had acquired could be maintained. I was conscious that I needed to recover fitness but to also allow my shoulder time to heal. It was just my luck that the easiest exercise to return to was my least favourite, turbo training in the garage. How something so dull can induce so much sweat is beyond me – they should introduce one into every prison cell, crime rates would halve instantly and there would be a huge uplift in towel sales.

Warren 'Ironman' Potts – laughing in the face of adversity

It was seven weeks from the accident before I returned to the pool. To stop myself doing something stupid I imposed hard cut-offs of twenty minutes regardless of how good the shoulder felt. I think the first session covered just 400m and a little more in the subsequent swim but nothing broke, nothing snapped, there were aches but confidence was growing.

I took a few liberties with exercises that required upper body strength but in August (month eight) I was following the training programme in its entirety, all be it with very much extended targets. I did lose too much time in a key part of the programme to let me get the finish times that I would like, but I will absolutely finish.

During training, many others in the group have suffered **adversity**, mine was a little more demonstrable, others have had colds that cannot be shaken, have backs that are maybe a little old, have tenderness from incorrect saddles, all have been overcome through determination to succeed. I don't know if you have to have that drive to enter an ironman, or entering an ironman gives you the drive, but the positivity of everyone involved is infectious.

With respect to the question: "wouldn't it just be easier to buy a sports car and a Hawaiian shirt?" Yes it would, but it would be nowhere near as much fun or satisfying. Where is the challenge in getting out the chequebook?

The Message: Adversity should be considered as a detour: not the end of your journey.

CHAPTER 13

"Journeyman" *By Chris Petrie*

I'll start by stating this – I'm the Office Cycling/Running Guy (OC/RG). You've almost certainly met him (or her) and if you are reading this book, there's a solid chance you are that guy. OC/RG is easily identified, he's the one splattered with mud heading for the showers in the morning, or the one furtively glancing at a very conspicuous orange Garmin wrist watch at 11:59 when that meeting looks like it's going to over-run. He's the guy with the bike "you can lift with one finger", and, if he got a quid every time he heard "you could buy a car for that" he'd have a much nicer bike.

Often, when colleagues see OC/RG return from a lunchtime session they will ask how far he's gone – "just a couple of K, not especially fast" is the usual response. "You should join me sometime if you like?" he'll add just on the off chance. "Oh no, I can't run! It's too hard/hurts my knees/I'm not fit enough" (they usually stop asking after that).

You see, to ordinary office Joe, OC/RG is a different species altogether. He's not an Olympic athlete (the cake consumption and resulting waist measurement makes that abundantly clear) but he's definitely doing something normal people wouldn't ever consider. OC/RG quite likes this, but the secret is… it simply isn't true. 80% of the people he has this conversation with will be 80% as fit/fast/slim/strong as he is. But they'll never know.

My relationship with and attitude towards sport (*and by extension, masculinity*) is (*as is often the case*) a product of my upbringing and background. I come from a long line of winners; however, in my family the definition of winning is somewhat different to most. Coming first, second, third or dead last (well, maybe second last) in any sport is largely irrelevant. Being a winner is about being able to have a convincing stab at any given task and never turning down an opportunity to try something new. Employing the services of a plumber would be viewed with the same suspicion as an enthusiastic fondness of disco music.

The men in my family are all keen cyclists, reasonable runners and competent yachtsmen. We have a couple of 50m swimming badges between us but certainly no trophies. None of us would pass up the opportunity to have a go at any sport or outdoor activity. I was disappointed when I tried golf and found I couldn't do it, but that's a game, not sport so technically doesn't count. If you were to draw a bell curve of sporting performance across a population, you'd find us lot right in the middle. Mr Average. My dad has a drawer full of marathon medals but he'd struggle to remember his PB. Even my late big brother (who certainly wasn't a runner) still managed to turn up to a cross country relay race with zero prep (*and as it turns out, with undiagnosed terminal cancer*), ran as fast as he possibly could (pretty slowly) and puked his guts up on the finishing line. *Legendary winning behaviour.*

As a juvenile I was into cycling in a big way. In fact, it's probably fair to say I was into bikes a little more than the act of actually riding them, but I was still hugely keen on the whole scene. I'd read whatever books and magazines I could get my hands on. My Apollo racing bike was regularly disassembled, reassembled and improved and most daylight hours were spent riding with my friends.

I joined Musselburgh Road Cycling Club and tried a few races, criterium, TT's and a bit of track, my claim to fame is that I was comprehensively beaten in an individual pursuit by a young Sir Chris Hoy (back then he was just Chris) but ultimately racing left me cold. I just don't have a competitive nature. I did love club runs, chain gang and the social stuff, but the desire to be first just wasn't there.

Over the years that followed I've gone through cycles of getting really into cycling or running, going out most days doing the same old route at the same old pace, quickly reaching a (pretty low) plateau, not entering any events and so not setting any targets, getting bored or distracted by work or life and before I know it I've not done anything for a month so struggle to get back into it.

In 2012 I was getting towards the plateau stage in the well trodden cycle. I'd lost a couple of stone I'd put on since having a family and got back into running with a group of semi-regular running buddies at work (which always helps) when I read a post on a popular mountain bike forum I frequent (*which as it happens seems to mostly be populated by other slightly chunky middle aged IT workers who talk about bikes more than ride them*). It basically read "fancy trying a big triathlon? Call this guy".

Now I've always fancied doing a triathlon. I'd never learnt how to swim freestyle properly which pretty much ruled out doing so, but the idea of a multisport event where the challenge is a personal one rather than a race against other people really appealed. I was feeling pretty good with the running I was doing and in a moment of wild optimism, I sent off the email.

When the response came back some time later, the enormity of my error became clear. The big triathlon was a full iron-distance event. A quick check of Wikipedia confirmed what I already knew – **that was a really big bastard of a challenge**.

I'd been asked to book an appointment to attend the University sports science lab for an assessment, which would include a VO_{2max} test. This was very exciting as I'd always wanted to do this test (*at time of writing, having done several and knowing how much they hurt, I never want to do another*) but it also presented the very real possibility that I'd pass, and in that event I'd have to do an actual ironman, which seemed simply impossible. I didn't want to waste anyone's time, but I didn't want to quit before I'd started, I was a winner after all. A short phone call with Dr Roberts was all I needed to convince me. He reassured me that the training would be progressive and it was absolutely possible, and that I would be the type of person they were looking for. I was in... **game on**!

I've always been of the opinion you should always be careful whose advice you take, but if you take it, follow it to the letter. Justins' experience spoke for itself and anyone discussing training with him in person would be left in no doubt this guy knows his lactate thresholds. Having such confidence in the plan meant I could disengage my own brain and get on with completing the sessions.

Training was for the most part pretty easy, in so much it was really progressive so you never felt daunted by a week's training. It was also easy to stick to because I was committed and I couldn't be the one to let the side down. Having a prescriptive programme took all the guesswork out.

My first major stumbling block was (predictably) swimming. I've never been a great swimmer. I can do a pretty convincing breaststroke and I can do it quickly over a decent distance however I've never mastered front crawl. It was clear this wouldn't be appropriate for Barcelona so I took my usual approach to acquiring a new skill and read whatever I could get my hands on. Books, online guides, YouTube videos etc. I went to the pool for the first time and... disaster! I just couldn't breathe. I was looking for some mythical pocket of air behind my bow wave that just wasn't there. I was certain I was doing what the guides instructed, but several abortive attempts in the pool followed by re-reading the guides yielded virtually no results. I could manage a pretty quick 25m length (effectively without breathing) but I was exhausted by the end.

Fortunately, the great thing about training with such a large group, is there are so many experts willing to provide assistance. I arranged to swim with Jamie (a top swim coach) one lunchtime and he had identified my issue within ten minutes (I was turning for air, reaching the air, not believing it was there so turned further, dropping my opposite shoulder effectively sinking below the surface well out of the air) by the end of the session I was comfortable breathing. I could do 1000m within a week and full iron-distance within eight weeks.

My second stumbling block was also swim related. By August I was pretty confident the swim would pose no significant problem. It took me a few weeks to sort out a wetsuit so by the time it arrived I was a few weeks behind my cohort buddies. I was looking forward to my first swim at Histon Lake in Cambridge on a Friday afternoon, and even as I pulled on my wetsuit at the boot of my car in the Holiday Inn car park I was looking forward to the experience. This lasted right up until the point I put my face in the water. **PANIC, DISORIENTATION, DIFFICULTY BREATHING** it was like being in the pool back in January, but with the added threat of man-eating fish (*it was around this point that I remembered I have unresolved childhood catfish issues*).

Once again it was the HURTS community to the rescue. Sharing my issues with the community revealed that many people were experiencing the same sensations, which was enormously reassuring and again experts were on hand to offer helpful advice. Within a few weeks I was covering the full distance in the lake and I finally completed a full sea swim in September. I'm still scared of fish.

The name's Petrie, Chris 'Ironman' Petrie

Releasing only a few weeks' training at a time with a set of clear goals for each block was a masterstroke. I'm sure I wouldn't be the only one to be put right off had I seen details of 7hr brick sessions back in January, but every block was entirely manageable, the goals easily achievable and above all the sessions were enjoyable. Even the turbo sessions. Recalling the early long sessions now it seems amazing that a long bike session was two hours (and required two stops for food) but the level of stretch for each new block was always about the same and soon the really long sessions became easily manageable.

The toughest part was finding time to complete the longer bike rides as the sessions grew to five, six and seven hours. With a busy family life, a working wife, two small boys and an energetic dog not to mention an often high-pressured job, most would consider anyone in my position simply doesn't have time. The truth is there is plenty of time, but that time is 4:30am when any sensible person would be fast asleep.

At the time of writing, it's three days to go until the start of my ironman challenge, I don't know what time I'll finish in, but I'll give it my best shot and I know I can finish and just knowing that's possible is simply amazing.

Whatever the result, I'll be proud to be office iron guy – even if just the once.

I am the journeyman.

The Message: No time to train for that big event? Nobody has time, and yet… people seem to manage. Switch off the TV and get out there!

CHAPTER 14

"Practice makes Perfect"

By Melanie Miller

Challenge Barcelona 6 Oct 2013

So where do you **begin** or… perhaps end at the **beginning**. Begin I hear you ask; a triathlon (swim, bike, run) is no mean feat in itself as far as the ordinary punter is concerned. Triathlon takes three forms: super-sprint, sprint and standard. Most will have attempted one of these three during their training before "the daddy" sorts the men from the boys. This is ironman material. A 2.4 mile swim, 112 mile bike ride with a marathon (26.2 miles) to finish – that sorts out the men from the boys. Times vary by region: Kona (Hawaii) is one of the more rigorous (with very hilly terrain) events 17hrs to cut off; Barcelona (predominantly flat) has 15½hrs to cut off. That may seem plenty of time; reality puts you hard against the clock.

How did I get involved? By replying to an advert put out by Dr Justin Roberts, eminent nutritionist and four times ironman contestant.

It read: *"Recreational athletes wanted for ultra-endurance challenge research study, must be in training for <4 days a week".*

That was it. The rest unravelled like a never-ending treasure hunt: you were given clues but left still searching for elusive treasure *(but won't I treasure that moment forever when I cross the finish line).*

Before "play" commenced everyone had to meet strict fitness criteria. Pre-screening involved pedalling a stationary bike to maximum possible effort while ones bodies' vital stats were scrutinised. Fortunately for me, cycling plays to my strength, I was told there and then I had made the grade – little did I then know just what I was letting myself in for.

Phase One: A detailed training programme, of increasing intensity took up the first six months with us all required to keep diaries, recording our training, diet, injuries/illness.

Regular observation workshops at the Uni sports lab put the cohort through a battery of tests to observe evolution of fitness. The tests varied from functional (measuring limb movements) then running on a treadmill, riding a stationary bike while hooked up to heart rate and other monitors. Finally we peddled a stationary bike to exhaustion. This latter test measured VO_{2max} (the overall efficacy of oxygen uptake/utilization by the body).

Phase Two: The cohort was split into several sub groups. My group are called to a meeting the tone of which lightens considerably when we are told exactly what the testing involves (think urine, stool and saliva samples). Let your imagination run riot, I'm sure you don't want to know how the above are to be delivered.

Our group was then split into two subgroups: Experimental and Non-Experimental. I was in the experimental subgroup, and we were informed that we would be told our results immediately, whilst the others would not learn their results until the conclusion of the study. These tests had importance from a training perspective as one would discover a lot about one's diet and where any shortfalls may lie.

Own up; who eats too much bread? Who has bread for breakfast, a sandwich for lunch and bread they dunk in their soup for tea or supper? Does this resonate with some of you? You are not alone. Justin, on seeing my test results was giving my diaries very close scrutiny. I appeared to exist on a staple diet of BREAD. He made a light-hearted comment about it initially but underneath there was a serious underlying message: time to change your diet now and no better to cut out the addictions of all addictions BREAD. All this was explained to me following my July time trials.

Ten days previously I was on a triathlon holiday in Southern France – the bread capital of Europe. No one makes bread like the French, with a *Boulangerie* on every street corner, freshly baked to perfection every morning. The odours literally ooze out of your nostrils, making you salivate to the point where you're drooling like a dog. How was it possible to resist a piece (baguette) of the nation's favourite food?

The second time trial came in August. Although I haven't managed to cut bread completely out of my diet I have switched to rye, which in small amounts has no deleterious effects.

Our extended winter had now become summer, the sunshine at last blasting down. My training went up a notch (several notches in fact) although my swimming was still weaker than desired. Lake swimming now beckoned; others were also now taking to lakes. One fine June day I pottered down to a local lake in Shepperton. Swimming in a lake I discovered is totally different to swimming in a pool. Without lanes for guidance you literally have to feel yourself round the lake, which can be disconcerting at times. A feeling of seasickness was also never far away.

I had been struggling in the pool the lake proved far more of a struggle, the water seemed to hold one back – or maybe it was just me fighting the water. My devotion to the lake had been absolute to the point where I would almost worship it, not that it became a place for prayer, though I did pray my technique would improve and that group sessions I had been taking in the pool learning the crawl would not be lost on me. But to improve further I needed a coach. Haley proved very helpful, she taught me how to breathe – it being quite possible to lose your breath in awe of the whole lake experience. But... although I was making steps I needed to make strides.

I'd been going to Shepperton many times, each time trying on different wetsuits two, three, occasionally four times a week in search of that elusive swim and wetsuit fit Then one day, when Shepperton was shut, I searched online for a different lake and found the beautiful lake of Bray.

The difference between the two lakes is remarkable. Shepperton's largest loop is 750m Bray is 1200m but preferring to stick within my parameters of comfort I'd use the 750m loop figuring that was enough to get my head round for the time being. Another big difference was management. Bray is more relaxed, but also far more professional. I found a new coach, who is head of both Bray and Heron lakes; where I've also swam. Following coaching my swimming improved dramatically. I soon became known as *"the lady of the lake"*.

If anyone deserved a medal for [swimming] improvement I believe that medal would go to me. I had progressed from struggling to reach one hundred metres to swimming multiple laps of the 750m loop, albeit interspersed with a bit of breaststroke, all the time working on newly acquired techniques. I no longer fight the water but go more with the flow. I am getting there slowly but surely, persevering in the hope I'll get there one day. So long as that day comes by the end of the month, that's all that will matter!

My summer of sport

> *In my childhood days sport was a major player for myself at school: Gymnastics, Rounder's, Netball, Athletics. Long Jump got me to Crystal Palace albeit third place*

Cycling has taken me on a long journey. In earlier times cycling was purely recreational – some thirty miles per day interspersed with tea and pub stops and hoping it wouldn't rain.

I had entered the odd sportive; The London Bikeathon a fifty-two-mile loop from Ham House via Chelsea Embankment finished in less than three hours on a hybrid.

Triathlon brings cycling to a whole new level – my hybrid would just not cope. A road bike was purchased – then there was getting used to cleats, hoping one wouldn't fall off, but everybody does at first. I just didn't expect to knacker the handlebars on my first flip into the unknown. It could have been worse, the bike and myself escaped requiring major surgery.

Practice makes perfect. I had learnt a lot of the art of road riding from Mike, a bike mechanic who coached me to success after I struggled with my first two sportives; southern half of London MITIE (eighty-four miles from Windsor to ExCel). I was not mad enough to attempt both halves at this stage, the first being one hundred miles over the Chiltern Hills before overnighting at Windsor. I could only look up in awe at Justin sailing through the entire event while I was struggling to climb the Surrey hills.

It is only May, time is still on my side. I hadn't yet gained the experience to master such terrain although a lot was learned for my next sportive.

Nightrider – A 100km ride starting 11:00pm at Crystal Palace winding up through Docklands to Alexander Palace then back via Victoria and Lambeth to Crystal Palace where I finished just after 6:00am. Cycling at night I found confuses the body clock. I found it difficult to take my nutrition but overall it was a fantastic experience.

Prudential Ride London my major cycling event of the year came out of the blue. I had entered the ballot in February the year before but had heard nothing more, until my entry papers dropped through the letterbox in late June.

Ride London was a truly unforgettable experience the route being on closed roads and a close mimic of the Olympic event the previous year. At dawn, 4th August, thousands assemble at Olympic Park and make their way to the start waves. My wave is L, scheduled to hoof it just after 7:00am At the gun I (along with a few hundred others) are off, not too fast as the [timed] start is about a mile or two down the road. Crossing the start line I go there's no stopping me, except when I need nutrition, not having mastered the art of consuming energy gels on the hoof (something I am still learning to this day) The first pit stop is Bushy Park, but the sun is coming up fast and strong and I realise I've left my sunglasses in the car. I stop briefly to send a text. Fortunately John is able to reach Bushy Park in time but I have the unenviable task of crossing a road very busy with cyclists to reach him.

Valuable time has now been lost; I still have to reach the hills. The next pit stop is Newlands Corner, top of a very steep climb. I reach it at 10:45 where I plunk my arse down for a well-earned sandwich.

Do I want to move? No. Do I need the loo? Yes – so lose yet more time in what is a long queue but at last I am on way towards the infamous Box Hill. This I ascend with little drama, its not really that steep – just a long climb. At the top it's time for another breather and refreshment, but my stomach has shut down; I can't consume anything. With great reluctance I continue, running on empty and soon pay the price. At Headley there is a downhill then an immediate [steep] uphill section at which point my body says "No more" and I come to a halt. Fumbling in my pocket for a protein snack, it [now] goes down with little effort after which I make good progress to Leatherhead. This is the final last pit stop but fearing I may not finish with another stop I keep going. Some gels fortunately sustain us for the final leg into Putney, along Embankment, up Pall Mall and to the finish line just over 8hrs from the start.

The beginning of September we all had a weekend group training session. Saturday we attempted a 3.8km swim, this turned out to be my first 3km swim, which was applauded by all around. Sunday we had a 160km cycle ride, four laps + a short lap around Windsor Great Park. I only completed 120km but was told it was a tough course far tougher than Barcelona would bring. Directly after (just like the real thing) we had a run. This was a mere walk-in-the-park compared to many [saddle sore] hours on the bike. After the first lap I chickened out – it was Sept 1st (my birthday) the first time ever I haven't put my feet up on that day.

My stepfather had given me a card featuring a guy on a bike with the words: 'Birthday wishes', with inside 'Max Out to the limit'. Little did he (and I) know how true those words would ring on my birthday.

The following Sunday I ran the Baachus Half-Marathon. Yet another nutrition lesson was learned, I almost bonked out in sight of the end. A protein snack saved the day although not without a stomach stitch – lessons still to learn.

The next weekend (is this girl crazy) I ran The Bupa Great North run, finishing in 2hrs 45min in horrendous conditions. Later, I was staggering about like Pinocchio on crutches and remained so for the next two days.

Barcelona now beckons – bring it on.

But first: What has been learnt from this experience?

(i) *Preparation is key.*
(ii) *Rest days are essential.*
(iii)(and most important) *Nailing one's nutrition strategy.*

I'm still learning, but have learnt more in a year about the mechanism of my body than in my entire lifetime.

Sadly Barcelona failed to come off as hoped – the swim proved to be a step too far. More important lessons have been learned:

D on't mess with the sea
I t is a powerful force
S how it your utmost respect
T est it to full **distance** a month before your race
A lso, don't forget to breathe
N ever be afraid of asking for help
C alella was a hard bolt to crack
E ven the strongest of swimmers found it tough

What of the future – was Barcelona the big finale?

After investing what seemed to be my life savings on this incredible journey and pouring all that time and energy into something many of us came into from the cold it would be stupid to call it quits right now.

Mel giving it her all – she will be back for more

On the agenda include a short 10km run called Run in the Dark in November at Battersea Park and two 100km cycle sportives in May 2014. However the highlight has to be Chantilly (France) a triathlon featuring a lake swim around a castle. So I leave you with this final message.

The Message: Practice makes perfect – if at first you don't succeed just TRI again.

CHAPTER 15

"The Unhappiness of Thor"
By David Wilkey

The omens were not auspicious.

The whole anticlockwise tube service out of Liverpool Street was shut due to a signalling fault at Aldgate. Fortunately, the delay was only temporary, and I was soon trying to lump my bike bag up and downstairs in full battle with the normal commuters. Gatwick airport was uneventful, only a slight delay to the outbound flight... which seemed to extend whilst in the air to a 30 min delay on arrival. This had become a full hour's delay once the bike bag finally arrived... Still, I'd paid extra for a shuttle service to the hotel, for which I simply had to meet a yellow-shirted operative at the Tourist Office. Sadly, the only yellow-shirted operatives were not from the nominated supplier. Apparently I had to get to the other terminal, contrary to the written instructions I had been given to follow exactly.

Some minutes were lost in search of the shuttle service to terminal 2B – apparently the Shuttle service in Barcelona is a fast air service to Madrid. I finally found the bus, and was in T2B shortly. A long trek with the bike bag to the appointed meeting point where I eventually met the right yellow-shirted operative, fully decked out in matching fleece (it being a balmy 28°C at least, and me rather warm from bike dragging exertions). Apparently, my bus to Calella would be along shortly. Another trek to the bus park, where the bus was indeed waiting, and after only a short delay for a few other passengers, we were on our way… Back to T1, where more passengers were embarked, as the minutes ticked by. Getting to the unofficial but nevertheless quite important pre-race briefing was looking decidedly sketchy. Was the one hundred minute allowance for the 50k to Calella inclusive of airport terminal dalliances, or, for that matter, Friday night commuter traffic?

The answer was no.

A stag party, provided a moment of levity still in the early stages of inebriation, cheering on the groom in what was probably his first outing on roller blades, and definitely his first outing in a black leotard.

We eventually arrived into Calella, up and down a not very flat looking coast road, a little before seven, rolling past the hotel where the briefing was, and continuing slowly north in the fading sun and lethargic traffic. A quick check-in at my hotel, and my warm-up run was the jog back into town to hear the last of the 'race briefing' and more on strategy. Still, it was warm, and the forecast suggested we'd seen the last of the rain. As the briefing moved into Q&A, the thunder started, nearly drowning out the PA in the basement room. All thoughts of walking down to the Finish area to see the pasta party and band were washed away.

Dinner was spent marvelling at the physiques of some of the Oktoberfest guests, who also appeared to be feeding an iron-appetite (or possibly just an iron-thirst).

Saturday dawned bright and blue – perhaps the sunshine that made this coast famous would stick around, much like the aroma of all-day breakfasts and 'doner kebab' from the many cheap eateries that abounded the backstreets.

A full day of race prep beckoned, so after a DIY breakfast of porridge and mixed nuts with special extras of goji berries and flax seed (see the austere diet of a triathlete, none of the hearty fare mere runners partake of!) it was time to head for race registration, the official briefing, and "expo". Justin, our tireless leader, researcher, provisioner, nutritionist and all round tri-god had warned us that the Challenge team were sticklers for punctuality and timekeeping. And to start with, they were. No-one was getting into the registration hall until 10am on the watch of the doorkeeper, a formidable lass who was almost certainly to be seen that evening at the Oktoberfest, manhandling large quantities of beer, whether in steins or in Germans.

Registration itself was fairly straightforward, not least as there were only around 1100 amateur entrants, and at least some were sensible enough to turn up and register on prior days. A sign indicating where to purchase the compulsory licence would have been useful, but that was swiftly dealt with. The registrars, despite asking for, and being given, my shiny new licence, proceeded to ask my name and race number – clearly written on said licence... And then after being given the magic envelope containing not quite everything I'd need for race day, and a fancy backpack containing different items but still not quite everything, I was free to peruse the random assortment of stalls whilst waiting for the English briefing clearly scheduled for eleven. The Cervelo stand had the most tempting goodies, include a "test ride" offer – I suspect a credit card and passport required as deposit. The ADF, who appeared to be the local forestry protection organisation, also had a stand (lots of pictures of trees, and butterflies) but sadly no english translation of what they do.

Nutrisweet had a promo for a drinks bottle pre-filled with their nutritional beverage... After queuing for a while, they ran out of water required to reconstitute their tasty beverage. I spent longest at the "official merchandise" stand, although that seemed to be mostly official as far as the supplier were concerned, and their marketing would have been bettered by most on the Apprentice. Selling old event shirts may be of interest to completists, but no-one competing in an iron-distance event is going to want to buy a 70.3 branded item…

Eleven came around not a moment too soon, and we eagerly took our seats to receive the pearls of wisdom. After an intro in Spanish, the main agenda, also in Spanish, appeared… And the presenter launched in to the contents in earnest. Quite promptly, considering the generally reserved traditions of the Brits, a voice enquired as to whether this was not supposed to be the English briefing. "Not according to my schedule" came the prompt reply… A copy of the event programme was produced, which confirmed the timetable on the door as correct. But she would not budge. A revised time of twelve was agreed. I sat through the Spanish one to get a feel for the contents… It was fairly easy to understand the key points: swim a long way, cycle even further, run 4x10km loops.

As this all took less than thirty minutes, I decamped back to the expo to stretch my legs… Returning at five to twelve to discover the English briefing in full swing. Fortunately I'd not missed much. The most important bit was really the weather info at the end, which I'd not followed in Spanish. It was something of a let down. The presenter confessed that she wasn't a weather girl, and that whilst she could tell us what the weather was doing now, she had not the faintest idea of what the weather would be like tomorrow.

Still, I had most of the essentials required to compete, so it was back to the hotel to assemble and test ride the bike (and discover whether I d brought all the tools), and to try to plan the contents of the Red (for Bike), Blue (for Run), and Green (for Going home) bags. The race guide booklet wasn't a lot of help – whilst the Run and Bike bags were fairly straightforward, quite what we were supposed to put in the Green bag, and when, was an exercise left to the triathlete. Were we supposed to turn up to the start in our wetsuits? Or would there be changing facilities at the start/finish (which was 1.5km down the beach from the bike park). Anyway, it was something to consider over dinner, the remains of a loaf from the local baker, and a pot of what was supposed to be honey, but which turned out to look suspiciously like laxative. Next time I race in a foreign country, I'll bring a language guide.

Race day

The day hadn't dawned – at 6am it was pitch black. Another round of porridge and magic berries, without the 'disappointingly not honey' topping. It didn't counter the nerves. I repacked the bags again, fetched the drinks bottles out of the fridge, and with nothing else left to do, struggled down to the bike park with Red bag, Blue Bag, Green Bag, bag full of bottles and gels for bike, pump, and helmet. The sun was just starting to break over the horizon – a golden-ruby glow above the calm, grey, leaden sea. Gels strapped onto the bike, tyres pumped, red and blue bags dropped off, and a walk down the beach to the start line. Goggle choice could prove to be critical – it might get sunny, and the main leg was northeast facing. Time to get the wetsuit on – baby oil helped immensely, especially as the shaved legs made it a lot harder to put on – who'd have thought leg hair was useful? A fellow competitor had never seen this approach before – I'm not sure the phrase 'baby oil' translated very well, judging by the look he gave me. He wished me a good race, nonetheless.

The race waves were only a few minutes apart, so with ten minutes to go, I was down at the start pen. The sight of a thousand people all in neoprene with coloured hats is a scene ripe with comedy potential, although I wasn't really in the mood for that. As we were ushered into the start area, the full enormity of what I was about to start hit me. Nine months of sweat and sacrifice, 6am starts, double sessions on a workday, and long and lonely weekend rides were biting hard. The sand was cold and damp, the sea grey and limpid. One of those moments when time seems to stop, just briefly… but there is no turning back. Commitment is absolute. Age group forty to forty-five entered the arena. The cannon fires, and into the maelstrom we dived.

There's no two ways about the swim, it was a long, cold, grey slog. 100m out, turn right, 800m south, turn left 100m, turn left again and 2300m up the coast. The main-end buoys were so far apart they were hard to see from the beach, never mind in the water. Sighting was mostly about following the people in front, and trying not to be put off by the waves from behind swimming over me. At least when running I can step to the side of faster people behind – when swimming, you don't know they're there until it's a grab at the foot, or an elbow in the back… I tried to pace the swim, honestly I did, but I lost all sense of time in the salty greyness. As we slowly crawled up the back straight, the waves started to grow, and the swell induced nausea… but as we neared the final buoy, the water flattened and the sun came out. The last 100m into the finish chute took an age, and suddenly I could stand up (or was I being hauled up). A cruel 200m of soft sand into T1, and past the first casualty, shivering uncontrollably in a foil blanket.

A T1 helper was on hand to get me out of my wetsuit and into my bike gear – no point bothering with the towel to dry myself, there's a race on. I stood up to try to put my helmet on, and promptly collapsed onto the bench, knocking my special 'anti-salt' beverage (flat full fat coke) all over my helper. "*Tranquillo, tranquillo*" was the response. I think that translates to "don't be collapsing on my shift". I wobbled out to find my bike (unsurprisingly not very hard), spilling more coke, and finding that trying to run with the bike and the bottle and not take my shins out on the pedals was too much for my swim-addled brain. Another 200m until the transition line. I somehow managed to get on the saddle without falling off, and once the gyroscope effect of the wheels got going, began to feel almost comfortable. However there was a sharp stabbing pain in my right thigh with every pedal stroke. My carefully attached gels had slipped, and a turgid tube of finest gunk was rubbing my leg. Unfortunately the first km or so was a narrow technical route through Calella's backstreets to the main road, so was unable to fix… and anyway, most of the photographers seemed to be in this initial section, and pictures of me with my hand up my shorts or in front of my crotch weren't going to look pleasant. Finally out on the N11, southbound to Barcelona, and a chance to sort the gels out. But oh, what's this. A hill. Justin said Calella was flat!

Hills were my nemesis in training – not being a cyclist, I'd spent hours grinding up Leith Hill, Box Hill and the sharp inclines in Richmond Park, not to mention some others I'd got lost on in random routes in Oxfordshire. Out of the saddle, and up we go. It actually wasn't too bad, and I soon found Jodie, one of my HURTS teammates. It would have been nice to chat, but we'd been warned about drafting, so after some polite encouragement, I pushed on. A little later, another incline, and then another. I think there were about five in the first 10km, and then it settled down. Onto the tri bars, up into the uncharted territory of the fourth and fifth cogs on the back wheel, and head up to keep the aero helmet optimised.

The first hour ticked by quite nicely, and the next. So where exactly was the turning point? Nature was starting to call, and whilst it wasn't exactly 'built up'; it wasn't exactly 'countryside' either. And then I heard bagpipes. This was all getting a bit much. And there he was, a piper in an underpass, making the most of the closed roads. Finally, the turning roundabout, and a small crowd. It seemed a long way out. And now I had to go back, and do it all again. Head down, grit teeth, and keep the faith.

Heading up the hills into Calella, out of the saddle again, it felt ok. Over two hours in, and my knees weren't burning at all, this was a good sign. Lots of cheering at the inner turn point, and then back out for round two. I backed off the pace a wee bit, but promised to dance up the hills. By the time I got to the outward turn point on the second time, the crowds had gone, just a couple of guardia civil. We waved, solitary executioners of our respective destinies.

On the return leg, the sky over Calella was turning dark. By the time I was halfway back, I could see the rain in the distance, a grey haze over the road. And suddenly Thor's vengeance was upon me. The lightning whistled and cracked, the thunder made the ground roll, and the rain, well, it was like an African monsoon. The drains were engulfed in minutes, and soon the road was inches deep in water. My glasses steamed up, the only time they've let me down, but even at 14mph the rain was stinging my limbs so the glasses stayed on. Discarded bottles from the feed stations floated like mines across the road, searching for unwary rims to trip. If Hell was wet, this is what it must be like. The rain lasted no more than fifteen minutes, but the roads were soaked, puddles were huge, and overtaking was seriously unpleasant due to the spray coming off the tyres. The supporters at the Calella end seemed to have dissolved in the rain as well.

Leg two complete, now just the short leg to go. It hadn't felt that far on the way out, but slogging out to the roundabout at Vallendres, only about 15km, seemed to take forever. By some stroke of good fortune, I only seemed to have spent six hours up to this point… I could just about read the Garmin now the rain had eased, and I might be on for 6.5hr time… this would balance out the near two hours the swim had taken me, and put me back within reach of my stretch target of a 12hr + time. On the homeward leg, I had some racing to do – a few stragglers were there for the picking off, and my legs were holding up for the hills. The feed station team had given up with the dancing and shouting, and were morosely plodding around in their cagoules as I heaved myself up the last incline, then straight over the roundabout and into the warren of backstreets.

Running into T2, I had to fight to rack my bike… but at least there was plenty of space in the tent! A quick change, no point worrying about not having dry socks, and suddenly a series of explosions. Initial panic turned to surprise when I realised it was the fireworks celebrating the Elite finish… and then I was off out into the sandy mud and the first short leg. Lots of cheering now, as the run was in full swing, and the first couple of kilometres were deep with people. First loop around the start/finish area, and a degree of mental effort required to calculate that from that point it was in fact four laps… and so I cracked on.

The first lap went quite well, I was averaging just under 9.30minute/miles, and whilst this felt good, I wasn't sure I could keep it up. I tried to back off a bit, but kept wanting to catch people. By the time lap two was complete, it was dark, and the crowds were thinning. Then it started to rain again. Lap three was tough, I was starting to tire, and it was difficult to hold my pace at anything, and a few laps drifted down to 11minute/miles, and I had to do some walks at the feed stations. The one upside was the fruit – sweet orange quarters, and charming children handing them out. At the end of lap three, there was a band playing at the finish line, and having spent the entire day without music, even a cover version of Queen's 'One Vision' provided a much-needed boost.

I'd taken a gel at each of the first three hours, and figured I might as well throw everything on the fire for the final lap, so broke out the emergency caffeine gels. It tasted like rocket fuel, and seemed to do the trick. I felt my pace increase, and thought I'd try and hold it for half way, and see what happened, mindful that by this stage on my previous marathons I'd usually hit the wall. Garmin reckoned I had about fifty-six minutes to do the last 10km and get inside thirteen hours..., which was about the time I'd taken on the first lap. This was going to be tough. I kicked off once more, and just focused on keeping a steady tempo. By this time, a lot of the remaining runners were looking distinctly the worse for wear. I'd already seen one chap collapse at a feed station, and passed another who was doing a creditable impression of a zombie. I'd given up trying to play tunes in my head, even the motivational ones, and my mind was just rambling. At 36km, I figured I had about thirty minutes to get round, so I was still just about on track, but it was going to be really tight. I then managed to miss the next two markers, and I was suddenly at 39km. I'd given up trying to work out the pace, so I just tried to time myself for the next km. That next km took nearly nine minutes... but the 40km marker was conveniently at the bike park... maybe it wasn't entirely accurate? I knew I had a little over 2km to go, and I had about sixteen minutes in which to do it... but I'd just spent nearly nine doing half that distance.

Time to up the pain level, and just go hard.

I now know what people mean when they talk about tunnel vision, I was just totally focused on the path in front of me, and passing people without getting caught up. As the final marker came into view, and I hit the red carpet for the final time, I tried to recall the advice our research lead had given about looking presentable for the finish photographers… I think I managed to get my arms up for about two seconds, before collapsing first into the arms of Justin, who'd managed to get a role giving out medals, and then being gently passed to Kimberley, our honorable 'iron-mother'. And that was it. Twelve hours fifty-two minutes and some frankly irrelevant seconds. I'd managed to pace it just about right, not over or under-do the nutrition, or get sick, or break a wrist, or a bike, or worse. I'd hit the target, and even managed to pull off a negative split on the run.

What an epic day.

The Message: It's all about the goal. Nine months of early starts, double-shifts at the gym, weekends sacrificed to the road,

David "defying Thor" IRONMAN Wilkey

relationships stretched to breaking point, and for what... a day of prolonged physical pain, yes, but then a lifetime of knowing what you can really achieve when you put your mind to it. Do you have it in you?

CHAPTER 16

"Nerves" *By Jason Baker*

Why do an ironman triathlon? To compete with the pro's? To win a medal? To prove I can do it? For me it was the chance to try something new and mark my thirtieth birthday with something to remember. I was approached by a colleague, named Eva Fleming, who asked me "you like to exercise right"? I said "yes, I do, I love it, but an ironman triathlon… that's really pushing it and I'm hopeless at swimming".

Her next words were:

"Go to this screening, they are still looking for people, if you get in I will help you with the swimming".

That's where it all started. I arrived at the last screening for a research study by the University of Hertfordshire based in a lab set up with stationary bikes and people being motivated to push harder and go faster while data was being taken all over the room by researchers in white coats; resting heart rates, height and weight, ECGs and fitness assessment. I had no idea at this stage whether I was eligible. From what I could see, it looked fun. The lab team asked me if I was a runner?

"I hate running" I replied.

"Great!" said the team.

After my cycle test I was told my results, I didn't understand it. "Does that mean I'm on the study?" "Yes!" said the team. Feeling happy about their answer, and a few words with the project lead, Dr Justin Roberts, I left the lab on the cold winter night thinking… "Holy shit, I got to learn to swim!"

I returned to work and spoke to my colleague Eva and told her the good news of my making the study. Eva had also been chosen. We arranged an early morning 7am pool swim together, I was hopeless and realised I had a long way to go after watching Eva doing her tumble turns and length after length gliding through the water making it look easy. Eva was to become my training partner and swim mentor.

Training started in January. The first month didn't seem too difficult apart from swimming, as I was a regular gym member; I loved the functional training and core exercises set out by Justin. Week by week trying to push that extra bit further or increasing the weight or repetition. I always found it funny watching other blokes in the gym huffing and puffing with loud groans of pain while weightlifting… Surely I can do this without making all that over-the-top nonsense!

As part of the study a nutrition diary and training diary was required. How easy this is going to be I thought, I'm just going to bang it in my phone, then record it on paper before we need to hand it in. Breakfast was normally quite easy as it was always the same. The little snacks throughout the day were a bit picky for the diary but it was definitely a good indication on how many times I attacked the office biscuit tin post lunch… Note to self: cut down on biscuits, buy extra next week for colleagues, and realise I am greedy biscuit monster.

Eva and I organised weekly swimming sessions and talked regularly on our progress or troubles. The group Facebook page became an instant tool for motivation from others on the study, sharing ideas on making training easier or advice on our training woes and a reminder of the weeks we had to go, until October 6th.

At times things were slightly stressful choosing the right bike, warnings of injuries, juggling training with work and life, and reaching the new benchmarks in order to feel ready, was challenging. I'm glad the team Facebook page also had regular comments on something we could all giggle at. Soon, weekly swimming sessions with Eva became easier with the introduction of the pool buoy and flippers… "I can swim!"

"You have to push the water back and bring your head just above the water for your next breath, don't come up so high, your technique is getting better" said Eva.

I walked the process through in the pool, thinking if I can get the basics right and learn how to deal with these freaking leg cramps, "I can do this!"

My lunch breaks soon turned into one-hour running sessions over the fields of Totteridge. I always used music as my motivator and felt I couldn't run without it, never starting a run without a good tune in my headphones to get me going, until one day my colleague arrived at work to inform us of sad news of a child who had been diagnosed at the age of twelve with cancer. I left the office and went running. The whole time on my run all I could think about was this poor young boy and what him and his family must be going through. I returned to the office to realise I had completed my first run without my MP3 player.

After three months I loved running sessions and the steep hills on my running route became easier, every run was done without music. My run sessions also became a time to de-stress and think things through. I soon started to try using gels during my running sessions in order to create and practice my strategy on feeding on the day of the event as we were advised to. I had never used gels before and I soon got to realise that they were not a popular option for me as I was out running in the middle of nowhere with a stomach about to explode… must find toilet, must find toilet, run faster, need toilet.

Eva and I began early-morning cycle sessions at weekends, some beginning at 4:30am, cycling around the back roads of

Hertfordshire. The early mornings were beautiful and Eva continually kept me entertained with how her week had been and we discussed issues we might have on the day…

"Jason, when we are on this event and we are on the bike, what do we do when we need to pee?" We had heard rumours that the professionals just continue riding and pee at the same time. We were both wondered as to how this could be done.

"Eva… I really don't think I am going to be able to pee and ride at the same time" I said. The months went by, and the training distances and hours increased, we all knew it had to be done in order to get to the starting line, ready for the challenge we had all been working towards. A group training session had been organised for us in Windsor: a 3.8km swim in Bray Lake on Saturday, and 180km cycle and run on Sunday.

Eva, Bradley and I arrived, suited up ready for the plunge. Around the first lap I went, I was a slow swimmer and often had to flip on my back and paddle for a bit before I continued with front crawl. Remembering what Eva had taught me I continued on to my second lap and all of a sudden attack of cramp in the left leg.

"Shit shit shit!"

I stopped in the water feeling sick, squeezing my leg, and looking around for the next orange buoy. I continued slowly on, knowing I had another lap to do after I had finished this one. After ten minutes the cramp disappeared only to show its ugly head again a short time later in my right leg. Determined not to let it stop me as it had done on our sea swim in Bournemouth the previous weekend I continued on to complete the distance, thinking if this happens on the day, I have to be able to deal with it. I made it to the finish to be helped out of the water by Eva and Bradley.

"Jason, you did it in two hours"!

Exhausted, but happy with the result, I had managed it.

We returned to Windsor for the cycling on Sunday I was quite looking forward to this, we were all about to set off and after not being able to clip out of my pedals fast enough, like a falling tree "Timmmbbeeerrr" still clipped in my pedals I fell… second time… I'm used to it by now. No harm done.

Eva, Jamie and I set off on the cycle route around Windsor only to realise after thirty-five minutes we had ended up back at starting point all over again as we had taken a wrong turn.

We were one month away from for Barcelona Challenge and the countdown was really on more than ever with the constant reminders on the group Facebook page. I was getting excited and already nervous and Eva was ready to take on the challenge:

"Jason, I could do this event tomorrow you know, I'm really ready for this and we have to watch out for those damn jellyfish, when we are swimming in Barca and I hope we don't see any sharks" said Eva.

"Don't worry, Eva, you swim so fast you will be one of the first out of the water, no sharks will be after you". I became so nervous I started avoiding thinking about last-minute things I needed to do before leaving for the event to the point I left my packing to the night before I was due to go to the airport, along with a list of things I was going to pack, and reading the group Facebook page I felt better knowing I wasn't the only one.

"I procrastinate at the worst of times"

I was travelling to Barcelona alone, and having friends meet me out there, I was wound up and anxious leaving the house en route to my local tube station. I had my bike all packed up in a bike box in tow with me, and I was thinking the train staff were going to stop me from taking it on the tube because it's too big. I wasn't ready to be dealing with this today.

I arrived in Calella three days before the event. I went for a sneaky peak down at the beach where I ran into John also from TEAM HURTS, it was good to see a familiar face. We looked at the choppy sea.

"Let's hope its not like that on Sunday," I said.

5th of October, one day left before the big one, nerves slightly astray, going through packing the right things to each bag, I was glad my friend Kayne kept me calm while I was doing this, as my order of contents to each bag for running and cycling had gone out the window. How am I going to sleep tonight I thought, I still have to have dinner, have I drunk enough today, what have I forgotten, I need to meditate… I wish my brain had a set of brakes.

Sunday 6th October Challenge Barcelona day has arrived. 5am the alarm clock rings its usual church bell charm. I pause before swinging my legs out of bed and nervously start to have breakfast which consists of a large portion of muesli, a banana, two doughnuts *(editors' note: really… doughnuts!)*, supplements and the usual morning electrolyte drink. Beginning to feel anxious I decided to tell myself that I was going on an early morning training session with Eva and today was just going to be a very long training session. Once I thought about it this way, I was able to walk out the door, down to transition for final checks on the bike, and bag drop. The weather was looking good, no breeze, and the sea calm as I past the beach… phew!

Mingling near the starting line I exchanged good luck messages with others from TEAM HURTS and a quick pat on the back from Justin before it was time to line up. Music was pumping from the speakers with a compere to get everyone in the mood. I looked out in front of me to the first yellow buoy. They were to become my new best friends.

"I can do this" I said to myself.

Bang goes the starter gun. Before I know we are all in the sea flapping like ducks in a big mass of yellow swim caps and black wetsuits. I try to position myself out of the way of other swimmers; anybody that touched me as they passed me stopped me in my tracks. I continued on looking ahead for the next orange buoy I could see in front of me. Each one I passed filled me with confidence that I could get to the next one. I was on the 2350m stretches and I could feel the beginnings of cramp in my toes. Hoping it wouldn't move to my calf muscles I said to myself...

"Please not today, not now".

I continued on to the next buoy, I had a boat pull up beside me and tell me I had ten minutes. I continued on, arms becoming tired, another boat pulls up beside me to tell me:

"The swim is over you must get in the boat and we will take you to the beach".

"Everyone finishes!" I yelled back. (*Editors' note: that's the spirit, Jason*)

These guys don't know how long it's taken me to get to this point. I'm not letting them stop me now I thought.

I carried on to the beach with a guide behind me. I could see there were a few others still in the water as well, my arms were almost ready to drop off, and I stood, scrambled to my feet to run through a cheering crowd. I had made the swim!

Onwards to the cycling area, although I had my timing chip removed I was determined to keep going and was trying hard not to have a melt down as the wetsuit was stripped off me. Out to the bike cheered on by friends I was soon on the road. Cheered on by other non-racing TEAM HURTS members from the road side it was just what I needed as I started the hill climb. It was so great to see other TEAM HURTS members, I thought I was so far behind I wouldn't see anybody.

Then I hear "Jaaaaason you're my hero!"

Eva went zooming past on the other side of the road...

"Go Eva!" I shouted.

A refill on water at one of the stations and I was off again. It hammered it down with rain on the second lap, but I just enjoyed it and there were local supporters on the roadside still cheering, it really makes a difference.

Jamie on the super bike passed me and asked me how many laps we were supposed to be doing, this made me laugh. Needing to pee, I tried for a good hour to just pee while I was still on the bike and it just wouldn't happen… I thought this would be easy, why didn't I try this during training?

I gave up and found a bush.

I made my way through my food slowly as I didn't feel I could stomach any more gels just yet. The rain eased but soon started again even heavier than before. Visibility was poor. The roads were beginning to reopen I caught up with Martin another member of TEAM HURTS. Martin seemed deflated as he had also been timed out on the swim too:

"We have to keep going Martin, *everybody finishes.*"

We rode back into Calella together still being cheered on by passers-by. A quick change into running gear and I was off. The same race marshal who I spoke to after coming out of the water that morning seemed surprised to see me. I was even more motivated than before to finish this. Only 42km to go. It was great to see all the supporters again and the atmosphere was brilliant. I managed the first and second lap well, and the feeding stations with sliced orange were welcomed. All the gels I had taken that day had finally caught up with me and it was time to find an unoccupied toilet at the other end of the beach, however there were none; but I did find an empty restaurant. Into the cubicle I go to do my business and the lights on the sensor went off as soon as I hit the seat and refused to come back on as I waved my hands in the dark.

"I can't f**king believe this, this is really the wrong time to be happening" I shouted. Feeling around for bog paper in the dark I managed to clean myself up, stood up, took one step and the lights came back on.

Back to the running route to continue roughly 14km until I could finish. I saw the fireworks in the sky. I caught up with Eva on her last lap looking so happy with the biggest smile on her face. I was soon back past the starting point, and on to my final lap, singing my favourite tune until I forgot the words; I kept a steady pace. Nearing the finish line, on to the red carpet the music pumping and the remainder of the supporters of TEAM HURTS joined to make a tunnel for me to pass over the finish line at midnight. I felt amazing as I completed my first ever Ironman Triathlon.

Perseverance got me through this. I believed I could do it, no matter how hard things became I told myself: "I can do this". I really stick to this theory and encourage others to just try it when things are getting tough, and the nerves are getting to you.

Overcoming the nerves: Jason 'Ironman' Baker

The Message: We all get nervous from time to time. Believe 'you can', and persevere to the finish line… no matter what.

CHAPTER 17

"Doubt" *By Peter Benson*

Doubt
daʊt/
noun
A feeling of uncertainty or lack of conviction.

Doubt and His Unruly Friends

There he is, the sneaky bugger. I'd been nervously waiting for him to turn up. It was late this time, quite unusual – punctual without hesitation normally – just as I lay my head. It starts like the quiet ticking of a misplaced watch, slowly building as you try desperately to ignore it. "*Shhh be quiet, please, leave me be.*" No chance, it only grows, caught in a vicious circle spiralling out of control. The more I try to subdue it, the more fuel I put on the fire. Oh dear, doubts delightful little brother, Tension, has turned up. Why not bring your cousin in too – let's have a party. Anxiety.

"Have I trained enough?"
"My calf's tight, is that an injury?"
"What if my goggles snap in the swim?"
"The taper was too long, I've lost fitness, and I'm going to struggle!"
"What if I can't deal with the pain?"
"What if I give up and let everyone down?"

I ran through the emotions, thought of every disaster, the fear of disappointment and letting people down. How heavy a weight expectation is.

"What excuse will suffice if I don't complete, what will disappointment look like in the eyes of those well wishers?"

"Christ, now I can't sleep."

Doubt, Tension and Anxiety didn't invite the Sandman, they came alone, just to play with me. How kind.

This is a time of complete loneliness, it's you that let these intruders in, and only you that can hear them and only you can deal with them. No one will understand the fear they cause and the mess they make. The door is slammed shut in the face of reassurance, and those that try to offer it. The party is on fire! Now they've let the butterflies loose… I've had this feeling before, it shouldn't bother me. *"Stop being a fool, you've done enough, trained hard, and followed the programme. Have I though?"*

It's a funny thing, *'The Night Before'*, it's like a Hollywood saga played out on the back of your eyelids. It's far better than 3D too, it operates on every plane, from your big toe to your little finger through to the deepest recesses of your mind… Each part of this epic saga plays out in vivid detail, profiling a journey of anguish.

The scene is set with Denial – denial that you're capable, denial that your training was right, denial that you've done enough to finish. This unfettered questioning facilitates your brisk move through to Anger, angry with yourself for having that beer, missing the long run, avoiding the swim because it was too cold. Anger gets your heart racing, no chance of sleep now. Bargaining comes next.

"If I take it easy on the swim, have a gentle bike, I can walk the majority of the marathon. I should be able to finish then, surely. If I make it to run, then I'm happy."

That's my success… Oh, now the fourth chapter in this epic rears its ugly head, Depression. This is the saddest part. You knock yourself here, disappointment grabs hold of you and it reeks. Like a bad smell that won't shift. You get used to it though, now it doesn't smell anymore, that reek is the new normal. Your new normal. We now welcome our final chapter in this long saga, Acceptance. Acceptance allows for peace. A calm serenity comes over you and you can feel sleep knocking on your door. What will be will be. Comfort at last, sleep.

05:00hrs and the alarm goes off – it's D-Day. Coffee, breakfast, shower. Wow, I feel good, I feel happy, lets do this.

I was ready.

The journey of the night before was a long one. It wasn't particularly enjoyable either, but what it did do was give me a renewed strength of character. I ran through every possible situation that could ruin my race, knock me off course, derail my dream, but thankfully and unbeknown to me was that my old friend *Sub-Conscience* had locked himself under the stairs, listening to the racket Doubt, Tension and Anxiety were making, and took notes. Developing my Plan B.

I can safely say I've never doubted myself as much as I did that evening before the race. It was a new and humbling experience, facing the unknown. It gave me plenty to think about after the race, introspection is a powerful thing. I learnt more about myself about that night. I learnt that doubt is as powerful as it is inevitable. I learnt to embrace it. The theologian Georg Hermes put it well,

Peter ready for action

> *... the starting-point and chief principle of every science [and endeavour] is not only methodical doubt, but positive doubt. One can believe only what one has perceived to be true from reasonable grounds, and consequently one must have the courage to continue doubting until one has found reliable grounds to satisfy the reason...*

And so, onto the path to glory...

The Message: Plan B is just as important as Plan A – make sure you embrace your doubts, fears and anxieties to better prepare for what an Iron-Distance Triathlon will throw at you.

CHAPTER 18

"Gestation" *By Nicki Combarro*

The gestation period of an 'ironman' is nine months/forty weeks – well that is how long it has taken for my transformation!

Having never trained or competed for anything like this before the only significant challenges that I have faced in my life have been the two pregnancies associated with the birth of my children, Olivia, seven and Rafael, five. Strangely enough there have been a number of similarities between both events along the way! For example both events started off with a romantic gesture...

My husband has never really been a romantic soul; although I am sure he would strongly disagree, so I was pleasantly surprised when just before Christmas last year he suggested that maybe for 2013 we should do something nice together. It was going to be our tenth wedding anniversary in October and also my thirty-ninth birthday, so the suggestion was made that we should go away then. It all sounded like a lovely idea, as the kids were getting a little bit older they were more than happy to be looked after by Grandparents and the thought of a child-free weekend in the sun was very appealing.

As Christmas day drew closer and the conversation turned to what we were buying each other as presents, my husband could often be found flicking through bike magazines looking at the 'ladies' bikes and trying to engage me in conversation about them. I make no apologies for my lack of interest in bikes! The last bike I owned was a beat up old three-speed mountain bike that reliably got me to lectures on time during my first year of university, before I realised that having a car was far more convenient! So a road bike was completely off my radar, there was no way that I had the balance to be able to stay upright on those thin fragile looking tyres and as for those hard pointy saddles… the less said about those the better.

So imagine my surprise on Christmas Day when I saw that Santa had not only left two children's bikes under the tree, but also a very nice Boardman Ladies road bike! To this day I still can't tell you anything about the spec – apart from the fact that it is white and pink and has a matching helmet! *(Editors' note – this was a strangely common theme among the ironladies).*

Over the next few weeks it appeared that the goal posts of our romantic holiday were beginning to change. There was talk of taking the bikes away with us to help with the sightseeing and, in fact, there was a Challenge bike race in Barcelona in October, so he felt that this could be a good fun location to go to and an activity to do while we were there! I could feel the romantic weekend slowly slipping away…

It didn't take long for the whole 'Challenge Barcelona' ironman study truth to come out and being easily swayed it didn't take long before I had been convinced that it would actually be a great challenge for us to have this 'journey' together. As with most spontaneous decisions I didn't stop to think about the long-term commitment that this was going to be, the impact it was going to have on our family, especially the children and how on earth I was going to fit all the training into my already chaotic lifestyle!

As a physiotherapist working with athletes from a variety of sports I did have a genuine interest in the study, and decided that taking part would allow me to be on the receiving end of the testing for once, and would be a truly educational opportunity. As for my previous sporting achievements, I ran the New York Marathon in 1998 in 4hr 30minutes, vowed never to run another one and have since been running 8km for fitness a few times a week. I had once been a comfortable swimmer who would happily swim forty lengths without too much trouble – however since having kids my time in swimming pools had been restricted to catching children as they launched themselves into the pool without armbands on. As for my cycling… well the less said about that the better!

So with my eyes wide shut, and my common sense temporarily departed from my brain, I signed on the dotted line and signed away the next nine months of my life!

~.~

From my memories of 2006 when I first discovered I was pregnant I went through a wave of emotional responses, denial, excitement, apprehension and finally acceptance, acceptance that this was going to be a long journey and there was nothing I could do to change the fact that at the end of the journey there was going to be a significant, life-changing event that I needed to face! It didn't take me long to realise that although the ironman event was not going to be quite so life changing it was a challenge that I needed to embrace and embrace it I did in a similar way to how I had embraced pregnancy… by shopping!

So I already had the bike, which was fortunate, as just walking into a bike shop was as big a minefield as walking into Mothercare to buy a pushchair. Every salesman a bike expert, tirelessly trying to convince you that unless you purchased this superlightweight carbon bike you were going to be a bad triathlete. I clearly didn't look like an ironman in training and couldn't help feeling a little bit like Julia Roberts in the *Pretty Woman* scene when she is trying to buy clothes in a stylish boutique. However, upon mentioning the magic word 'ironman' people suddenly became over-helpful, I can only guess that they presumed I had cash to burn! Did I really need a watch that told me how many minutes my heart rate had been dangerously high, or beeped at me if I chose to slow my running down, and a bike computer that allowed people at home to track my ride and then come out and join me? Apparently I did! There were bearings, cassettes, derailleurs, rear mechs, bottom brackets, deep rim wheels, TT bars and tubeless tyres, and if I didn't upgrade all the components on my bike I really wasn't going to give my best performance on race day. And as for all the clothing I needed to buy, well let's just say I was getting the hang of this ironman lark!

Over the first few months I learnt more about myself than I could possibly imagine, my flexibility, exercise tolerance, running efficiency, heart rate, bone density, percentage body fat, VO_{2max} and lactic threshold were all precisely measured. By the end of each testing session I felt like a science experiment. We had been pushed on the bike to our maximum whilst having our fingers pricked for blood testing all in the name of science. The encouragement that we received from the testers was amazing as they helped us push ourselves to new limits.

Desperate to do the right thing and to give my body the best chance of becoming IRON I tweaked my diet, stopped drinking alcohol and tried to get some early nights. I was making the same conscientious choices that I did when I was pregnant and was insanely jealous that my husband, who was also training for the same event, continued to entertain corporate clients and indulge in rich food, red wine and late nights and was still able to get up before the crack of dawn to squeeze in his training sessions before the children woke up and my training started!

Regardless of the relentless training programme and trying to balance it with the rest of my life, this journey for me held two major challenges; the first was road cycling. Having never been on a road bike until this year the thought of trying to balance on thin slick tyres was bad enough without the additional worry of my feet being clipped into pedals. It was definitely a steep learning curve as I cycled my first very slow ride around our village on a rare sunny day in January, with the children running alongside me shouting instructions on how to change gears. To this day I am not entirely sure whether my husband shouting "go up a gear" means going onto a bigger or smaller ring – however trial and error and I found what was comfortable in the end.

My first significant 20km ride was fairly memorable for all the wrong reasons. Still lacking in confidence and balance on the bike I hung onto the handle bars for dear life for the entire hour, the drop handle bars were completely wasted on me! I had nothing to drink for the duration, as I was too scared to even attempt to take the water bottle out of the cage. Every junction I relied on friends telling me the roads were clear so I didn't have to turn my head or use an arm to indicate, I was every car driver's nightmare! I powerfully climbed the hills in Hertfordshire with little effort – the training programme was obviously working, however then applied the brakes as I crawled back down the other side. Speed was not my friend. I gave every parked car a really wide berth and avoided anything that looked like a hole. There was no fear of me drafting or getting close to the cyclist in front, it was like being a learner driver all over again – I needed time to make decisions on the bike and therefore needed to see the open road ahead, not the back end of a fellow cyclist. I finally made it back into the house unscathed on my maiden road journey; relieved, I unclipped my left foot from the cleat and put it to the floor then promptly wobbled and fell to the right before I could get my right foot out! Laying on the pavement with my bike on top of me, all I could think about was how sore my arms were from hanging on so tightly, my legs however felt fine!

Due to a completely irrational fear of open water my second challenge was the swim. I am a confident pool swimmer, maybe not the best technique in the world, but even at the start of the study I was able to comfortably swim 3km in a pool. However the thought of swimming in a lake or out of my depth in the sea really worried me. It wasn't the fear of having problems with my swimming it was the thought of being in the water with other things around me, those things namely sharks! My rational brain told me that I was unlikely to find sharks off the coast of Barcelona and there were definitely none in Denham lake, however just the thought of getting into the water made me feel sick.

My first lake swim was on a beautiful summer's evening with a few of the other study participants, I had been at work all day with my mind not completely on my job, definitely a little preoccupied. I was already feeling sick when we arrived at the lake and tried to eat a bagel in the car to settle my swirling stomach. The process of arriving, signing my life away on a waiver form and squeezing myself into a wetsuit for the first time seems a distant memory, however even now thinking back to me standing on that lake side makes my stomach churn. Watching all the other swimmers confidently jumping off the jetty into the tranquil lake just made me feel like a complete novice as I slowly climbed down the ladder lowering myself into the water. The first few minutes floating in the water felt like ten, slowly letting water into the wetsuit and getting used to the buoyancy of the suit. With my goggles firmly in place I rolled onto my front and put my head into the water.

Although not cold the temperature of the water really affected my breathing and when I started to swim I just couldn't catch my breath. All I could see in the water was a brown haze and I couldn't even make out my hand in front of me let alone what might have been swimming underneath me at the time! Needless to say I swam that first 100m pretty fast with my head out of the water trying to control my breathing and trying to think 'nice' thoughts. Apart from occasionally spooking myself when pond weed brushed over my bare feet and squealing loudly when two ducks came into land on the lake and skimmed over the back of my legs, the experience in the end was not too traumatic, although was mentally more draining that I had anticipated. I decided that I definitely needed to learn how to control my imagination in the water if I was to conquer the sea swim!

My fear was not something that I had to conquer on my own. The HURTS team were like my own little ironman 'antenatal' group. We were a bunch of people from all walks of life thrown together with one common link – however in this case it was an ironman not a baby. We were always there for each other, whether

First lake swim
(from left to right: Jamie, Neo, me, Kimberley and Helen)

to just provide company on a ride or run, to answer a silly question like "what do you do if you need to go to the loo whilst on the bike?" or to reassure me that sharks were not going to be an issue. Our ironman antenatal group provided well-needed support and guidance along our iron journey and as a result many lifelong friendships and bonds have been created.

By the beginning of the summer my life had turned into one big spreadsheet. Everything had to be fitted it and was planned well in advance, there was no flex in the system. On one occasion I had even convinced my daughter that despite her feeling a little peaky she would be fine and packed her off to school, so I could go out for my 20km run. Only to get 10km out and a phone call from the school asking me to come and collect her as she had been sick. Feeling a little guilty, I turned up at the school an hour later all hot and sweaty, bad parent but pleased that I had managed to fit in the day's training!

So as the planning for the big day continued we were told to start thinking about our nutrition and race plan for the big day. Memos were sent out highlighting the importance of 'the plan' and how we needed to review our options to find out what would work best for us individually. I couldn't help thinking that this sounded like the 'birth plan' conversation that we had with the midwife in our antenatal group before the birth of Olivia. Well I wrote a plan back then and on the day just ignored it so I figured that I could probably wing it on this occasion too.

Nine months seems like a long time away when you are busy waiting for an 'event' to arrive, the journey seems endless and the days tick away so slowly. If it seemed like a slow journey for me – I can only apologise to my friends and family for whom it must have been unbearable. Every testing session, every training session somehow impacted on them, whether it was that I had become an ironman bore and had started telling them about the forthcoming heart rate zone training session or had left the kids with them for five hours while I got out on a sunny day to do a brick session. I had stopped chatting at the school gates when dropping of the kids in the morning in favour of trying to cram in a long ride before pick up and praying that my timing wouldn't be messed up by some bike mechanical or a puncture. It was without doubt an all-consuming nine months that had completely taken over my life and the lives of my family around me.

So, on my thirty-ninth birthday, just before my tenth wedding anniversary, I flew out to Barcelona with my husband to face the *biggest challenge of my life!*

Although the weather forecast looked changeable for the weekend I had not prepared myself for the size of the sea waves that would greet us upon our arrival in Calella. Trying to face my fears I thought that a walk along the beach would help to settle the nerves, however as I stood watching two Spaniards repeatedly getting thrown back onto the beach by the waves, my confidence was fading fast. It looked like my first challenge was going to be getting into the water!

Race day was an experience not that dissimilar to labour, the inevitable day had arrived and there was nothing that I could do to stop it. I am not really sure that I truly remember a lot about race day and I think my mind has been playing tricks on me since. There are a few points however that are still very vivid, standing on the side of the beach thinking thank heavens that the sea is calm, smiling and waving at people as I got onto my bike in transition so thankful that the swim was over, without the appearance of any sharks and running past some HURTS' supporters offering to sell my wetsuit and bike at a good price! As the rain lashed down during the bike ride flooding the road and then continued to soak me to the skin as I ran, I definitely remember thinking never again, never again! However, by the time I finally crossed the finish line with a final burst of effort I had already started to forget the pains of the day and started celebrating with my gold and red medal!

I can honestly say that apart from the birth of my two children, Challenge Barcelona has been the biggest physical challenge that I have faced. Mind tricks have left me describing race day to friends and family as a fun and an amazing experience – however I am pretty sure that they are not the adjectives that I would have used to describe my experience mid-event. I have been really fortunate to spend the last nine months sharing the experience with a fantastic ante-natal iron group who have provided support and friendships during my transformation into an '**Iron lady**'!

On my return home a few days later my children greeted me like a hero and my finisher's medal may as well have been Olympic Gold. As I emotionally gave them a big hug, trying to ignore the exquisite soreness in my legs, a little voice piped up "mummy we really are so proud of you". What more did they need to say... job done!

Iron-mummy and daddy Combarro

The Message: Training and completing an ironman – not that different from having a baby really!

CHAPTER 19

"Inferiority" *By Gary Smith*

Where to start? I'm hoping that this chapter may both be profound and funny… note that doesn't mean it will be profoundly funny – that would be pushing it!

When I first started on this aspect of the project (the book that is, not the soul-destroying, body-sapping, mind-numbing, race training), I thought it would be:

a) *Easy* – I can talk for England! If there was a Kona, i.e. an Ironman World Championship for talking, I could probably win it;
b) *Completed months ago* – This will come as no surprise to anyone who knows me. For example, I once decided to build a garden office to work out of, I diligently started it in the summer but I didn't start working in it before Christmas! We needed to get some fitted wardrobes for the daughter's room, pay a carpenter how much? No way I'll build them myself… I succeeded, but it did take me over three months in which point my daughter's room looked like someone had burgled us;
c) On a previously agreed topic, ***Why?*** – Yep you guessed it, turns out I wasn't really sure "why" so that pretty much screwed that as an idea. In hindsight "procrastination" may have been a better choice.

So here we are, I'm finally writing, and yes, in case you are wondering, there are a million other things I have agreed to do, which aren't being done… If anyone reading this has asked me to do something, which I still haven't done yet, would you mind terribly much forming an orderly queue and taking a number?

Right, back on topic, my chosen word is **Inferiority.** Now if you know me personally you will probably see the self-assured, confident and occasionally arrogant persona, but in reality what drives me to be all of those is a deep-rooted *inferiority complex.*

Wikipedia tells us that this is "*a lack of self-worth, a doubt and uncertainty, and feeling of not measuring up to society's standards. It is often subconscious, and is thought to drive afflicted individuals to overcompensate, resulting either in spectacular achievement or extreme antisocial behaviour*".

Not sure about the anti-social behaviour aspect, unless that's the opinionated and arrogant aspect? It is true I have been known "not to mince my words" and it is true that at a recent interview my employer asked other people about me… The result, I, ladies and gentleman apparently am the human form of Marmite! (Good news was that my new boss is also like marmite, so that didn't scare him away)

You see, most of us compare ourselves to others, and in the modern world of always-on media, we are subjected to a constant stream of the most beautiful, athletic and talented people and the social-networking revolution also allows you to interact with these people. Unfortunately, this can lead you to believing you know these people, I mean after all you know when they are sad, when they are happy, where they shop and what they had for breakfast, lunch and dinner and what do we do with people we know? We compare ourselves to them! Not a good recipe for those already with a possibly slighted view of themselves.

So what's my story?

Well mine stems from childhood, a young Irish boy growing up in South Africa… yep we arrived in sunny Durban when I was the tender age of eight. As a skinny, translucent child with no redeeming sports qualities and a very strange accent, popular I was not. A real crowd puller was the twice-weekly PE class of swimming, yep the South African children learnt how to swim around the age of three to four and I on the other hand could not swim. I suspect an eight-year-old wearing armbands was something of a circus show for the other kids, combined with school-issue budgie smugglers, I made the previously "uncool" children feel like kings – guys if you are reading this I feel your pain and I was happy to take one for the team!

Unfortunately it didn't stop there, I never really seemed to get with the programme and whilst I managed to eventually represent my school at swimming, rugby and shooting, my friends went on to represent the school in our first teams, represent their province and some even, eventually, our country. Yep, I was athletically challenged by South African standards, but what I lacked in ability, I made up for in enthusiasm and passion, two qualities that have stood me well throughout the rest of my life.

My grandmother told me at a very young age "If at first you don't succeed try, try again" and my dad, who wasn't athletically challenged having played rugby for a major Irish club and English county cricket, always said "if you don't buy a ticket you'll never win…" I think it's these two statements that have had the biggest impact on my life, firstly persevere and never give up and secondly, if you don't give something a chance or a go, you will never be good at it!

So in short my high-school period was dominated by hanging on the fringes of the "jock" crowd, hoping that they accepted me while my real friends, who also weren't "jocks" just accepted me for who I was. Funnily enough I'm not friends with the jocks anymore, but I am still friends with the guys who just accepted me.

I left school; I study part-time and begin my articles at an accounting firm in the city. My driven nature to succeed, allows me to gain ground from a career perspective and I am carnivorous in my appetite for power, respect and money, even in my fledgling state as an articled clerk. Unfortunately I develop a similar appetite for Nandos and Pizza – I reinvent myself, I'm the cool kid, I drink, I party, I run a restaurant part-time and when I finish my two-job day, back to back, I load as many waitresses as possible into my 1967 Cal-look VW Beetle, and we party the rest of the night finishing with a garlic cheese pizza at the roadhouse on North Beach watching the sunrise.

… And then it happens, my, then, fiancée gets the news that her parents are leaving to live in the UK, and I have to make the biggest decision of my life, leave everything I know and move continents? Leave my own family behind?

At first, I'm reluctant, South Africa has been good to me, I'm doing a job I love, I enjoy my life and it is a tropical paradise, BUT I sleep in a small annex in someone's garden, I have bars on all my windows, there is only one entrance point into my bedroom at night and it's locked. I sleep with a 9mm CZ 75 Compact semi-automatic pistol under my pillow; I have a spare magazine next to my mattress. Only twelve months prior I left a client stock taking in the city where they were held up and killed before I'd had time to park my car at home some fifty miles away.

A short pros and cons list later, a large study loan of R70k (about an 18mths gross salary) and a very attractive Pound/Rand exchange rate and the decision was made, on one condition – we go it alone. Her parents were going back to

Wales and quite frankly, I didn't want to live in Wales and research told me there weren't any job prospects either. So two backpacks, £1000 and a list of friends and we made our move.

It was a scary initial period in London, more specifically Kilburn, near the tube station; to be honest whilst I fortunately never had to discharge my gun, I felt naked without it... which is funny since one night I went out clubbing in Durban, checked my gun into the safety deposit box at the nightclub, had a little too much to drink, forgot it and then rather embarrassingly with a hangover had to go back and pick it up in the morning. This in a significantly more dangerous place than Kilburn, clearly drinking does numb the senses! However, more scary than Kilburn was the rent FFS, we spent half our money before we'd even been in the country two days. We then adopted the Safeway Supermarket Survival Strategy – bread bought at the end of the day at a reduced price, own brand beans at nine pence per can and cheap tea bags, French lager and cola. This naturally was a short-term plan, particularly since we would run out of money soon, I needed to find a job and unfortunately my demons had come back to haunt me – yes I was back on the bottom of the ladder, I was once again inferior and scared.

The Job, ah yes the first job, a large teaching hospital in London as an Internal Auditor for a very respectable rate per hour, so respectable in fact that I was earning as much in a week as I was in a month in South Africa, things were looking up. The working location left a little to be desired, it was clear that the National Health Service valued the Internal Audit Department GREATLY.

We were positioned next to the morgue! At 10:30 every morning the whole building shuddered when the medical incinerator was fired up, add to this my first encounter with limescale in my tea, and a sight I wish I'd never seen (the bottom of that kettle still haunts me) and you could say that the working conditions left a lot to be desired. To top it off, at the end of my first week, I was "warned off" by the "boys" for making them look bad! You see an internal audit is normally a three to four week project minimum, something they were taking six to eight weeks to do, AND not one a week as I was doing! Yep, I was warned off for making the full-time civil servants look bad! I needed a new job, despite being a cushy little number and every Friday off (as I could only work 35hrs a week) I wasn't challenged and therefore I couldn't really succeed and wasn't able to feed my demon.

So as much as I liked the working hours, the shit tea, the corpses and smell of a fresh BBQ every day at 10:30, and the student doctors and nurses bar on a Wednesday night, I had to leave... it was at this point I began working for a large global company where I still work today and that was sixteen years ago.

I've held a number of positions within that company; some made me feel like a king, some a minion. The worst wrecked me emotionally and mentally as the competitiveness of a big corporate environment and the more sinister side of human nature seeking to fulfill its own needs over those of others, told a firm grasp of my career. One thing remained constant though, which is that coming from a background of feeling inferior, what doesn't kill you really does make you stronger, and it gives you the internal engine to want to do better – the flip side of course is whilst you could recognize this trait, the engine occasionally needs maintenance and you often wonder how long before it blows a head gasket?

The problem with my career, and I am sure is the case for many of you, is that it is sedentary. No matter how much I succeed in my work life, I continued to wish I was more athletic and sporty and no it wasn't a mid-life crisis (I did buy a Porsche though which was nice!) It was a simple case of somehow not being the person I wanted to be or felt I should be, but I had become seriously overweight.

How serious? Well at one stage I was wearing size 44"–46" trousers and a 48" suit and weighed just under 19st. The final straw was going to Topshop one evening and when looking for a shirt for a Christmas function being told "I'm sorry Sir we don't cater for people of your size". I was devastated, having an inferiority complex and then using food as a coping strategy clearly wasn't the route to my desired "Adonis" like physique! My God man what have you done?

I think I joined Weight Watchers the very next day… And after nine months of dedication managed to become a shadow of my former self, weighing in at 14st. Elated with my new body, the attention and clothes, I slowly started to allow old habits to creep back in and I started to gain weight; and on the back of a failed first marriage I began smoking and eating badly again – not good!

I let my weight balloon back to 17st and despite the weight gain my girlfriend, now wife part deux, never called me a fat git… (Note she has called me many other things!!). Unfortunately the BUPA doctor at my company medical hadn't got that memo and figured the best solution was to call me a "clinically-obese walking heart attack"; a little harsh perhaps but it did make me think! Well I thought for four months before doing anything about it; I joined the gym got a personal trainer and decided to run a marathon. Yep, back to that old chestnut couldn't just follow a normal route to healthiness, could I?

Hmmm, marathon training day one was interesting couldn't run for a bus and couldn't wait for a cigarette when I finished… I would have probably taken them with me, but running gear doesn't make pockets big enough for a packet of twenty and a lighter! (Take notes NIKE!) Anyway it's fair to say I was unfit, not in the marginally unfit way, in the way that older smokers look; you know the ones having a fag while they cough up a lung?

Did my running get better? Yep.

Did I stop smoking? Fuck no.

In fact I smoked for another year, I even managed smoking while training for the Great North Run, and finished it in 2hr 18, took a bloody age to get my bag from the baggage bus and finally be reunited with my beloved cigarettes. It wasn't until I was leaving for the Mighty Deerstalker, a ten-mile mountain race in the Scottish border town of Innerleithen that I finally made the decision to quit. I'd been on the anti-smoking medication from the doctor, and surprisingly, despite my obvious self-esteem and mental shortcomings and the pills which notoriously caused suicide, it never crossed my mind… they did make me very bloody sick though AND like a REAL TROOPER I managed to struggle on smoking throughout the course of tablets!

In fairness, the tablets did allow me to both cut down and change to a lighter cigarette (girlie ones with white filters, which matched my iPhone), which ultimately made it easier to give up in the long run. That week I had a really bad cold, a hacking cough and a lot of undesirable "content" exiting my body, I wondered if I could race at all but bloody-mindedness suggested and decided otherwise. On Friday it was time to leave and Martha said, "You've left your cigarettes behind" my response was "no I haven't, I'm giving up!". That was it, and I haven't smoked since. (Incidentally Martha gave up that weekend too, so that when I returned home we could be stronger together against the dreadful addiction that had been part of our lives for so long).

So now onto the race itself; starting and finishing in the grounds of Traquair House in the Tweed Valley the organisers had a wide choice of countryside for the evening's shenanigans including some very LARGE hills, numerous stretches of river and lots of mud. Billed as 10km Adventure run, the 10km is somewhat misleading, with various GPS devices putting the event at somewhere closer to ten miles and the MC for the evening actually telling the crowd this year it was 17km! Lining up at the start line, along with another 1619 idiots, in the spring twilight, I was glad to see that most people were donning their tweed with pride and everyone was smiling, something that the course would strip them of very shortly, either the smiles or the tweed BUT very possibly both!

Personally I had decided to opt for very technical running gear and saved the kilt for après course wear (in fact I'd been wearing the kilt since arriving at the venue 6hrs earlier). After more than a week of being sick, I just couldn't see how me and fancy dress could both reasonably make it to the finish line and settled for no fancy dress and a finish instead – turns out that this was a very wise idea, although SealSkinz waterproof socks turned out to be a seriously bad idea... but more on that later.

The start was uphill for seventy to one hundred yards to a straw wall, two? Or was it three bales high? Anyway, a bit of a pile-up ensued, but I got over it albeit a bit slow. A jog downhill followed, which led us out of the estate onto a country road, with a brief detour back into what can only be described as a muddy field. Fortunately my keen vision spotted that in the middle of the track there were a lot of short people, no wait they're not short they're stuck up to their asses in mud! I managed to skirt around the bog and began my journey towards the first of the two hills – turns out later that my team mate, who finished in an impressive 2hr 08 was one of the short people, and lost a shoe delaying his time by around five to ten mins and putting his entire race at risk had he not found it!

Anyway, the trail headed skyward, zigzagging up Innerleithen XC mountain bike trail, with the gradient easing after a few hundred yards on to a forest road. Unfortunately, for me, just as the gradient eased into something, which might have been runnable, the trail headed away from the road, straight up the hill. I think this might have been the point I had an extreme coughing fit and my body finally let me know, that really had I asked for medical clearance to do this race, I would NOT have been granted it!

Not one for DNFs, I decided to compromise by agreeing with the "saner" part of my personality that I would WALK all the uphills and run whatever else I could – time was no longer important to me but finishing was. Through the dense woodland, I slowly made my way on the trail which then seemed to double back and rejoin the road only about one hundred yards further up. No sooner than that had happened, were we then back off the road, up a steep stony gully and heading upwards across a clear-felled moor. Footing was distinctly dodgy here, rough, weather-beaten outcrops of heather; hiding tree roots, stones and stumps and then back into the woods via singletrack. Still going up we come across some obstacles – a few balance beams and then a cargo net tunnel – not too difficult except my head torch got caught in the netting which tried my patience slightly and wasted about five minutes – exit onto the road again and finally the turnaround! I think it was about this time that I heard the firework go off, which indicates that the first runner has summited the second mountain and lets the town below know that the "deerstalkers" are starting to come home – that was at fifty-two mins FFS!!

It was now that I was able to consider moving at speed for

probably the first time in an hour and it was a fast descent following a wide mountain-bike trail; complete with jumps, bends and tabletops. Running them was pretty scary; I wondering what that would have been like on a bike, pretty mental I'm certain! The track continued down a very steep and densely-wooded hill, it was fast, narrow and slippery and that's when I started to really eat up some places. I was enjoying myself so much, I just felt reckless and careered down through the trees, bumping and cutting my hands as I tried to slow down on the trees. Suddenly I could hear music and then flashing lights, Snap's 'Rhythm is a Dancer' was pumping out in the middle of the forest in the dark! Ingenious!!! A bloody nightclub in a forest, my smile just got bigger! Flat road and then riverbank felt odd after all the up and down in the woods. The first dip in the river came soon, short and sharp, knee deep, not too bad I thought and then the second came… by this point I'd realised the FATAL error in my kit choice, with regards to socks! You see waterproof socks and shoes do their jobs very well EXCEPT when you completely submerse your feet i.e. once filled with water, the clever material you pay a fortune for doesn't let the water back out, since, in fact, it was designed to stop it from coming in, in the first place!

So now running is a very strange experience indeed – If I'd brought Bob the Goldfish with me, he would have been very happy sloshing around in the nice Scottish stream water encased in my shoes, however personally I was less convinced about running with two water balloons at the end of my feet knowing that I was probably only a little over halfway around the course and one mountain left to climb (please note there is a certain irony in that very thought coming soon!) I'd guess at this stage we went about half-a-mile upstream, yes we're actually running in the river now, knee to thigh high in ever glorious Scottish river water in March (i.e. it was bloody freezing). You didn't know where your feet were going so slips, trips and falls are now common place, but don't worry since this is the section of river that runs through the town, EVERYBODY is watching you make a fool of yourself… The town folk were awesome, massively supportive and encouraging and by the end of the half mile my spirit had been relifted and I could get on with the job at hand (even though by now a combination of the really refreshing Scottish mountain water, temperatures approaching zero and waterproof sock encased feet has resulted in a running version of an upside-down ice lolly – good news though is that pain from freezing appendages is quite hot, so that was a plus…)

A bit more running through the town and now we are off up a hill again, grassy, good going, back to more walking than running, but progressing well. I think it was at this point I could see the full extent of what lay ahead as the head torches of the runners illuminated the mountain – staggeringly beautiful, but menacing at the same time, the sheer steepness of the rope of light draped over the mountain cannot be described or photographed, it can only be experienced. It was at this point that the scree started to become visible and ever present – to start with it was mainly across the hillside and started to limit everyone to traversing in single file. A few people tried to nick some places, but it just wasn't worth it, since the hill just forced them back down onto the same single track, but now with a concertina effect… much to the frustration of the rest us.

It was pretty much like the muppets you get on the motorway charging up the outside lane, only to have to wait to come back in when they realize the lane is closed, adding more time to everyone's journey. Next came the bit that previously had only been visible as a line of illumination up the side of a mountain, it was "the straight up" bit, there's no other way to describe it, you have to see it to believe it. I estimate about 550–650ft of hands and feet, vertical ascent, climbing over scree of all sizes (I mean all sizes, from stones as big as golf balls to boulders the size of small cars, all loose and it MOVED, CONSTANTLY!). Let me paint you a picture, a conveyor belt of rock, no wait, ever tried walking UP a DOWN escalator? Right, picture that, in the pitch black with a head torch, the escalator is 600ft. long, at an angle so steep that hands and knees are your only option, the steps vary in size, bits of the steps above keep dislodging and sliding towards you, occasionally you need to move to the side very quickly as a result and all while you're cold and freezing.

Perhaps you grab the handrail, except it's not a handrail, it's some Scottish firethorn plant which immediately draws blood and stings like mad and you make a mental note not to be fooled into that scenario again… I've no idea how long it took but it felt like FOREVER, and it was HARD, but weirdly ENJOYABLE – nope, I haven't worked it out either, perhaps one for the psychotherapy chair at a later stage of my life.

Anyway, the summit is just ahead and then, wait, what's that, another cargo net? Are you f**king serious? After all of that? You think we need yet another psychotic cargo net? Much f'ing and blinding later, I get stuck in the cargo net again, yet you would have thought I would have learnt the first time… oh well, at least I can feel my feet again. Don't worry Bob would still be safe, the water is still very much there, but now my body has warmed up the water and it's a bit like travelling with a private bath at the bottom of each shoe. Now it's down, down and down – I went fast, it was reckless abandon, it was a "feet in the clouds" moment, I was elated, my head torch picking spots I hoped my feet would find, hmmmm maybe I could get used to this fell-running malarkey, it certainly had its highs in more ways than one.

After I little bit of flat terrain, where I managed to regain some composure, we had a mud slide, well I don't quite know how else to describe it? Basically the side of the hill where the tree line now started, except it was very steep and as I approached it I heard the marshal say: "use all three ropes". I decide to grab the one on the left, since it seem to have less people using it, perhaps they knew already what I was about to find out... About two-thirds of the way down, Houston we have a problem – the rope stopped! Whereas the middle and right hand ropes clearly went all the way to the bottom, the left hand rope just stopped. The band of merry warriors behind me decided that despite the steepness of the hill, they were now going to try and traverse onto the middle rope – my issue with this was that if that were possible, why did we need to use ropes anyway?

I decided to go for the far more sensible option and not try to traverse to rope two, but rather to throw myself down the mountain in a sitting/sliding position, this worked very well! I reckon I reached the bottom in about five to ten seconds and made up about twenty-five to thirty places! Result!!! We then had a very slippy, muddy, single-file track along the river to encounter and strangely for the first time in the race I'd found some clear space to run (all due to my ingenious slide down the hill tactic) which eventually released me onto tarmac road. I can categorically tell you that I was pretty relieved at this stage, knowing that I would now be heading back through the town to the finish. Once again the people of the town were fantastic, giving me the energy and boost I needed to dig deep and finish in style, well some sort of style anyway BUT the fun wasn't quite over yet, there was the small matter of another few river crossings, including a storm-water drain tunnel underneath the road (GOOD NEWS – it was only just above waist deep!).

Whilst in the tunnel I tried to get a bit of a sing-song going on with the rest of the competitors, but alas it was only me singing "I love you baby", perhaps they didn't know the words?!? Maybe they were just shy? However, it did bring it home to me how much I was loving this, the mud, the madness and the sheer insanity of it all. The rest of the run was pretty much flat, muddy and therefore slippy, just then a noise filled the trees and I realised I could hear the arena... I'd made it, I was there, Gary Smith you are a "Deerstalker". It was at this point that reality kicked back in and I remembered that those bastards at Rat Race had decided to put a few extras in the finishing arena, a 20ft pipe, a cargo net and TWO six-foot walls to negotiate in the last one hundred yards or so, but fortunately they happened without further incident and I crossed the line smiling in a rather more tortoise-than-hare-like time of 3hrs and 3mins.

Elated, exhausted, excited and very, very dirty!

I did go to the doctors on Monday and they confirmed what I already knew which was that I had a severe chest infection, needed antibiotics and to rest. Not great marafun training which was now fast approaching, having entered into the Edinburgh Marathon Festival towards the end of May. In short, I recovered in a couple of weeks, started training again and I thought, "My god, what has happened"?

Exactly a year to the day, since I went from not being able to run for a bus, I was officially dipping my toe into the world of endurance! I say that, but in reality many average people run marathons nowadays, it's pretty much commonplace – so why was I so bloody scared?!? Was it the continuing bouts of illness and injury that have seen my marafun plan become somewhat of a joke? (It certainly makes me laugh every time I see it on the fridge door!) Or, was it that somehow winter has lasted an eternity, with temperatures battling to reach double digits, but yet somehow this week a mini heatwave has arrived and the UK is now hotter than Ibiza?

I'm not sure which one it was, but I think both of them were bothering me… I did my final run on Wednesday of that week, a cheeky 5km in twenty-six degrees Celsius – it was twenty-six minutes of pure hell, I reckon probably a bit like running in a sauna with a tracksuit on. Even when I stopped running, I continued to sweat, I had a shower and continued to sweat, ice bath? Yep, I continued to sweat!

Yep it was a little annoying, although it was probably more annoying for any twitchy-curtained neighbours to see my half-naked torso sitting in the back garden trying to get cool. Probably also an appropriate time to mention that despite various attempts by a well-known gas company to fix our central heating boiler, they continue to fail. Basically the boiler and central heating system in general had two settings: 1) OFF – no heat and no hot water, you can't have one without the other 2) ON – you get hot water, but it's so hot you can use it to slow-cook food (or children) and it's positively tropical (even if zero outside).

As you can imagine, in a week where the outside temp is tropical, a malfunctioning boiler is a real treat, how about some heat with a dollop of hell on the side, whilst eating a bowl of raw habaneros? I digress… Basically it wasn't the perfect end to my less than perfect training, which is now going to be put to the test in the Scottish version of the Marathon Des Sables (*yes, yes, Justin minus the real desert and blisters and lack of toilets and general hardship and sand dunes and hallucinations and aliens and camels etc.*). What was nice was friends continuously sending me texts wishing me luck. Many of these also include the following useful gems of information:

1) *Take it easy out there it's going to be hot*
2) *Just a word of warning Edinburgh ran out of water last time it was hot*
3) *Good luck, but be careful people die running marathons*

REALLY !?

1) It's a marathon FFS – it was never going to be "easy" and yes amazingly after six months of grey skies, howling winds, running in snow, rain, hail and sleet and a few times where the backdrop to my runs looked like a scene from *The Wizard of Oz*, I did notice the big, bloody yellow thing in the sky – but thanks anyway
2) Useful to know, terrifying but what the hell am I exactly going to do about it? Funnily enough, this was from the same friend that when I previously suggested training with a hydration bladder said something along the lines of "you don't want to do that mate, carrying just a couple of kilos of water will add 6 mins to every 10km and wear you out early – best to rely on the water stations"
3) Great, excellent thanks for reminding me, I was completely oblivious to that, but now that I know, I'll be sure to look over my shoulder every mile or so and at the first sign of a large fellow in a black smock claiming to be Mr. Death, I'll let him through!

Another thing about that glorious weather, and all the advice you read on clothing is as follows. Make sure that run in clothes you've run in before, are comfortable running in, trained in, done your long runs in… Hmmm, slight problem with that, it was WINTER until the weekend before! So all my training was done in winter kit, layers upon layers.

Options: run in the Edinburgh desert marafun in:

a) Tried-and-tested winter training gear
b) Summer training gear that I have never run further than five miles in!

I opted in the end for the base layer winter training kit. If there was ever a time for these technical sports apparel companies to put their money where their mouth is on how breathable and temperature regulating their apparel is, it was then! I finished Edinburgh in 4h45 despite attempts by the local sprogs to steal the water… Some rather valiant efforts by local law enforcement, the army, volunteers and generally anyone with a modicum of common sense, ensured that they never did actually run out of water – it was very, very hot though, and I waddled past a number of people for whom the weather and distance had all just got a bit much. At times like that it's quite humbling to realize just how much of a risk endurance sports can be, something that I reflect on every time I "toe the line".

Overall it was an amazing event, and I thought the organizers did rather well given the weather was proving to be a challenge. It was all a bit of a mad rush after the finish though, the buses back into the City of Edinburgh were a twenty-five minute uphill walk from the end of the marathon at the Musselburgh race course, and then the bus took about an hour to get back to the city, and then it was about another forty-five minutes to get to our hotel. SpeedoDave (my friend and fellow endurance lunatic) had managed to book the hotel right near loads of establishments offering "full massage, sauna and steam baths" and I have to say that having run 26.2 miles and probably walked another five or so, that sounded quite appealing BUT looking at some of the attire the "spa assistants" were wearing, I don't think they would be on any marathon's approved supplier list of post-race sports therapy! All I say is thank god, the wives and kids decided to let me and SD race on our own, the opportunity for suitably embarrassing questions would have been on an epic scale not seen often outside of the House of Commons.

One thing I did realise later that night on the train home was that I wasn't that sore... Well trained or didn't try hard enough? To be honest I thought the latter! A week later, I found myself in a very strange position... having entered my first triathlon earlier in the year, it now dawned on me that it was only two weeks away, and if that wasn't enough... some other "friends" were trying to twist my arm into running the relay leg of a triathlon on the 1st of July. The day of the triathlon arrived, it was bright and sunny but VERY early, something I started to realise is common place with triathlons... very early starts, I guess when it's an ironman I understand it given the size of the challenge ahead but why on earth registration needs to be so early when it's a sprint distance is well beyond my comprehension.

Let's be honest, doing a triathlon is sadomasochistic enough, does it really need to be combined with getting up in the middle of night, driving cross-country and then diving into a sub-zero lake to be truly enjoyable? To be honest I don't know the answer, but if I ever find a triathlon that starts at some sort of sensible time I'll be sure to let you know! Anyway, I raced for the first time in pirate colours; a very proud and exciting moment and I seemed to be the only pirate in attendance. If you don't know who the pirates are I recommend reading *Can't Swim, Can't Ride, Can't Run* by Andy Holgate or visiting the website (http://www.pirateshipoffools.co.uk) Wearing the pirate kit immediately seems to grant you a fair amount of automatic support from Joe Public, well actually both support and abuse, but nonetheless the experience is fantastic and kids seem to love the "Pirates". As the only "Pirate" in the field, I got the full experience and managed to finish the race in 1hr 30, which wasn't too bad for my first sprint-distance triathlon… well I was pleased anyway.

I'm not going to bore you with even more of my misadventures in racing of which there are many, or talk more about inferiority as by now I feel you should know me relatively well and I will be back later in the book to talk about the weeks leading up to the biggest race of my life – and so back to inferiority, I shall leave you with some pearls of wisdom:

> *The one permanent emotion of the inferior man is fear – fear of the unknown, the complex, and the inexplicable. What he wants above everything else is safety.*
>
> H. L. Mencken

> *While one person hesitates because he feels inferior, another is busy making mistakes and becoming superior.*
>
> Henry C. Link

It was Eleanor Roosevelt, who said *"No one can make you feel inferior without your consent"*.

Now there is a lot of truth in these pearls, but the reality is this:

1) EVERYONE feels inferior about SOMETHING.
2) NO ONE is actually PERFECT
3) Inferiority only becomes a COMPLEX if you let it
4) Don't limit your own ability and self-beliefs based on fiction
5) GIVE IT A GO, you might surprise yourself

"If I can, YOU CAN… Make Time"
(Gary 'The Ledge' IRONMAN Smith)

The Message: There is a very well-known IRON-DISTANCE TRIATHLON saying –

> Anything is possible… (And I would add)… You just have to take the first step!

SECTION 3

A Reason to Shine

CHAPTER 20

"Inspiration" *By Alex Smith*

According to the inventor who had the original "light bulb moment", Thomas Edison: "*Genius is 1% inspiration and 99% perspiration*" and throughout this ironman training programme, 99% perspiration has been an understatement!

But what was the spark that inspired me to start on this triathlon adventure.

Genius?

Ambition?

Stupidity? *(All of the above?)*

I'm not sure, and the dictionary definition of inspiration didn't make things any clearer, as there were multiple options:

1. the process of being mentally stimulated to do or feel something
2. a sudden brilliant or timely idea
3. the drawing in of breath

Well, I've certainly drawn in plenty of breath during training, and at times I've been certain that this wasn't a brilliant idea, so it must be the first, but that still doesn't really answer the question – what inspired me, an overweight, non-exercise couch potato to sign up to a research programme to compete in an ironman.

Eleanor Roosevelt is quoted as saying "*do one thing every day that scares you*" and when I looked at the proposed lifestyle change that the ironman programme required, there was no doubt that I was scared shi…

But what is my inspiration, my light-bulb moment, my reason for taking on this challenge?

The answer is simple when I *really* think about it… because 'I CAN'.

I grew up in a sporty family always encouraged to take on sport as a way of life, to enjoy both team sports and individual pursuits, tennis became 'my thing' and I was pretty good at it, getting up to a competitive regional standard in my early teenage years but boarding school and the lure of a heady mix of girls and alcohol ended my tennis aspirations.

Here began the next twenty years of my life, very irregular exercise, an awful lot of hedonism and a life that revolved around me and me alone.

When I was thirty-five and drunk again at a family BBQ the challenge was put down to run the London Marathon for a friend who had recently been diagnosed with Leukaemia and needed a bone marrow transplant. In my drunken stupor I agreed and set about training. As is often the case with people who still think they are sporty after years of inactivity I injured myself trying too hard too soon and never really recovered.

The day itself was special, to be there with my brother and sister preparing for our biggest challenge yet I knew I was going to get in a spot of bother with an injury (hip flexor) at some point and popped some pretty heavy-duty painkillers just before the start. Everything was going okay and I was on 4hr(ish) pace up until the halfway mark at Tower Bridge when the painkillers wore off and the pain really set in. For the first time on any run in training and until that point, I stopped. I was half prepared to walk off the course imagining the distance still to go ahead but I was immediately joined by a fellow runner who asked if he could stride out with me.

Here started the next thirteen miles, it turned out my companion was a seasoned marathon runner, this was his seventh London event but had decided this year to do no training and just turn up. He continued to tell me just how relieved he was that I had stopped as he was also considering walking off the course at the same time. We took on a walk/run strategy for the rest of the course, went through all our 'Top Tens' best films, best songs, best chat-up lines etc. etc. He met my family on Embankment, I met his, we ran through the finish line together, man hugged, thanked each other for getting through it, and that was that.

In all honesty I don't think I was ever really in shape to do it, effectively I 'blagged it' and got it done on the day, completing it injured in five-and-a-half hours hurting most of the way. Not a fun day!

With ten weeks to marathon race day my family's world had also changed forever when our eldest son Harrison was diagnosed with the fatal, life-limiting condition Duchenne Muscular Dystrophy. Duchenne is a muscle-wasting condition that robs every skeletal muscle in the body of the ability to produce dystrophyn, an essential element that all muscles need to grow and repair. I was numb and heartbroken but also still fully committed to helping my friend in need.

It took me almost a year to recover from the injury slowly gaining weight up to seventeen stone (I hold it well ;-)) and falling back into the old habits of a bottle of wine or more often than not two bottles every Thursday, Friday and Saturday. I founded our charity Harrison's Fund to raise the money needed to find a first treatment and eventual cure for Duchenne whilst also holding down a full-time job and having my best stab at being a good husband, father and friend.

I thought my life was super busy; I had no time for anything else surely?

Until, one day in late 2012 a good friend mentioned to me about a triathlon study she had applied for, to take recreationally fit… (hmmmm me?) people up to an Iron-Distance standard.

It was instant… Harrison loves swimming, Harrison loves running, Harrison has just learnt to ride his bike. This is for me!

Why can't I learn to do all three of these sports well?

Why can't I take on an epic challenge, something you absolutely can't blag?

Why can't I have a six pack? (*still waiting on this one!*)

How do I get this past my wife?

The stark reality that the three sports Harrison loves will be taken away from him before he has the chance to complete any type of sporting endeavour hit home… hard! I cried, no, I sobbed about him eventually losing his muscle function, his ability to give a hug, scratch an itch, breathe even, but Alex I thought, you CAN do all these things.

You can put one foot in front of the other… *check*

You can swim… *kinda check*

You can ride a bike… *check*

You know what pain feels like, that pain that is deep in your soul, the pain a parent feels watching their son slowly die in front of their eyes.

You can do this for him, you can be his muscles, his lungs, his heart and you can take that pain and use it to drive you forward.

Unlike many of my fellow ironman virgins I've been blessed with an incredible team helping and inspiring me along the way from my Personal Trainer, JP deVilliers to Gary and Chris at Anatomy in Motion, Carlyle at Prohab Performance the awesome duo at Ooey Custom Paint who custom painted my Tri bike. It's emblazoned with the Harrison's Fund livery and adorned with a photo of Harrison on my top tube to motivate me on the day and throughout the long training sessions. My brother JJ is also on board, a Team GB performance psychologist and psychological mentor who helps me get my game face on and focus on the goals at hand.

But none more so than Gary (aka Smithy2) and Justin (aka The Dr), fellow contributors to this book and whom I had not met before being part of the ironman cohort. I now count them among my close friends. They took my cause and essentially me under their wing, driving sponsorship, sourcing free top-of-the-range kit from Castelli and HUUB, helping me find my first bike, an epic eBay bargain. Both will be part of my life and endurance challenges for years to come.

You see ironman does that to you, brings you closer to people, and introduces you to like-minded focused individuals that become friends and supporters for life.

Ironman is a lifestyle, a bit of an extreme one for sure but most importantly, it's a family.

Training has been hard, the time element is incredible… up to nine sessions a week, six sometimes seven days' takes its toll but I cannot tell you how much I have enjoyed every second of it… I have found that the limits I used to set myself are just there to be broken and surpassed. I have chosen to be and do something extraordinary and live my life without limits.

My first triathlon experience was in July 2013 and as is my way it seemed like a good idea to do a half-iron event as my first… If you are going to do it, you might as well go large. Gary and I and two others from the Cohort entered the Vachery Middle Distance event to finally put all our training into practice, run by 'Brave Events' and the awesome team that welcomed Harrison's Fund in. So the distances themselves were 1.9km swim, 80km bike and a 20km run. Our wave went off at 7:30am with a swim in the very nice (apart from the lilies and weeds which seemed to be trying to drag me down)

Vachery Lake. I'd never swum in a pack before but found it really helped with swimming straight, a first for me! And managed to get it done in an easy forty-one minutes. After a 400m run into transition and a pretty slow stop – NOTE TO SELF: – practice getting aero helmet on, I have a GIRO Selector and kept on pulling off the bottom fairing as I tried to get it over my wingnut ears! Took me nearly seven minutes to leave T1. Not quite as long as Gary who had got the kettle out for a cuppa – it was out onto the bike course…

… A very technical 40km loop in the Surrey Hills to be completed twice, including the infamous Leith Hill **TWICE!!!**

Unfortunately no more than 1km in I had a rear puncture, cue mild panic as I am not the most able tyre changer, especially a rear one, twenty minutes later back on the road to stop 7km further along with another rear puncture, another twenty minutes stop and thoughts of my day ending early were almost overwhelming!

So, now right at the back and seemingly by myself out on the roads I buckled down, got aero and put the hammer down. The first 40km loop was finished in a disappointing 2hrs 10 minutes but managed the second loop in 1hr 20… the downhills were taken at quite a lick… topping out at 75kph at one point!

Into T2, pretty much alone to get ready for the run, and a familiar grumble downstairs reared up which led to a mad dash to the portaloo, in the end it took me over ten minutes to leave T2. The run itself was great, a fantastic lift to see and 'High Five' Gary out on his run all be it a good 7km ahead of me. The first 10km was great, felt strong… no stopping and pretty much on my 4hr30 desired ironman pace. The wheels came off a little as the gut played up again at about 13km necessitating a dash into a field to get naked another time… I can confirm hay works quite well for wiping up but can be a little rough on the delicate areas! ;-)

Note to self: *At 4:30 in the morning, in your kitchen when someone offers you Imodium, don't laugh at them, don't take the piss, you may find yourself naked, squatting in a field next to me.*

Anyway, back on it and after more high fives and lots of encouragement from fellow competitors the finish was in sight and I came in having finished the half in 2 hrs 15 less the 'unscheduled stops'. A total time of 6hrs 56 or 6hrs 16 without the bike mechanicals would be my preferred time.

I'm writing this chapter with thirty-nine days to go till race day. Last weekend I ran 30km in three hours, swam 3.8km open water in 1hr 23, this is almost a standing joke now as I don't seem to get any faster however fit and strong I get, and rode 180km in just over six hours. I'm now 14.5 stone and feeling pretty fit, even as a guy I can't get enough of people telling me how good I look, although my wife is finding this role reversal a tad on the annoying side!

Will I get the Ironman done?

Yes I will, no doubt... my game face is on, I visualise myself crossing the finishing line every day, to be honest it makes me well up just thinking about it. My children are my life, Harrison and William are my inspiration, I want to save Harrison, and I want William to keep his brother and best mate.

Ironman is a sport that grabs you by the short and curlies, (if you don't succumb to the full body-shaving thing... I still keep asking myself why?) and becomes a massive part of your life. So much so that I am already entering my second iron-distance event before completing my first. Next time, however, I will be taking Harrison on the journey with me, dragging him in a boat on the swim, riding with him on my bike and then running with him in a racing wheelchair... an

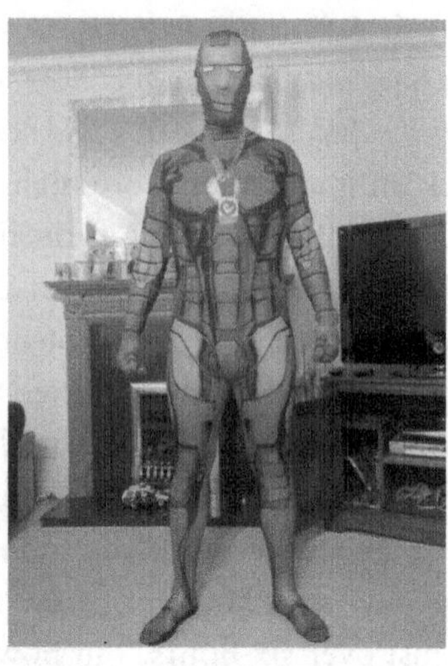

Alex Smith – aka the real Tony Stark
– aka the 'real deal' IRONMAN

epic challenge known by me as 'doing a Hoyt' inspired by the incredible endurance team, Rick and Dick Hoyt www.teamhoyt.com

Whenever doubts arise in my mind about what I am trying to achieve and the difficulties that lie in the way and I need reassurance that what I am doing is right, I re-read Theodore Roosevelt's "Man in the Arena" speech. These words inspire me, support me and give me strength:

> *"It is not the critic who counts; not the man who points out how the strong man stumbles, or where the doer of deeds could have done them better. The credit belongs to the man who is actually in the arena, whose face is marred by dust and sweat and blood; who strives valiantly; who errs, who comes short again and again, because there is no effort without error and shortcoming; but who does actually strive to do the deeds; who knows great enthusiasms, the great devotions; who spends himself in a worthy cause; who at the best knows in the end*

> *the triumph of high achievement, and who at the worst, if he fails, at least fails while daring greatly, so that his place shall never be with those cold and timid souls who neither know victory nor defeat."*

Or as the International Triathlon Union puts it

"*Swim 2.4 miles! Bike 112 miles! Run 26.2 miles! Brag for the rest of your life*" ® ITU
@AverageManToIronman WILL be an Ironman!

The Message: Life can throw a curve ball or two, but choose to live your life without limits, and you really can reach for the stars.

CHAPTER 21

"LOVE" *By Shaun Hunt*

L.O.V.E. – Yes, Lots Of Volume Exercise I hear you say… Well you wouldn't be too far out if thinking that, but you need a little of the other as well in order to achieve it…

My sporting story begins back in the early eighties at the age of eleven or twelve, distant memories at thirty years old but I think the experiences that help make you the adult you become are often the ones that stick most vividly in the mind. By background, I come from a farming family with hard physical labour a normal part of life, even as a schoolboy cleaning out cowsheds by hand and feeding the animals were duties put before schoolwork or any other hobbies that I would want to develop.

At school I had by luck surrounded myself with good friends who all participated in and were passionate about various sports. A wide choice of sports so often available at schools such as football, rugby and cross-country running, but coupled with a dedicated and enthusiastic PE teacher (the old fashioned type, tough but well respected, fun with an ability to draw in students to really enjoy sport) gave a shy farming lad the confidence to get stuck in and take part in any sport he could, an attribute that has stood me in good stead for where I am today. Like so many young lads, football was my main sport at school; every break time spent kicking anything round; tennis ball, sponge ball and even sometime the luxury of a football! Evenings and weekends were occupied with squash, snooker, golf and rugby where possible. One of my lasting passions, this one rugby, was also started here. I played for the school and county with a bit of football for the village team thrown in for good measure. Another passion that started around this time was for anything with two wheels and preferably an engine. My trusty bike took me to and from school, between sports and round a very big paper round and led me to a hobby that became a big part of my twenties…

Around this age I also became aware of the thrill of competition, what it meant to get involved, not necessarily to win but the thrill of trying and having a go. Whether I was a natural, or rubbish, I have always enjoyed participating in sports and competing. Trying to be the best you can is an immensely satisfying way to live, for me at any rate!

At sixteen, having been allowed my education quota, my parents encouraged me to 'get out and get a trade'. Fancy universities or polytechnics were not to be a luxury afforded to me! Leaving school allowed the two-wheeled hobby to develop, I am a dirt-track biker, this upbringing of mud, biking in all weathers and battling with the bike to stay on top around the undulating and unforgiving race tracks has reinforced the traits in me of enjoying physical activity and developing a strong mind committed to finish a job no matter how hard or tedious a task. I think these traits may have a little to answer for come Barcelona race day! They also took me through a carpentry and joinery masters apprenticeship, not a profession that I still practice but skills that I use on a regular basis and am proud to have to my name.

My twenties saw a return to competitive sport with the local rugby team, competing in the first team in the Wilts and Dorset League in which we were moderately successful. Great people were met and friendships made but still my 'ideal' sport had not been discovered. Motocross racing stepped in to provide a needed buzz and adrenalin-fuelled hobby. It was also one of my father's passions and bikes had always been around the farm when I was a child but we splashed out on a race bike (a 500cc four-stroke motocross bike for the interested) and weekends were spent training or racing round the country for nearly ten years. Out of racing season the speed of bike slowed to a mountain bike but although cycling was not what I would say a natural sport to me my determination has led it to become probably my strongest discipline now and got me to the national qualifiers so maybe I don't do myself justice by berating my skills…

I should mention that I got married during this period of my life as well, not the L.O.V.E. to which I allude in my title but rather an ill-fated mismatch with someone whom I shared no common interests, least of all sport. A lack of interest or understanding of sport, its ethos and what it meant to me became an increasingly apparent division between us. No interest or support was offered; rather it became a cause of friction between us. Luckily I have always had the love and support of my parents for my sporting events, even if the concept itself was not encouraged.

This was all humming along quite nicely until 2003 when a major change was thrown my way… Rainy race days were not unusual but when the bike and I parted company soon after the start of the race on a particularly nasty bend my racing fate was decided. Thankfully the other competitors whizzing by like bumblebees missed making my day worse, but it soon became apparent that my foot was pointing in the wrong direction. I have respect for anyone who gives their free time to help others but the St John Ambulance that day must have missed the anatomy class in training and with a helpful Wiltshire "don't worry it's not broke, you've just twisted it" whipped off my bike boot to assess the damage. Unfortunately twist was quite an apt description and the boot, which had been helpfully holding my lower leg together looked on as my foot flopped to the wrong side… "Ah, maybe you have broken it" was helpfully offered (*I shall omit the eloquent swearing which was at this time streaming a little from my good self*) and then I received the news, that due to the wet weather, the Ambulance had already left with another casualty. This was not the best day so far.

Luckily, a good friend who was watching the race was on hand to provide the longest and most agonising drive to a hospital that I have ever made. After gently hopping through the hospital doors (you get a much grander entrance with the blue lights…), assistance came in the form of a wheelchair and I was lined up amongst the great (and mostly obese) number of others waiting in this Swindon hospital waiting room. I feel a few were there simply to get the sick note out of work in the morning but luckily I didn't need to satisfy my curiosity to find out as, of my limited memories, I was soon wheeled to x-ray. News of a bad break was kindly broken by the doctor who then promptly knocked me out to straighten it. This was probably a good thing as I have a deep dislike of hospitals and so given half a chance would probably have tried to drag myself home before anything was injected or administered but luckily the next I knew was waking up on the ward alone, terrified and waiting for the next day's surgery. The parents couldn't visit, as they were busy clearing up the mess I'd made with my bike at the track and the other part of my life informed me that as it was "my own fault" I had to suffer it as such.

The next morning the surgeon did a fantastic job fashioning me an ankle out of wire pins and two titanium plates. However I think he had a dislike for motorbikes due to the addition of a non-weight bearing plaster… Not really, but the nature of the break made for a long and inconvenient recovery, and put my motocross career on hold for at least a year. Once healed it took a lot of 'discussion' before I could get back on to the bike but, apart from the hell it created at home, the fast times that once had come so easily now eluded me. Realising that the bike leathers would be hung up for the last time I had a last fling at Weston-Super-Mare beach race and walked away happy, albeit with a freshly broken rib, but it carried me round eleven race laps and so for me it bought 2003 to a good close.

With the bike sold I now needed something else to do... Things were falling apart at home and so I threw myself into my running and mountain biking once again. Sport is an integral part of my being but was not unfortunately part of my home life. I tried to get the whole family involved in the same ways that had made me so happy, but sport itself was resented and me more so for bringing it into the home. I did what everyone with a passion for sport would do when faced with this and threw myself into it more. I created a small local running group of friends, colleagues and family members and whilst our runs became an established and fulfilling hobby, even taking us to local events, the rest of my life deteriorated further.

But how did I get into triathlons and what is the relevance to the ironman and this book I hear you say? In 2008-2009 a casual comment from a wild-haired great friend of mine, Stuart Crowhurst, culminated in our first entry to a sprint triathlon; "I fancy one of these multi-discipline races" were the words, and there it began...

The Malmesbury Sprint Triathlon we competed in was a buzzing affair with a raucous 200 entries, not quite what we'll be faced with at Barcelona, but I was there and I got involved. The bikes were racked and serious looking Wiltshire folk paced around in fancy Tri suits... I borrowed my brothers' mountain bike as it had road tyres unlike the humming off-road beauties on my bike and off I went. I can't say I was confident about all the disciplines as swimming is not something that I had really done much of before but just to be involved started to give me the buzz that I had once had with Motocross… Was this the event that I had been searching for? So how did the race go I hear you ask?! Well, I managed a fantastic first length of front crawl and completed the rest with an out-of-breath steady breast stroke, being the last to exit the pool… onto the bike and I felt a little more in my element, passing several of the competitors who had no doubt been worrying about my health and safety only moments before. I passed more on the run and I was hooked! It was so thrilling and without the week of motorbike prepping beforehand, perfect!

From here I got myself a second-hand road bike and invested in some adult swimming lessons. It is never too late to get involved and learn a new trick and regular trips to the pool meant I was soon clocking up the lengths. In eight or nine months I had become like a duck to water, well almost! The local triathlon scene soon picked up and I was involved in developing a small club of other like-minded people of mixed abilities and all ages. Triathlon is a very friendly and social sport, with new enthusiasts always made to feel welcome and able to give it a go.

Where one part of my life was really going well, the other was not so, and 2011 saw the end of my marriage. Luckily, I have a great family and network of friends around me who were on hand to support me through these hard times.

So where are we now? To skip forward a little and my life is very different. I am loved and respected immensely, and supported in my work and home life. As with my parents' love and support when I was younger, with my beautiful partner and her love and support I am now about to compete in what is to me, the ultimate sporting event; an Iron-Distance Triathlon. All of us that are competing in this event will understand the volume of training that the L.O.V.E. stands for but also hopefully the other side that allows us to achieve it.

Alison motivates and encourages me, as I do her. Having rowed for the youth GB team and herself enjoying triathlons (when not pregnant…) she understands the passion for sport. Mostly, she understands me.

Barcelona?… well I'm a regular subscriber to Triathlete Europe (the emailed webshot version for general skiving and distraction whilst at work…). I read an article about this dude Dr. Justin Roberts wanting to conduct a triathlon study culminating at the Challenge Barcelona. I seemed to fit the criteria so I fired over a quick email with almost instant reply. Ali and I were quite excited even though there was a long way to go, but I am sure we were quite confident that we would be there in Barcelona. As like all on this study, after the pre-screening everything fell into place. Justin was so welcoming, we felt confident, reassured by what, we heard from Dr. J, was going to be an exciting journey! As the emails started coming I felt the need to get my good friend involved for the journey as well. I kept on and on about how good this was going to be and when a few of the initial participants dropped out I seized my chance to put Stuart forwards to be involved. I am sure he thanks me for it now?!

But I am very glad we have made the journey this far together. The exercise programmes rolled (and rolled) in and just kept coming. But I loved it and told everybody I met, training is so often unstructured and after years of this I had a structure to follow. Training days could be moved around to accommodate the odd social event in the early days but generally I followed the programme day by day, and word for word. I must admit that over the first few months my head was in slightly different places from time to time, I wanted to be totally committed, but struggled with the sheer amount of time that the training consumed and what else had to be put on the back burner in order to achieve it. The light-bulb moment came in a comment from Ali. She insisted that I follow the training programme for my own safety! I hadn't thought of safety as a factor but the words "yes I want you to do the event but without having a heart attack" can ground one and focus the mind a little and she was perfectly right, this was now more than a personal quest, this journey affected the whole family and I needed them to help me get through this, but at the same time they needed me too! Every step taken was watched and encouraged, turbo sessions sometimes involved our one-year-old son sat on the aero bars with excitement. Runs were accompanied by outriders, children in trailers and children on bikes who complained about hills with little offer of encouraging words but this was no problem as the simple fact that they were out with me was encouragement enough as we were doing it together.

The testing started and the consumption of facts and figures that followed only made you want to do more. All around us were interested in our gains, our highs and our lows. The race was entered, the flights and accommodation booked! The mighty beast was rolling, but not uncontrollably. Ali encouraged me, whilst Justin and the cohort family guided. You are never alone, even on a long solo bike ride my head was full of thoughts and people from the family cohort, the trials and tribulations, the facts and ideas from Facebook all bounce around in your head and allow you to pluck out the content that you need. At no point did I feel questioned in my ability to do it and at no point did I hear a sigh from Ali when I mentioned that again I would spend our weekends biking or running just "well what time did you do?" "how do you feel?" it was always great.

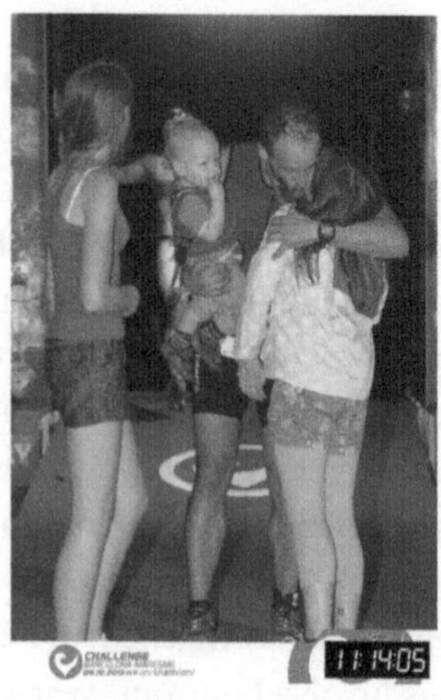

Sharing the finish with family: Shaun "Ironman" Hunt

So as I sit here, a week before the big day I reflect on the people I have met, those that I've probably bored to death and I have only positive thoughts. My body has changed, and my mind and will to finish are strengthened. I feel ready now. I maybe won't win but I will be doing my damnedest to finish!

It is the love that has made me who I am, and the love of the best woman that has driven and understood me. Equally it is the love of the family Hatfield that will see us all over that line in Barcelona and I mean the finish line!

The Message: Triathlon – it's all about the person and the people who love you!

CHAPTER 22

"Pursuit" *By Mark Jex*

Humans are designed to run. Well, technically we've evolved to run, but either way prehistoric man had good reasons to run. He was either chasing something or being chased. Either trying to catch food or avoid becoming it. Modern man doesn't generally need to run to Morrisons to catch a Chicken Tikka Masala and I haven't spotted any sabre-toothed tigers recently. The evolutionary pressures, which gave us the ability to run, have pretty much ceased.

We didn't evolve to cycle; instead bikes are designed to fit around us – some more comfortably than others. If there is an evolutionary branch of humans who are adapted to swim, the aquatic apes, then I personally come from a very different ancestry. The water is an alien environment to me in which I need to fight my primitive instinct to get out and go and sit on a sun lounger.

The cumulative impact of the discovery of fire, the age of enlightenment, the industrial revolution and the invention of the takeaway pizza has meant that we can survive just fine without running, cycling or swimming. So what motivated eighty of us to join an iron-distance triathlon study when we could have just gone to the pub instead? For me, the motivation still comes chasing some things and from running away from others.

Ok – one of the things I'm chasing is that little man on my Garmin GPS training watch. If I catch him, I can't eat him, but

I chase him anyway. I set the pace for my "virtual partner" wrong for a race in June and ended up running a personal best trying to keep up with the little digital bastard. But the "virtual partner" on my watch didn't make me sign up for this study. It's much more about the ticking of the big hand on the clock.

Most recreational athletes will have seen a back of the envelope formula to calculate your max heart rate. It's something like 220 minus your age. It's the "minus your age" bit that gets me. Every year older is another beat off my max heart rate and there's nothing I can do about it. I can improve my VO_{2max} or lactate threshold with training, but the upper limit is coming down all the time. For twenty years I did no exercise and I lost twenty beats off my max heart rate. I'm not going to let another year go by without using my full range of heart rate zones.

Sometime in the last ten years my hair turned from brown to white – the salt overwhelmed the pepper. I can't bend down without making a noise, which sounds like Maria Sharapova serving. I'm getting older and I'm not happy about it. I'm sure the Germans have a compound noun for the day when a father is beaten by his son for the first time. My ten-year-old son can already swim faster than me and ski better than me – the moment when he can beat me at running and cycling can't be much further down the line. The only ace I have up my sleeve is sheer bloody-mindedness. If age means that I can't run, cycle or swim fast, I'll just keep on doing all three slowly until everyone else gives up and goes home.

When it comes to motivation I'm in the Forrest Gump camp. I just keep going until I see the stop sign. In that sense endurance triathlon is a very simple sport, despite the jargon, complex kit, transitions and nutrition strategies. Triathlon is mainly about doing the same things over and over again for a very long time.

Just to be clear, *I'm not an athlete.* I used to run when I was a kid, but I did no meaningful exercise for the twenty years between 1988 and 2008. In 2008, my Dad retired and I took some time off work so we could go trekking in Iceland together. He had been living in Hong Kong for over twenty years and the trip gave us a chance catch up after a long time apart. I needed to get fit for the trek and so I bought myself some trainers and started going jogging in the park. The trek was tough, but we got through it together and I felt healthier than I had done for a very long time.

Fresh from Iceland, and feeling inspired by my feats of Viking intrepidness, I entered the Herts 10K race. This is probably the pivotal point for me. I discovered that having a race to train for gives me the motivation to get out of bed and go out running.

The Herts 10K is a fantastic community race and raises money for Grove House, the local hospice charity. It has a great atmosphere and is the perfect first race for someone starting to run. It got me completely hooked on racing. Not because I did particularly well, nor because I actually have any chance of winning anything, but just because there is something wonderful about running with other people in a competitive environment. It's like the migration of the wildebeest across the Serengeti, but with a lot more digital watches.

I did a few more 10Ks and then the odd ten miler. Before long I'd done a couple of half-marathons and the big 26.2-mile challenge was calling. I managed to get a charity place for the London Marathon in 2010 for the Alzheimer's Society. The training went really well but I pulled my left quad muscle two weeks before the race and needed a lot of physio and acupuncture to get me to the starting line on my thirty-ninth birthday. It was a great experience, and the support from the London crowd was unbelievable. I finished in a fairly leisurely

3hr53mins. Although I vowed at the end that I would never to do another one, I still felt I had some unfinished business.

I bought my first road bike one week after finishing my first marathon. The plan was to use it to keep fit without putting quite so much strain on my knees. I don't think I had any intention of doing a triathlon at the time – the fact that I couldn't swim meant that I didn't really consider it. However having bought a bike it was fairly inevitable that I would end up doing a couple of duathlon (run-cycle-run) races. Then I made the fateful mistake of buying a Triathlon magazine. Inspired mainly by looking at all the cool kit, I took the plunge and entered the Blenheim sprint triathlon in June 2011. I also took the plunge of having some swimming lessons to get me through the 750m swim.

There are two things that have kept me motivated from my first attempts at jogging in 2008 through to this iron-distance triathlon. They are races and the gadgets. I love races. I don't really care about where I finish, but I still love racing other people (rather than just the little digital man). I'm not trying to beat anyone in particular – I only really care about beating my previous time and not making a fool of myself. But when the race starts I'm off like a whippet chasing a rabbit. The herd mentality kicks in and what would be an impossibly-fast pace in training seems suddenly easy in a race – at least for the first half a mile.

I have some little motivational tricks to keep pushing myself during a race. There are small bugbears I have with other people's running kit, which gives me the kick I need to sprint past them. For example, anyone wearing a replica football shirt in a race needs to be beaten. Anyone wearing knee-length rugby socks is asking to be overtaken on the next hill. Fashion trainer wearers deserve to see my heels disappear into the distance. Wearing just one calf sleeve? Get thee behind me!

The best race motivation comes from finding a nemesis. Usually about half-way through a race there is someone who has been going at roughly the same pace, but then decides to put on a little burst of speed. I'll step up my pace to match them and without having to say anything we both know it's now a race between the two of us and the rest of the field doesn't matter. This usually ends in a ridiculous sprint down the last 200m to see who gets 234th place.

The gadgets are also important. Without the gadgets I wouldn't be a runner, let alone a cyclist or a swimmer. The gadgets are what keep me training. If it isn't logged it didn't happen. That's become my philosophy to training – every run, swim, ride, weights session and even the odd Pilates class needs to be recorded and logged for future reference. I need to know my speed, heart rate, GPS route, stroke rate, and how many Strava trophies I've picked up. I wouldn't go running without my GPS watch and heart rate monitor any more than I would go swimming without my goggles or cycling without my helmet, sunglasses and gloves. The first thing on my mind when I come back from a six-hour cycle ride is to plug my cycle computer into my PC and upload my data. I need to check if I've beaten my PB up Wheathampstead hill.

I started logging all my training on the wonderful Fetch Everyone website in 2009. Fetch Everyone was recently voted the favourite running website in a Guardian poll and it's being an integral part of my transformation from an exercise agnostic to triathlon evangelist. The ability to analyse and digest my training data has been instrumental in getting me out the door even in the foulest weather. It's made me put in that extra effort to beat last week's 10km time or literally "go the extra mile" to hit my distance target for the week.

I think my data obsession is something like the gene that makes trainspotters spot trains and stamp collectors collect stamps. It's reached the level that whenever I travel somewhere new I have to go for a run into order to "collect" the GPS route. You haven't seen Sydney Harbour unless you've run over Sydney Harbour Bridge and logged the GPS route to prove it.

Historically this part of my personality has been kept private and not shared with the wider world, but last year I discovered the Strava website and realised that I'm not alone. Strava is a cycling website which allows you to compare your performance with other users on particular stretches of road which have been marked as "Strava sections". You upload your GPS data from your watch or bike computer and it tells you where you are on the leader board for each section you've ridden. I'm currently 308th out of 888 people who have logged times up Wheathampstead Hill, but I shaved three seconds from my time at the last attempt.

The idea behind Strava is breathtakingly brilliant. It takes data obsession out from behind closed doors and lets it run around in public with its tongue hanging out going "Wahhhhhh". It's also completely addictive. There must be scope to apply the same leader board motivational tricks to other areas of my life. Maybe if there was a Strava for sex I might put in more effort to attain the bedroom King of the Mountain accolade.

It was September 2012 when I first heard about the research study at the University of Hertfordshire. I think my wife, Anna, spotted it on the Welwyn Wheelers' website and mentioned it to me. So she is at least partly culpable for me joining the study. My kids were quite disappointed that it wasn't the kind of ironman research programme where you get a gold titanium alloy superhero suit. But I think they are still a little bit impressed that I'm actually doing it.

2012 was a tough year for me. Against the background of the London Olympics, I went through a major upheaval in my work and family life. To borrow a Triathlon term – I "*bonked*".

Bonking is the dreadful moment when you run out of energy in an endurance race. If you don't get the nutrition and hydration strategy right, you use up your energy reserves and then you slow down and end up doing the painful ironman shuffle.

I'd had a successful career in the City for eighteen years but in 2012 things started to catch up with me. I wasn't looking after myself. I was working long hours and skipping breakfast and lunch – maybe only grabbing a sandwich to eat on the train home. I also ended up doing the "weekend warrior" thing where I would then try to squeeze a week's worth of running, cycling and swim training into two days.

I think it would have been quite obvious to anyone looking from outside that my lifestyle wasn't sustainable, but I was stubborn and blinkered and just kept ploughing on. I got ill. Nothing serious, just persistent sinus infections, chest infections and stomach bugs. I stopped sleeping. I was running on adrenaline and not much else and I started to get very anxious. My heart was racing and I couldn't concentrate on simple tasks. My job was highly technical, highly mathematical and required keeping a calm, clear head. I simply could not do it anymore.

I ended up leaving my job and taking a "career break" and spent the summer recovering. One of the things, which really helped me get though a very tough period, was cycling. I don't mean cycle training – I just mean getting out of the house and going on a bike ride. Getting out of town onto some quiet country lanes for a ride allowed me to feel calmer and raised my mood. It also helped me to become physically tired so that I could start to sleep better.

When I found out about the University of Hertfordshire study it seemed like too good an opportunity to miss. I was starting to feel better and for the first time in my adult life I had some free time. I was also in desperate need of something to focus on to help me recover. Where I live in St Albans is an 8km run from the Sport Science department at the University of Hertfordshire – so it's effectively right on my doorstep. The study provided a chance to prepare for Challenge Barcelona with a structured training plan and with monitoring and testing. But what I hadn't realised at the start was how important the support of all the other triathletes would be in getting through this. I don't think I would have been able to get through the training on my own without them. I also didn't realise how much time I'd end up spending on Facebook discussing every detail of our collective journey.

I very nearly didn't make it to the first hurdle. Having got through the initial testing and been accepted onto the programme, I got ill again. I ended up in hospital with severe abdominal pains and then bizarrely my face became paralysed. November and December were pretty awful – I spent Christmas Eve waiting in Watford General Hospital for a brain scan. But I recovered over the New Year, and just got back on my feet in time to start the training programme at the end of January 2013.

The training is all about peaks and troughs. Justin's training plans have medium weeks, followed by hard weeks, followed by recovery weeks. You push yourself, but then allow your body time to recover and adapt. It's been fun, but I certainly haven't found it easy. Running is my strongest of the three sports and although the volume of running is less than I have previously done in training for a marathon, I've still been troubled by small injuries and niggles. The cycling is still something I'm learning. I've been able to increase the cycling distance well enough, and I'm now capable of cycling for over a hundred miles, but I'm still much slower than I'd like to be.

The swimming has been really hard. Two years ago I

couldn't swim two lengths of a 25m pool. Now after months of intensive training I *can't* swim 3.8km.But the swimming also has been the biggest transformation for me. Before this year I really wasn't the sort of person who would go wild swimming in a French river or spend my Saturday mornings dodging swans in Denham Lake. But I do sometimes wonder if I have gone a bit too far.

It's early on a Sunday morning and I'm in the sea. I've got seawater in my goggles and my neck is red raw from where my wetsuit has been rubbing. I can feel the warmth draining out of me into the cold water. I know there is an orange buoy somewhere in front of me. I raise my eyes out of the water but I can't see it. I swim a few more strokes and try to "sight" the buoy again. This time it is just visible for a split second above the waves, but it seems to be no closer than it was five minutes ago. I lift my head out of the water and look around me – none of the 200 swimmers who ran into the sea with me nearly two hours ago are in sight.

I feel a momentary sense of relief – I tell myself I'm having yet another Barcelona race-day nightmare and I'll wake up any moment. But the stinging in my eyes and the rubbing of the wetsuit snaps me back into the moment. I'm not in bed, I'm somewhere off Boscombe beach in Bournemouth taking part in the aptly named "Long Swim". When I entered I had the idea that I would confront all of my sea-swimming heebie jeebies before Barcelona – but right now the heebie jeebies are winning.

There is a strong tidal current running along the beach. I'm on the last far leg of a three-lap course swimming against the current. I've already worked that you lose much more time swimming against the current than you gain when you swim with it – right now the current seems to match my swim speed and I'm swimming just to stay still. My form has gone out the window and I'm flapping around like an Arsenal goalkeeper. Then I remember my mantras. "Hugging a fat man" – to remind me to swim with my arms wide and not cross over my body. "Over a barrel" – make sure my hands slide into the water with the fingers pointing down. "Smiley face" – push right to the end of the stroke, imagining there is a smiley face drawn on the palm of my hand and I'm showing it to anyone behind me. Not that there is anyone behind me. I'm pretty sure I'm the last person in the water. I repeat the mantras over and over in my head – I'm hugging a fat man with a smiley face over a barrel – not a particularly nice mental image, but it seems to be doing the trick. The buoy has edged a little nearer next time I look up.

Eventually I get round the buoy and swim back to shore. I can see Anna and my two boys are standing on the beach waiting for me. Open-water swimming is not a great spectator sport, as all wetsuits look the same and everyone is wearing the same orange swimming cap. I'm forty minutes beyond my expected finishing time and they've been getting increasingly worried. It turns out I'm not last, there's one person behind me, but I've still put my family through an ordeal. I've got a whole new set of heebie jeebies to worry about, but I think I might just be stubborn enough to get through the Barcelona triathlon.

I could probably improve my triathlon swim times considerably if I just stopped apologising. Swimming with a large number of people in close proximity means that there's going to be the odd collision. I've done one triathlon with a mass start of over 1000 people. Despite being at the back of the pack it was still like being in an industrial washing machine. I'm not yet able to ignore the melee and just swim. Whenever I inadvertently touch someone, even if it's him or her kicking me in the face, I feel the need to stop swimming and say sorry.

I'm trying to get all my rookie mistakes out of the way before Barcelona. In June this year I took part in the Outlaw Half-Triathlon and managed to come up with a checklist of mistakes, which I'm aiming not to repeat.

My key Outlaw half lessons were:

- If you've locked your bike onto the car roof rack then remember to bring the keys;
- If you've taken the front wheel off the bike for transport remember to re-attach the brakes before cycling off from T1;
- The toilet queues before the race can be very long;
- Body Glide stops a wetsuit rubbing and allows it to be removed quickly in T1. It works best when applied to the ankles, wrists and neck. It doesn't work well if it's left in the bag.
- Warming up and acclimatisation is a good idea before the swim. It's not such a good idea to rush from the toilet queue straight into the swim;
- Slapping yourself in the face and shouting "Toughen the f*** up" at the top of your voice seems to be an eventual cure for the panic attack and hyperventilating which is a result of rushing from the toilet queue straight into the swim;
- The thought of posting a DNF (Did Not Finish) after only 10mins of the swim doesn't feel very iron;
- It's impossible to put on compression socks with freezing hands;
- Ten minutes in T1 flies by if you're trying to find a missing contact lens in one eye. I didn't even have time for a cup of tea;
- It is possible to complete the cycle and run with only one contact lens;

- Sunscreen works best when applied to the neck, face, shoulders and arms. It doesn't work so well when left in your bag on the first really sunny day of the year;
- It's a good idea to put energy-drink powder in your water bottles before you leave home – but you also need to add water at some point;
- There's a limit to how many Rhubarb and Custard energy gels you can swallow. That limit is one;
- The only Cervelo bike I overtook all day was on the motorway on the way home; and
- There are lots of horse trials in Nottinghamshire. I don't know what crime the horses are accused of.

Since I started running in 2008, cycling in 2010 and triathlon in 2011 the exercise bug has been contagious. My wife and has been a self-proclaimed non-runner for all of her life, but has recently completed her first Olympic triathlon and is seriously considering her first half-marathon. My boys, Edward and Oliver have both recently joined the local Tri-Force triathlon club and have completed their first triathlons this summer. They are also both members of the St Albans COSTA swimming club. Their swimming genes come from Anna who has some aquatic ape ancestry.

All I need to do now is convince the rest of the triathletes to wear fashion trainers, Arsenal shirts, rugby socks or one calf sleeves for the race and I'll be flying.

What I've really been running away from this year is my old life. I have no intention of going back to the lifestyle I had before I started this. The triathlon is part of a reboot. What I'm chasing is the new version of me – Ironman Mark 42. But I think just by starting this study I've already caught up with him.

Postscript

Unfortunately my reboot ended with an air boot on my right foot. With just a week to go to before the Barcelona Challenge race I saw a consultant and had an MRI scan on my foot which showed some stress damage to three of the bones. On top of that my neck, back and right shoulder all seized up in sympathy after limping around for a week. I went from being iron fit to being a physical wreck in the space of a few days. Although I couldn't admit it until the last minute – my iron-distance triathlon ambitions were over for 2013. I went as far as shipping my bike and taking all my kit over to Spain, but this wasn't a niggle I was going to be able to run off.

Having spent nine months visualising every aspect of the race and in particular crossing the finishing line, it was a real mental challenge to accept that it wasn't going to happen. I did not have a plan B for not making it to the starting line. Instead of racing, I spent the day supporting the rest of the HURTS contingent as they pushed themselves to the limit. It was an emotionally-charged day, which has made a deep impression on me. Hobbling along the run course with Gary Smith as he limped on blistered feet toward the glory of role of last man home was both uplifting and sobering. If you want to do an iron-distance triathlon I would not recommend watching one at close quarters.

I am very proud to have been part of an amazing group of people, some of whom realised their ambitions this year and some, like me, who missed out. Nine months of training for one day of racing is a difficult equation to balance. For me the challenge next year will be to get to the start line in a fit state. After racing and really enjoying the Outlaw half in June this year, I've decided to have another crack at iron-distance triathlon with the full Outlaw in July 2014.

Already gearing up for 2014 – Mark Jex

There are a whole heap of mistakes I made this year, which I will be aiming to avoid next year. The biggest of these was not listening to my body. The injuries, which finally kept me out of the race, had their origins much earlier in the year. My foot was first injured in February and my neck and shoulder surfaced as a problem in April. My aim for this winter is to heal properly and really work on my core strength so that I can come back stronger next year. Injury prevention is more important to me than speed.

The Message: nine months training for one race. Focus on injury prevention, going from Iron fit to Iron strong. Most importantly, never give up that dream…

Editors' Message: With great adversity, the real human spirit is observed. On behalf of team HURTS – Mr Jex, we salute your attitude, bravery and conviction – true IRONMAN spirit.

CHAPTER 23

"Human" *By Dan Searle*

Having a job in IT, I spend most of my working life sitting down and staring at a computer screen. I consider it pretty much essential that I do the opposite of that for some of the time I'm not at work. Knowing you should do some exercise, and actually doing it are different things though. I felt I wasn't born with the motivation to work up a sweat that other people seem to have. It's always easier to find excuses why you should stay indoors rather than go out in the rain/heat/cold, and exercise often doesn't seem to come very naturally. It can feel like an effort just to get out the door.

About fourteen years ago I read a book called *Survival of the Fittest*, by Dr Mike Stroud – the guy who did some of those crazy expeditions and extreme feats of endurance with his friend Ranulph Fiennes. In it he describes how as someone who's not particularly fit, he would use himself as his own test subject by putting himself through physical stresses most people would wince just at the thought of. The premise of the book is that 'humans evolved' for these sorts of endurance-based things, and it is only our modern undemanding lifestyles that make such feats *seem* superhuman.

I'm human, I thought, I'm not particularly fit, that must mean I can do these kinds of things! I was convinced, of the theory anyway. From then on I tried not to let my natural aversion to exertion put me off. I would have a go anyway. What's the worst that could happen?

At the time I read that book, I was a young and just about adequately fit soldier in the Territorial Army, based at a small outstation in Chertsey, Surrey. My little troop was without a Physical Training Instructor (PTI), which meant we couldn't do certain types of training that we needed to do. Army PTIs had something of a reputation for striking fear into you with their demands for you to run, march long distances, clamber over assault courses and generally push yourself until it hurt. Even the PTI badge features instruments of physical pain: swords.

One night at a dinner when we were discussing what skills and qualifications we needed in the troop, the subject of our lack of a PTI came up. I'd had a couple of drinks and Dr Mike's book was still quite fresh in my mind, and it dawned on me that even PTIs are human, so how hard could the PTI course be? I volunteered for it. The next day I quietly hoped that everyone had forgotten, but unfortunately not.

A few months later I found myself in a barracks in Wiltshire spending all day every day sweating my arse off. Sometimes I was acting as instructor, sometimes as student – either way it was knackering. I came within a few seconds of failing one of the critical fitness tests, but somehow I scraped through the two weeks and I passed. I could wear the crossed-swords badge (on a rather retro white vest with red piping). I was a qualified PTI. I could hardly believe it. I certainly didn't feel as fit as I had believed PTIs to be, but now officially I was, even if only just.

Although opportunities to don my retro vest and train people were fairly frequent, the TA is a part-time volunteer force – and it's generally not practical to do physical training for any more than about an hour every other week, which just wasn't enough to make a real difference. It quickly became apparent that a key aspect of a PTI's role, is simply convincing people to do some exercise in their own time. That meant actually motivating them, not just 'beasting' them. The problem was that for a lot of the recruits (especially the 'PlayStation generation'), the idea of running or loading yourself up with a 15kg Bergen (backpack) and marching was completely alien. Sweating was a sign that something was wrong, not that you were doing something right. They had virtually no idea what they were capable of. I found this frustrating, knowing that these people were human (the medical checks confirmed this) – and humans are built for physical endurance, Dr Mike said so. It seemed to me that to be an effective PTI, I would need good skills of persuasion. I would have to get a bit evangelical about it.

You can't be all mouth and no trousers, especially in the military. You have to try to lead by example. So when some of the more keen soldiers around me were trying to get people to join them in doing military challenges like the Lanyard Trophy (a forty-mile march, carrying 40lbs on your back) or civilian events like half-marathons, I felt I didn't have much choice but to enter with them. I had no excuse. I was *human* after all, and physical exercise hadn't killed me yet. Doing something as a team made things easier. If your determination lapsed, you had your mates around to support you. It also made the challenges more enjoyable, not least talking about them afterwards in the bar.

Over time, I started to become one of those more keen soldiers and it was me who was entering events and encouraging others to. I suppose it's a case of 'fake it to make it'. I wasn't particularly competitive at any of the things I entered, but I completed them and started to enjoy them. I liked the focus that a looming event brings, and the sense of accomplishment that outlasts the aches and pains you feel afterwards. Sometimes I didn't enjoy the event itself, but mostly I did – even if only in retrospect.

One such event that's not exactly enjoyable is Tough Guy. Held on a farm near Wolverhampton, it's the brainchild of an eccentric chap calling himself Mr Mouse. It starts with an eight "country-mile" off-road run, and then you're straight into a massive obstacle course. Now, I like obstacle courses, but this one is different. The event is held at the end of January – about the coldest time of the year, and many of the obstacles involve wading through, or *fully* immersing yourself in, mud and water. The race leaders often have to break the ice to get through. Ice-cream headaches, cramp and hypothermia all round. It's not so much a test of fitness, more a test of pain tolerance. Somehow, I managed to persuade enough people from my TA unit to enter a team of over ten, four years in a row.

Like a lot of people, after a completing a few half-marathons, the word "half" played on my mind a bit and I started to aspire to running a full marathon. I would watch the London Marathon every year and be inspired and moved by the stories of those running for charity. I also saw that people like Fauja Singh who completed his first marathon aged ninety-three. If he could do it, surely I could too?

Unfortunately, so many other people from all over the world also want to run the London Marathon that there's a ballot to get a place, and the odds are not in your favour. After three years with no success, in 2005 I decided to enter the Paris Marathon instead – it was about the same time of year, it was easier to get into if you applied early enough, and it was doable in a weekend, travel-wise.

I tried to follow a training programme and increased the distances I was running, but aside from that I didn't really know what I was doing. I generally didn't drink enough or take on enough energy during long runs in training, and I paid the price of that during the event itself. I was feeling quite good and was on-target for a 3 hour 45 finish until I got to about nineteen miles, and then I hit 'the wall'. The next six miles were a real struggle and started to alternate between walking and running. Even the locals' shout of "*Allez! Allez!*" could barely keep me moving. At about the twenty-three-mile point I noticed there was a drinks stop, but instead of cups of water, there were cups of wine. I was very tempted to just stop right there. I refrained from trying the wine, thinking it would just make things harder and I struggled on. At the finish the cheering from the crowds gave me a massive lift and I really picked up the pace for the last 200m, and I crossed the line in four hours and five minutes. I was disappointed at going over four hours, but elated at finishing a marathon.

Later that year, a friend overheard me saying I could barely swim, and informed me she was a swimming teacher, and offered me lessons. I gratefully accepted. For the next few months she would spend a couple of hours a week helping me go from what I would call "moving through the water without drowning" to something resembling front crawl. It was tough and frustrating at times, but slowly but surely I learned to swim properly. This was a revelation for me. Swimming was now something I could do! I wasn't going to win any races, but I could just about fool a casual observer into thinking I was a competent swimmer.

Keen to make use of my new ability to swim, I started thinking about what I could do with it. I stumbled across a local sprint distance triathlon. The swim was pool-based, and at 426m would be a good challenge for me to attempt doing all front crawl. I decided to enter it.

For some reason when you're new to triathlon you assume that it's really elitist, and by turning up to take part in one you're proclaiming yourself to be similarly elite. I turned up expecting to be an amusement to my fellow competitors, but instead I discovered there was a huge range of people taking part. It wasn't just the super-fit semi-pros with their strange carbon TT bikes (but they were there of course); there were people like me doing their first ever triathlon, and everything in between. When I was racking my bike in the transition area before the race, I noticed the bike next to mine had a basket on the front of it. Suddenly I felt like maybe I wasn't as unprepared as I thought.

That first triathlon went ok. I got through the swim mostly doing front crawl, and didn't make any stupid mistakes on the bike and run. Most importantly I really enjoyed it.

I decided to enter another triathlon, this time a slightly longer one – the Bananaman triathlon – mid-way between a Sprint and an Olympic/Standard distance triathlon – but this one had an open-water swim. I bought a wetsuit and ventured to my nearest swimming lake for a practice. Swimming in a lake took some getting used to, but I enjoyed the sense of freedom and not having to turn around every twenty-five metres. It was like the difference between running outside and running on a treadmill: unless it's freezing cold, or the weather is bad, outside is better than indoors. It was good to do something a bit unusual too; not many of my friends swim in lakes.

As well as the swimming, I tried to be a bit more focused on running and cycling in my training. I really started to like the variety in training for three different disciplines, and the 'all-round' fitness aspect of it appealed to me. I generally prefer to be a jack-of-all-trades to being a master of one.

The Bananaman was in mid-July 2006 and happened to be the hottest day of the year. My start time was 1pm and it was over 30°C. I had been nervous about the swim, but, waiting on the pontoon to start, sweating in my wetsuit, I was so hot I couldn't wait to get in the water. After what seemed like ages, we all jumped into the water and we were off. It seemed to take my forever to get around the square course, but eventually I turned the last corner and reached the exit point. I found out after the event that they'd put the buoys in the wrong place and it was a 1000m swim instead of an 800m swim. I'd never swum that far in open water before! I was relieved, and pleased to hit an unexpected milestone.

Completing an open-water triathlon in a heatwave gave me a new confidence, and the following year (2007) I decided to have a go at an Olympic-distance event (Windsor), and then the a middle distance (aka 'half ironman') event, called Cowman, near Milton Keynes. Cowman involved a 1.9km swim, 92km ride and 21km run. I didn't really have a training programme, I increased the time I spent doing all three disciplines leading up to the event, but I still didn't pay enough attention to the nutritional side of training and racing. Unsurprisingly the event went much like the Paris marathon. The run course was four laps, each lap being half on road, and half on a dirt track up and down a hill. I finish the first lap on target for a sub-six-hour overall finish, but by the time I got to the top of the hill on the second lap I felt like a flat battery. I tried to take on energy drink but it was too late to make much difference. The next two trips up the hill were a real struggle and my sub-six-hour finish slipped away. I crossed the finish line in six hours and six minutes, once again disappointed it had gone a bit pear-shaped, but elated I had completed a half-ironman.

At the time my son was seven months old, and I was enjoying family life, but it clear that it wasn't feasible to work full-time, have a family, be in the TA, and spend that much time training for and doing triathlons. I decided to put triathlon on hold. I could at least bask in the glory of my Cowman finish for some time yet.

Although I tried to remain active, and I was proud of my 'half-ironman' finish, the word 'half' played on my mind, just like with the marathon. Also, I owned a windproof cycle top that had the ironman logo on it, and I would occasionally get asked if I'd done one. It seemed like I was a bit of a disappointment when I'd say I'd only done a half. I became pretty sure that one day I'd attempt a full one. I had no idea when though, certainly not whilst I was in the TA.

In 2012, I decided it was time to leave the Territorial Army. I'd done over seventeen years and whilst it'd been a great experience, it took up a lot of time and I didn't like being away from my wife and (now) two kids. I knew I wanted to do something with some of the time that would be freed up, and I also wanted to get some of my previous fitness back.

A few months after becoming a full-time civvie, I was sat with my friend Gareth at a TA dinner. Gareth was a fellow PTI in the TA and sport scientist in his day job, and he wasn't averse to finding new ways to challenge himself. He told me about Dr Justin Roberts' ironman study and how he was going to go for it, and I was intrigued. Here was an opportunity to not just do an ironman triathlon, but tackle the challenge with other people and do it for science. I could be like Dr Mike Stroud! After years of telling people that as humans they are built for endurance, I could now put my money where my mouth was.

I decided to contact Justin and see if I could join the study. I was quite late in joining but it was ok. I turned up to the Human Physiology Laboratory at the University of Hertfordshire for pre-screening fitness testing. As expected, my five years without serious exercise meant I wasn't too fit to take part in the study.

I knew I wanted to do an ironman one day, but I hadn't really expected it to be so soon. A few days before Christmas, I signed up for Challenge Barcelona: the iron-distance triathlon being used for the study. There was no turning back now.

In mid-January the ironman training programme would start. I felt determined to try to stick to it as close as possible, and to pay more attention to the nutritional side of things than I had in the past. Week one got off to a poor start when halfway through my cycle home from work on a dark damp January, I got one puncture after another. Unfortunately I only had one inner tube and no repair kit. I ended up calling my Dad to come and pick me up in the car. As I sat in my Dad's car, with my bike laying across the rear seats, I wondered if a real ironman would run the seven remaining miles home (in cycle shoes) pushing the bike. In any case, there was a much longer journey ahead of me over the next thirty-six weeks. The following weekend I replaced my bike tyres with Kevlar-lined ones and thankfully I didn't suffer from punctures after that.

The times and distances required by the training programme steadily built up week-by-week, and it quickly became apparent that the hardest bit of ironman training is fitting it in. I'm certainly not unusual in that I work full-time, spend a couple of hours a day commuting, have a wife and two kids and try to have some semblance of a social life. I've found that by the time I've planned when I might be able to fit in the training, tried to get normal life out of the way, and got my kit ready, it's time for a training session. There I am with my kit in front of me, not having had time to think about what the training might actually feel like. I think it's better that way. Training sessions, when you think about them beforehand, are almost always worse than they actually turn out to be. I rarely regret doing a training session, but almost always regret not doing one.

I never used to do strength training, but now I have developed a bit of muscle. Before, I used to find I often felt lethargic when I got home from work and I'd just want to park myself on the sofa for the evening and watch TV, but now I generally feel more energised and motivated to do more productive things. I feel I can concentrate for longer periods and my thoughts seem to become more organised whilst I'm out running at lunchtime.

I used to pretty much fear the idea of getting up at 5:30am to do exercise, but having had to do it quite frequently over the last few months it's actually ok. I generally don't feel any more tired than normal during those days, and it's nice knowing I've got my exercise out of the way early. A few times over the last couple of months I have run the 30km from home to work, as that's been the only way I could fit the three-hour run session in. Amazingly I actually enjoyed it. It's a good way to convince your colleagues you're a lunatic too. They joke that I'm mad, but really I'd be mad to attempt an ironman without training properly, and replacing a journey you have to do anyway with a run makes more sense than doing the run another time.

The training has been challenging certainly. There have been periods where it just seems relentless, when you seem to be going sleep-swim-commute-work-run-work-commute-bike, and times when I couldn't remember what it's like for my legs to *not* feel tired. I have definitely needed the support and understanding of my wife, friends and colleagues. But overall it has been a fantastic experience.

So, here I am months later, with less than two weeks to go before the ironman, and amazingly I feel ready. Thanks to the slow, but steady, build-up of the training programme, I can think about the distances I'm going to have to do and both comprehend them and not panic. I've completed the swim distance a few times now and, although I'm slow, I don't feel exhausted by it. I've done the bike distance a couple of times too, and it hasn't killed me. Although I don't really know how I'm going to feel when I get to the run part of the race, I've done enough running on tired legs over the last few months to know that often when your body is telling you it needs to stop, it's basically lying to you. It can always do more. I've practiced the nutritional side too. I used to hate energy gels, but now I know that they work, every half an hour cycling and running its "gel o'clock".

I've tried not to have a target time in mind for the event and just stay focused on the goal of just finishing (after all it'd be a guaranteed PB!), but I can't help but think about it. So here it is:

- Swim: one hour thirty-five minutes. I'm hoping the adrenaline of the event will mean I can beat my training PB by seven minutes;
- Bike: six hours fifteen minutes. On good flat roads I can normally average 30 kph quite comfortably and I'm hoping to keep stops to a minimum (calls of nature only hopefully);
- Run: five hours. I'd like to run each 10.5km lap in an hour or less, but I'll be surprised if I can sustain that the whole way. My goal will be keep running, however slow that turns out to be.

Total, including transitions: thirteen hours. *Anything could happen though.*

Dan "IRONMAN" Searle as he finishes

The Message: If you're lucky enough to be human, with a fully functioning body, then all you need to do is train, and you'll be able to do things you never thought possible.

CHAPTER 24

"Denial to Opportunity" *By Mike Ashton*

"Granddad. Are you really an Ironman?"

These are the words I would love to hear. When things get tough, they are my driving force, when I imagine a young child looking up at me in awe. Let me explain why this is so significant for me.

Mid-forties. Surely a time for reclining gracefully on the sofa after a large Sunday meal, watching my daughter playing in the garden, coffee or a nice wine by my side. Why is it, then, that this Sunday the sofa is a long way away? A one-hundred-mile bike ride and a two-hour run will be completed before I see it again.

It's 7:30am in Windsor. I'm stood by my car in a field, dressed in Lycra, reassembling my bike, which is upside down leaning against the car. I have three water bottles in the car, and two on the bike – all are filled with sports drinks. Sports gels and energy bars are in every pocket of my cycling top and in the various bags attached to the bike. Inside the car, there is another set of gels in a hip-belt ready for the run, sitting alongside the protein milkshake ready for when this is all over. The spare inner tubes, puncture kit and multi-tool are all in a saddlebag. I hope I don't have to use them, but all have been used in anger in the last six months. The day looms ahead, yet the fifty people around me exude a quiet confidence. We swam nearly 4km yesterday, we will get through this today, and soon it will be the big event in Barcelona. I feel fit, and prepared.

A few years ago, I was in very different shape to what I am right now. My story is one of change, and turning denial into **opportunity**.

During my late twenties and thirties I noticed my weight creeping up. Not too much, but steady. I exercised less, and socialised more. My jeans went from being a 34" waist to being a 36". Then the 36" became tight. The warning signs were there, but I chose to ignore them. My father was very overweight. He had asthma from an early age and had been advised to avoid exercise, which he did in abundance. He now had Type II diabetes and the various complications associated with that. I convinced myself that I was a different build to him, that I took more after my mother, and so wouldn't end up like that.

My new job paid for a medical every two years, where I learnt about the BMI scale. The ratio between my height and my weight showed me to be quite considerably overweight. I tried to dispute the findings, telling myself that this scale doesn't differentiate between male and female, muscle and fat, by age. But deep down I knew I was getting fatter. There were also issues around blood pressure and cholesterol. I was advised to lose 10kg to get back into the right zone. I also had to see our HR department, to be told that my BUPA coverage may be affected.

Not good. But was it really a problem? I was only in my late thirties. I was happily married, had a beautiful six-month-old daughter, and a good job. I was still in denial.

My epiphany happened a few days after my fortieth birthday. My parents came down and we had a lovely barbeque. They loved playing with their new grandchild.

Two days later, my father died suddenly of a heart attack!

I looked at my daughter and realised that my father would never see her grow up, would never hear her speak, and wouldn't play with her again.

That wasn't going to be me.

It was as if someone had flicked a switch. I joined British Military Fitness, who conducted army-style circuit training classes in the local parks. They encouraged me to train faster and harder than I thought possible for me, but made it fun. The group training, and the variety, suited me perfectly. Suddenly I was taking part in small sprints, or doing twenty sit-ups before rushing off to run around a lake. All this took place outdoors, and I found the fresh air in the evenings exhilarating.

I trained hard, and the weight started falling off. I felt lighter. I could run across the road, without being out of breath at the other end. I had energy. I could put my daughter on my shoulders and run up a hill, to her amusement and my pride. Suddenly, I was alive. And the weight kept coming off.

I cut down on the chocolate – I realised it was easier to not eat the junk in the first place, than it was to exercise harder to lose it. And suddenly I became faster still. Soon, I could get into my 34" jeans. And people were noticing my weight loss. Friends I hadn't seen for months were suddenly telling me how trim I was looking. This just encouraged me further. I was on a roll, and wasn't going to stop.

At university I had never been particularly fit, but had watched from the sidelines as some of my friends raced in the mountain marathons. These two-day events involved competitors working in pairs navigating their way across a mountain range, carrying their tent and all their supplies, collecting as many checkpoints as they could. I decided I wanted to complete a mountain marathon. I hadn't done this in my twenties, but now, in my forties, I could do this. And I could probably do it before you could say "mid-life crisis". I quickly talked a friend into doing it with me, and set about training for the event. This involved running by myself – something I had hardly ever done – carrying a rucksack (another first).

I entered my first 10km race and did a respectable forty-seven minutes – my friend, suffering from a cold, did it in forty-two minutes. A few weeks later we did a half-marathon, and I was delighted to finish within ten minutes of his time.

Unfortunately, things then went downhill. I picked up a knee injury just before the mountain marathon. The physiotherapist pointed out that changing my trainers at the same time as increasing training volume and starting hill work really wasn't the wisest thing to do. She opened my eyes to the science behind running – what a sports watch does, how there are different styles of running, the importance of a strong core, the thinking behind 10% training volume increases. I had no idea about any of this.

I struggled through the mountain marathon, on a combination of painkillers and sheer bloody-mindedness, but was now looking for the next challenge. Ideally not purely running, as my knee injury was likely to be a long-term problem. But something that is difficult, otherwise it ceases to be a challenge. An ironman came to mind. But what would this involve?

Around the same time, two of my old university friends were busy cycling the length of the country, from John O'Groats to Lands End. At the end of that ride, they also mentioned they were looking for the next challenge. How about an ironman? There were some logistical difficulties. I didn't have a racing bike, and couldn't swim front crawl. But these could be remedied. My friends were in a similar position; none of us would be good at all three events, we'd all have to learn something.

I went to the local triathlon shop to look at bikes and to see if I could learn anything by looking at what was on sale. This proved to be an education, and not a cheap one. I'd never heard of a bike being fitted before – when I was young, you might change the height of the saddle every few years, but that was all. It was then that the extra costs hit me. "What, it doesn't come with pedals?", "I need special shoes?", "Cleats – what are they?", "Yes, of course I need all this lycra gear", "Yes, I'd better have some spare inner tubes, and a pump, and I'll need a saddle bag to put them in". I tried not to wince as I handed over my credit card.

Soon I had my bike, and what a machine it was. I'd never been on a bike like it. Light, fast, responsive, it was like nothing I'd ever ridden before. This is it. I'm now ready to work toward ironman. I joined the St Albans triathlon club, and discovered there was far more to running, swimming and biking than I'd ever realised. And transitioning quickly between them was a skill in itself.

The weeks passed, and my knowledge and experience built up. I did a couple of small triathlons with the club, with each one providing more lessons. But always ironman remained the driving focus, albeit still a long way away.

Another life-changing moment appeared.

Alone in the office at 8pm, during a pause in a telephone meeting I saw an advert, "Do you want to train for an ironman"? It was local to me, and offered a full training plan, along with the chance to train together with a group of people. The more I looked at this, the more I realised what an opportunity this was. With regular ECG and VO_{2max} tests alongside nutritional advice, structured training aimed at bringing an armchair athlete to iron fitness, this was undoubtedly my best opportunity to complete an ironman. And the medical research aspect fascinated me.

Getting accepted onto the study was another matter. I had to prove I wasn't too fit, or too good an athlete. It turned out I needn't have worried. After my test results came in, and I explained to the lead researcher that I was mediocre in every discipline, I was accepted.

Mike 'IRONMAN' Ashton taking OPPORTUNITY in his stride

And now I find myself a few days away from my first ironman. Perhaps one day, in the far future, my daughter will have her own children, and I will play and laugh with them, in the way that my father never got to play with his granddaughter. Of course, this may never happen because my beautiful little girl has told me that she's not going to get married, but will stay with Mummy and Daddy, although I'll understand if this changes in a few years.

Most of all, I want my daughter to be happy, and I want her to be proud of her father. This race is the *opportunity* to show how your life can be turned around, and how Denial can be beaten. To show how long hours of work and focus brings rewards. To show her and her children what Daddy did, and what sort of man he is. This is how I want my daughter and grandchildren to think of me. And if I ever hear a little voice asking their grandfather about his ironman, I will be delighted.

And finally, can I take this opportunity to say in print – Mia-Gabrielle, Mummy and Daddy love you very much.

The Message: It is easy to DENY. Every denial masks an OPPORTUNITY, and seizing the opportunity is so much more rewarding.

CHAPTER 25

"Ignorance" *By Charlie Fuller*

Ignorance… is bliss!

I am Charlie Fuller, twenty-seven years old living on the South Coast. When I'm not working I enjoy swimming, cycling and running. If I were writing a dating ad this would be it at the moment, and even that is an underestimation of the truth. Triathlon has completely taken over every aspect of my life. I even managed to convince my best friend to have a cycling-themed stag do so I could keep up with the training plan and, much to my girlfriend's dismay, managed to hire a bike when we went on holiday this year. At first I didn't realise this would happen but it soon became clear my life had suddenly got a lot busier to say the least.

When I applied to be part of the study, I didn't think I had any chance of being selected. I didn't consider myself to be fit enough and thought there would be many more people applying who would be more suitable for the criteria. So I put it to the back of my mind and forgot about it. Then the email confirmation came through. I had been selected for pre-testing. Awesome! Brilliant! Oh hang on, Oh crap; I may be doing an iron-distance triathlon next year. I thought about it some more, how hard can it be? A few tests at a university and fourish training sessions a week or so, I thought.

On the day of the pre-testing, I arrived and was greeted by the team in the lab-style testing room. I was weighed, measured, prodded, poked and that was all in the first five

Charlie taking it to the max

minutes. They still had a VO_{2max} cycling test for me to do. VO_{2max} is maximal volume of oxygen that can be used when working at an exhaustive rate, or so I've been told. I was put on a bike where Dr Justin Roberts and the team controlled the rate I would be working at and then had a very fetching mask placed on my face to measure my output. This can only be described as torture and the hottest and sweatiest nine minutes of my life, to that point. A VO_{2max} of forty-eight was the result (average overall). Then that was it, the lines were drawn and I was selected as one of the lab rats, I mean iron-person in training. The countdown begins: 351 days until Challenge Barcelona.

So what next, how to fit these four sessions into my life, it won't be a problem, drop football on a Monday and get up early on the weekends, no problem. I've done the London Marathon can't be much more training than that. This is where my ignorance came into play, where did I get four sessions from, wherever it was, it was very wrong. Double it and add a few and you are closer to the number. The realisation was sinking in that I was in for a long year, but in a strange way I knew I was going to love it, the highs, the lows and the realisation of a dream to complete an iron-distance event uncovered.

Over the last few years my experience of triathlon and the distances involved has been steadily developing. It started off as an interest, casually training, reading some of the magazines. Then became a hobby of actually taking part in events for each of the disciplines. Now I think all my friends and family would agree it's a fully-fledged obsession. Over the last year I have read countless books, autobiographies, and facts and figures and registered for every triathlon website under the sun. So much so I think my girlfriend, Amy, would rather catch me looking at pornography than another triathlon-related book or website. No chance there, triathlon and bike porn gives me far more kicks.

I've become obsessed with all data around the subject. It still shocks me that only twelve people competed in the first ironman in Kona, 1978, they only paid $12 to enter and the winner, Gordon Haller, completed in a time of eleven hours forty-six minutes, fifty-six seconds. Is it possible for me to break this time in October? Only time will tell. Also the rumoured average DNS (Did Not Start) percentage is triple the rumoured average percentage for DNF (Did Not Finish). That's enough talk about DNS and DNF, they are two subjects I wish not to have to discuss after 6th October.

Unsurprisingly lots of my conversations with people over the course of the year have been around Challenge Barcelona and the training involved. What has come as a surprise to me is the general lack of knowledge of what is involved in triathlon and that if you are doing a sprint or an iron-distance event the three disciplines are the same, and in the same order. A swim followed by a bike then a run; it's just the distances that change.

I had a conversation with a colleague around the start of the year regarding Challenge Barcelona, I could tell he hadn't quite grasped the concept but I was then surprised even further at the extent to which he hadn't understood.

He confidently said to me "if you want a real challenge once you've done this iron thingy you should try Tough Mudder".

*Tough f**king Mudder*!!! Does he have no idea what I am going through, the hours upon hours of training each week, the constant tiredness, the lack of social life? In one sentence this guy had highlighted and double underlined the general ignorance some people have to long-distance triathlon with the suggestion that a ten-mile assault course is more challenging. I am so involved with triathlon it seems alien to me that some people are unaware. It seems especially alien that those who are unaware would try to make suggestions to my training or aspirations. Needless to say I took great pride in talking about my favourite subject, triathlon, and making sure he was fully aware of Challenge Barcelona, ironman triathlon and the research study behind it all.

The day-to-day training for the big event in October became like a second full time job, I was either training, working, eating or sleeping and any free time I had I would train some more. The nice thing about training is that there is no pressure, generally it's just me; my thoughts and the elements; which over the summer months have been very kind; hopefully good preparation for the Barcelona weather. Even sticking to all the elements of the training plan I became conscious of the fact that no amount of training can mimic the adrenalin, nutrition requirements and the mental toughness it takes to compete in an organised event. So I've entered a few events along the way; Goodwood Duathlon in March, Cotswold 113 half ironman in

June, Magnificat 125 mile cycling sportive in July, Salford Olympic-distance triathlon in August, Bournemouth Big Swim also in August and the Portsmouth Triathlon fourteen days before the big one in Barcelona.

Not sure I ever thought a half-ironman would be considered a training event! But here I am mid-June, 156 days until Challenge Barcelona; if I am to stand any chance of doing sub fourteen hours in Barcelona I need to be hitting seven hours for the half distance. So there it was Sunday 16th June 2013 with the target set.

04:00 the alarm rings around my head like a clash of pans, "What on earth, this is too early" and still feeling dazed I stumble around getting my final few bits together, remembering not to forget the nutritional and important peanut butter sandwiches for the bike. I head out of the house and make my way to the venue for my 06:00 swim start; still not feeling completely awake. I had to forget the time and get my game face on; easier said than done with only four hours sleep on a blow-up bed. But with my wetsuit on, lube on my neck (to prevent any rubbing), goggles in hand and my face pulled so tight from the swim cap it makes me look like I've had a face lift gone wrong; I was ready.

Bang… we're off. 500 triathletes all at different levels and speed splashing our way to the first buoy. I find a space and start to find my rhythm, I'm in the zone, the occasional body would collide with me but that's to be expected with a mass start. Then out of nowhere a hand slaps down on my foot, again and again and again. Someone is swimming right behind me, drafting off me. *"Bastard, not only is this guy using me for a tow he is slapping my feet for good measure"* was the only thought running through my mind. This continues for what seems like the next five minutes. Right time to drop this pond snake, I up my speed and steer my body position to the left and give it all I've got. The slapping stops and I'm on my own again, and my thoughts return to the job in hand. Transition is getting closer and closer; a hand comes down to help me out of the water. Swim done, I look at my watch, thirty-six minutes. I remove my goggles and look again; thirty-six minutes was a shock, I was expecting fifty minutes minimum.

Now into transition, wetsuit off, helmet on and I'm off for the two-lap fifty-six-mile ride. The bike course is fairly flat with a 300ft climb half way round each lap. I do some calculations in my head and realise I need to complete this discipline in under four hours to stand any chance of hitting the seven hour target. Lap one flies by really fast, time now on the clock, 1hr 25. On to the second lap, my legs are getting increasingly heavy but still turning at a good rate, on to the climb for the second time. The guys on the Time Trial bikes struggle with the gradient and I slowly pass by on my trusty Trek. I laugh to myself under my breath; "*all the gear*". Transition is approaching again, as I start to loosen the Velcro on my shoes I glance at my watch again 3hrs 32 total time.

I'm tired, but this isn't going to stop me now. Only the run to go, breaking seven hours has now left my mind and six hours has replaced it. Could this actually be possible, all I need to do is run a two-and-a-half hour half-marathon. Three laps between the finish and me. Although I am starting to feel groggy I am surprisingly fresh; I cannot understand how my legs are still turning but they are and turning well. I complete the ten miles in 1hr 20. Now I am really confused; 4 hrs 50 down and only three miles left to run. My revised six-hour target is now irrelevant; what can I achieve, how am I doing this? My mind is drifting and I need to focus back on the run. The finishing shoot is in sight, "*leave it all on the course*" is a motto I live by. I start my sprint, legs burning, eyes and nose streaming, gasping for air. I'm there, across the line in a time of 5hr 21. "YESSSSS".

This is the first time in six months where I actually felt,

and noticed, the difference from the training. The times had been coming down gradually but now it was in black and white. My thoughts turn to October, what I can achieve, I will do this, Iron Will. 112 days until Challenge Barcelona.

Taking part in such a prestigious event as Challenge Barcelona I knew I would have to look the part; this includes everything from the wetsuit, the trisuit and possibly most importantly the bike. When I was accepted on to the study I had just purchased a Cervelo R5 frame. With this event now on the calendar I set about building a bike which fitted the bill. I had everything from carbon-fibre bottle cages; custom-painted Sram Red shifters and the aerodynamic Mavic Cosmic Carbone wheels. The bike took me ten months to build and cost a pretty penny but by the end of August the bike was ready. The training is well underway; I finally have the equipment I need, "What could go wrong now?" Unfortunately this is when the wheels started to come off, literally.

I seem to be struck down with injury after injury and to top it off my expensive rear wheel broke and buckled five weeks before the event on a big training ride. Major injury number one an inflamed bursa on my left hip or in simple terms it felt like I was being constantly being stabbed in the hip on longer runs. I didn't let this get me down. I booked several sessions of sports massage and physiotherapy, this would slow the mileage down in terms of running but I could focus on the swimming, biking and functional training. After a couple of weeks I felt like my hip wasn't getting any better but after taking a few beatings from the masseuse and a few sessions of ultrasound I noticed the pain subsiding and I was able to gradually increase my speed and mileage once again. This put me back in the right frame of mind. I managed a twenty-one-mile run in three hours and this was six weeks out from the event.

Lady Un-Luck then struck me down once again. Thirty-six

days until Challenge Barcelona and most of the study group met for the peak training weekend. A full iron-distance open-water swim on the Saturday followed by a one-hundred-mile ride and two-hour run on the Sunday. The swim went well for me completing the distance in 1hr 20 and I was looking forward to the Sunday. We set off on Sunday morning on the one-hundred-mile ride, the weather was sunny and I was making good time aiming to achieve a sub six-hour ride time. As I clocked up the miles I began to notice a pain developing in my right knee, it started off as a throbbing but soon it turned from an irritation to constant ache with every revolution of the pedals. Then at sixty-seven miles, whilst climbing one of the ascents, my ride was struck by further bad luck and came to an abrupt end.

With a loud crack the rear wheel buckled taking a spoke with it. A feeling of immense frustration built up at the initial disappointment of knowing I wouldn't be able to complete the ride; then having to solve the imminent logistical challenge of getting back to the car, to the further issue of having to fix, or worse, spend even more money on this bike and buy new wheels. Trying to remain focused and calm I set about walking back to the car with the injured bike. On top of everything now I could really feel the pain in my knee.

Finally some luck, a generous passer-by picked me up and gave me a lift to the car, thank you John for that. Once back at the car the pain in my knee was unbearable, so I did what anyone training for the biggest event of their life would do and went out for a two-hour run around Windsor Great Park and ignored the pain. I managed fourteen miles in the time but the stabbing feeling was back, and the knee was well and truly swollen. Onto major injury number two and back to the physio for me; she banned me from running and cycling for at least a week due to a dislodged kneecap. So at thirty-three days to go until Challenge Barcelona, I'm left with a dislodged kneecap and a broken wheel;

the biggest mental kicking to date. After a day or so of sulking and moping about I snapped myself out of it with the thought running through my head that *pain is temporary and glory lasts forever.*

I have learnt ironman training is not just about the physical side of it; you also need to mentally prepare yourself. You have the highs when everything is going well and you feel invincible but the expression what goes up must come down is very apt. You need to develop a sort of sixth sense to mentally pick yourself up, when the weather is bad, when your injury niggles or when you just can't break through the infamous 'wall'. I'm not going to lie; this was one of the biggest struggles for me. There were days where I couldn't face five hours of my own company on the bike but as with everything the mental ability grows. After a while these downers went from lasting days to a few hours.

I encourage anyone who wants to see what they are made of to compete in an ironman.

At the start of this all I was ignorant to the intensity of the training, the magnitude of what I was going to put my body through and the mental battering you will impose on yourself. In the months leading up to the event you gain a true sense of if you are a fighter. You will ask yourself "Are you sure you want to do this or are you going to take the 'easy route' and back out?" There will so many voices in your head telling you to stop, but if you only remember one thing from this chapter let it be *"Don't stop, keep pushing"*, you will achieve your goal if you push, push, push. Ignore the little bastard screaming in your ear; this is too hard, it hurts, I'm not strong enough. *You are f**king strong enough*, keep that finish line in your mind and when those thoughts of quitting become almost too strong to ignore, remember the iron will, with the right training and determination the body can get to where you want to be. I now think I am mentally more focused to deal with any situation a lot better than I would of a year ago. I hope this bodes well for

Charlie showing what it takes to complete an iron-distance

the 6th October in Barcelona.

There are really two types of individuals, those who say "I can't" and those who say "I can". For the select few taking part in iron-distance races they are firmly following the "I can" belief. What they have to do to get there is monumental by anyone's standards, even their own. The unknown is feared by all and come 8:30am on 6th October there will be an ocean full of it. This is also about limits, reaching them, understanding what yours are and stretching them to the absolute max. The ups, the downs, the physical and the mental determination it takes to become an ironman. It takes more strength than I ever would have imagined…

The Message: *"When ignorance is bliss, 'tis folly to be wise"*. Ironman is a journey of ups, downs, physical and mental determination. Do you have what it takes?

CHAPTER 26

"Countdown" *By Gary Smith*

Sadistic Sunday – fourteen days to go

Waking up early on a Sunday is something you get used to when training for an ironman, it's a perpetual state of tiredness and bewilderment that yet another night has passed and yet again someone let you get run over multiple times by the number nine bus… Getting up this morning was slightly different; it was going to be a whole new world of pain and suffering. Cycling? Err no… Running? Err, no… Swimming? Err, no… Another circuit-training session previously shunned be the SAS as being too severe, but adopted by Dr. Roberts for our pleasure anyway? Err, no…

Today my friends, four of us are going to be waxed within an inch of lives at the lovely Bliss Beauty Therapy in Hatfield, all in the name of charity. You see some time ago, a number of us agreed to have a full leg wax for Harrison's fund and interested Sadomasochists could vote to make the event a reality by pledging the princely sum of £30… very good value for money to satisfy what in retrospect seems to be a popular female fetish [*Note: Possible business opportunity right here*].

It was a fairly miserable, dank and wet morning in Hatfield as I walked through the deserted parade of shops in the precinct, but not long after arriving I saw the welcoming light of the beauty salon and a smiling Lynn Stevens. Lynn, the lovely owner, who selfishly gave up her only day of rest to wax four grown babies, I mean ladies, I mean men, for nothing. Kettle on, a quick trip to the Polish deli to buy something resembling milk (it had a green lid and a picture of a cow) for tea and soon the other reprobates started to arrive, namely Justin, Alex and Perry. A quick check of who was the hairiest, and we all knew that Perry was going to suffer IMMENSELY – of course, being the friends we are, we all reassured him it would be fine and that being hairier of course meant they could get more purchase and finish quicker… (we were lying through our teeth of course).

Admittedly, being a male who doesn't like body hair I am no stranger to going "*au natural*", albeit waxing is somewhat a new territory. I had my chest waxed twice, so I sort of knew what to expect, but never my legs, however regular shaving and "veeting" of my legs meant I was no longer as hairy as I once was.

I didn't remove my body hair because I was a triathlete or cyclist, more the fact that I choose to be a triathlete because I needed an excuse to justify my weird obsession… When people comment on my legs being smoother than my wife's or their own legs/wife, you can simply say "I'm a "triathlete" and people nod knowingly (they don't really understand, but they nod regardless). Similarly, other people automatically say, "you shave your legs, you must be a cyclist". This of course did mean I was in for a slightly easier ride than the others though. Since Perry had organized it, it didn't seem to be too unfair to "let" him go first while the rest of us continued to drink our tea and I'm so glad we did…

Words cannot describe our collective enjoyment or those of the thousands of YouTube viewers who have subsequently viewed the 30mins of comedy, pain and hysteria. Honestly, it wouldn't have been amiss in an *American Pie* movie, Perry didn't miss a cue… screaming, shrieking, shouting and swearing for the camera phone.

In reality it was a great, funny and immensely entertaining morning that bonded us even closer. There was no doubt that Perry was the star of the show and in reality we should have charged people to watch the video, we would have made a lot more money!

Moaning Monday – thirteen days to go

Everyone hates Monday don't they? I know I do, in fact I normally start anticipating Monday from Sunday – never a good thing. So there it is, it's Monday and I have to travel to the city for a meeting at HQ. Really nothing to moan about, your standard everyday Monday for 90% of the working population. The day was in fact uneventful until home time, why the world goes into meltdown when a train breaks down God only knows, and the journey home became interesting… Apparently trains from Kings Cross were operational, however a short walk and tube ride later, suggested otherwise. A packed Kings Cross, filled with frustrated commuters and a tempest was brewing, it was at this time that the first person pulled my arm to get my attention and then started rambling at me about the train service standards of "British Rail" which hasn't existed since 1997. I figured the person may not be of this earth, or possibly had some health issues and politely informed them that I didn't work for British Rail; after all what possible other explanation could there be? This is London; you barely make eye contact with Londoners for fear of an unwanted reprisal, never mind physical manhandling them.

Anyway we were now informed to make our way to Finsbury Park where there would definitely be trains running from, interesting concept?!? You see on weekends the trains for both First Capital Connect trains run from Kings Cross, so why you would take all the stranded commuters for one main line and move them from a main station like Kings Cross, to a smaller station like Finsbury Park and create a possible riot and overcrowding bemuses me somewhat, I can see why my "friend" believed British Rail were to blame!

So along with the other cattle I squeezed myself onto a northbound train heading for Finsbury Park. It will come as no surprise that upon arrival it appeared we'd arrived at a standing-room-only concert, minus the music and any sort of entertainment. I think I'd been there all of about five minutes, before someone appeared in front of me, confrontationally, demanding an explanation for the train delays and compensation for their disrupted evening. I mean did I know that they were going to be on business for the next two weeks and this was the last opportunity they would have to put their children to bed?? I explained that I wasn't sure what they were on about and that I was simply trying to get home from work, and No, I didn't bloody work for the train company.

Jesus, have I been transported to a parallel universe?

Another five minutes passes, another platform alteration and finally our trains start appearing on the board, and as you can imagine they are now very much "all stations" trains. It was at this point that someone now says the immortal *"Do you work here? I want to know when the next fast train is?"*

"Pardon? No, I'm sorry I don't work here but may I enquire why you believed I did, only you're not the first person to ask this evening...?"

"Terribly sorry, its just you're wearing a navy three-piece suit and looked quite official, so I made the assumption you were some sort of management from the train company."

The moral of the story? Don't wear a smartly tailored, vintage, navy three-piece suit. It may well shout "retro-cool", but equally shouts, "accost me please, don't you know I work for Bloody British Rail!!!"

Two's Tuesday – twelve days to go

Not every day is that eventful, but that's life isn't it? Some days are just days and we're in taper mode, the period before a big race where you allow your body to recover, rest and adapt to the rigours of training.

However, in my case having had whooping cough since the end of August and a *clawed* left hand as a result of an Ulnar nerve injury, training hasn't been exactly high on the agenda, or possible for that matter. In hindsight now, as I sit here writing this, I realise that I have been very disrespectful to the distance in that I didn't curb my terrible eating habits or appetite while tapering – enforced or otherwise.

My name is Gary and I'm a pizza addict, there I've said it... and next year I promise I'm going to do better, but on Tuesday night, the girls were out and that left me and the boy to fend for ourselves. I have to be honest and say that this isn't necessarily an unusual experience on a Tuesday. Two's Tuesday is a popular pizza franchise, any pizza, any size – buy one get one free!

This obviously isn't good if a) you're a pizza addict b) you're in training for a major athletic event and actually weight counts against you and c) this also happens to be a testing week and everything you eat leading up to the test needs to be recorded!

Oh well, I suppose Dr. Roberts did say we needed to carb load weeks before the event!

Whopper Wednesday – eleven days to go

Probably around now someone might think that my life revolves around food, you'd almost be right. We've talked about my weight in an earlier section of the book, so you already know that I have a certain penchant for the unhealthy which when you combine with extreme training, drives an insatiable appetite (*you can read that however you wish!*). So, Wednesday is typically our (me and the wife's) yoga night, which means no food until afterwards, which means no feeding oneself until later in the evening. It's times like these that I set myself up for failure, tired, hungry and not bothered to cook combined with a distinct lack of planning in the food purchasing department. I mean seriously? After nine months of constant training you'd think I would have worked out a late-night eating strategy for times like this? Err… no

Good thing therefore that a popular burger franchise runs "Whopper Wednesday" where one can purchase a Whopper for £1.99 (note recently increased to £2.49). In my opinion it's the perfect blend of protein and carbs, it even contains some salad!

My name is Gary and I also have a burger addiction… Christ no wonder I'm overweight!

"Tanked-Up" Thursday – ten days to go

Goodness gracious me, it's not turning out to be one the best of weeks, is it? So today at the office, we have a team meeting followed by drinks for a colleague who's celebrating thirty years of service. Phil, who I only met a month ago when I started my new job, is an inspiring individual, an ironman himself, he was then unfortunately involved in an accident which left him with a broken back from which he has made almost a full recovery. I say almost, since he is currently recovering from a second operation which hopefully will remove any remaining niggles and has every intention of returning back to training and completing a marathon in the new year. I personally remain in awe of the resilience and drive that I find common in people in this sport.

Anyway, it was an interesting evening of far too many beers (more carb loading!), good company, no food and a very late train home. I only had four pints, but when you haven't been drinking much for a year, it turns out that this is more than enough to get you slightly inebriated when training for an ironman.

On the train home, I reflect on the journey ahead, Phil's stories of race day and the hangover I'm bound to have in the morning – I'm also wondering how the hell I'm going to write up this week in my "food" diary!

Freaky Friday – nine days to go

F**king hell, who let the number 9, 221 and 240 buses in? Yep I've been run over by all three, a combination of regular medication; not being a morning person and a hangover are going for nothing short of a quite spectacular day. I'm not good when hung-over, generally speaking… I suppose this is not that unusual for anyone. To be honest there are three things synonymous with being hung-over in my book: headaches, horniness and paranoia. Not really a good combination and the wife normally gives me a wide berth accordingly. The paranoia is the worst; even though I can remember everything I still follow the same procedure:

1. Find wallet;
2. Find keys;
3. Find phone/blackberry/tablet;
4. Check wallet to ensure there are no unrecognizable receipts or ridiculous purchases; and

5. Check all mobile devices for calls, texts and emails sent after 8pm.

Throughout the day I'm questioning myself about whether or not I can do the race justice or even complete it? Has the recent spate of injury and illness that stopped my training pretty much dead in its tracks for the past three to four weeks going to undermine my ability to finish? Can I really do this? I know my fitness has declined as a result of the whooping cough, my breathing is laboured at times and my heart rate higher than ever.

I internalize it all, the fear is real and I have a weekend of testing ahead, I decide to let the testing dictate whether or not I am still able to compete, knowing that if my performance has seriously declined I'll find out soon enough.

Right now where's the wife gone?

Poo Testing Day One and DXA Scan – eight days to go

Well this will be the second time round for the poo testing which involved a series of tests conducted over three days to understand more about how our finely tuned engines are performing through the evaluation of biomarkers. How, you may ask? Well the next few pages may get a little graphic so if you're of a sensitive disposition you may wish to skip ahead… Basically every morning for the next three days, in the privacy of my own home I will be collecting and storing faeces, urine and saliva.

Ask any lab rat involved in this element of the study and they will tell you that by far the worst element of the test is collecting your own faeces – it's also the only one which stretches over multiple days. Anyway let's describe the process of what I need to do this morning. For starters it's 06:30 as I also have to go for a DXA scan (more on that in a bit) before most sane people have brushed their teeth, and I need to collect my range of bodily fluids before I can leave the house.

On the agenda today, all three… great! Life as a guinea pig is just fabulous… NOT! Anyway, I lock the bathroom door; lay out the "equipment" on the floor, to elaborate (process steps shortened):

Saliva – place mouth over the test tube, allow saliva to naturally drip into tube until you reach the 2ml line and store in freezer in biohazard bag – repeat every four hours.

Urine – Urinate into provided cup, then use provided pipette to fill supplied test tubes to fill line and place in freezer in biohazard bag.

Faeces – *Uggh*, fold small cardboard tray to collect stool sample then use supplied spatula to place a small amount into supplied test-tube solution container, being careful not to UNDER or OVER fill. Once collected, seal container and shake to a SMOOTH consistency – *grossed out yet?* Believe me that's the easy bit…

You see the first two tests, whilst less than desirable, are simple, the faeces test well is just plain horrible.

1. It stinks like poo, well that's because it is,
2. Have you tried to do a controlled poo onto a cardboard square about the size of a 6"x4" photograph?
3. Have you tried to stop squatting and then pooing long enough to remove the cardboard collection device before finishing?

4. Now quickly switch to urine collection, all while trying to maintain some dignity.

The collection passes without incident I fill in the poo consistency description (runny, soft, semi-soft and solid) place the faeces sample in the shower cubicle (the designated shit biohazard zone for the next three days) and the other two samples in the designated biohazard drawer in the freezer.

Next on today's agenda, I desperately try and make myself feel clean and fresh and I'm off to the Saracen's new rugby stadium, Allianz Park for the next test of the day – the DXA scan.

DXA stands for Dual-energy X-ray absorptiometry and is a means of measuring bone mineral density (BMD). Two X-ray beams with different energy levels are aimed at the patient's bones and when soft tissue absorption is subtracted out, the BMD can be determined from the absorption of each beam by bone – in short the fucking thing basically confirms for those interested the following two things.

Firstly, despite telling people for years that I'm "big-boned" I'm actually pretty average and secondly, despite the huge amount of training throughout the year I'm still as fat as ever (note to self, pizza and burger addiction might have a role here). I arrive for time slot and am soon joined by Perry, Eva and Jason; my choice of underwear (anime tattoo design briefs) adds a touch of light heartedness to the proceedings and when it's Perry's turn to be strapped to the scanner we line up an excellent self portrait with Perry's briefs in the background. After last week's waxing session, Perry and his briefs have become quite popular in the "socialverse" and Eva and I think it's only right that we shouldn't disappoint his growing throng of groupies. If you're bored and fancy a laugh check out the Facebook page, where all can see video footage of the waxing and associated photos of Perry's gear

The rest of the day passes without incident, thankfully!

Portable friends – seven days to go

Another day, another series of tests… on today's gorgeous menu:

Starter – Urine measurement and sample, measure the first morning urination and retain a 40ml sample for lab at University, followed by day two faecal extractions.

Main – On arrival at the University testing facility hand over AM sample, drink sugar solution and begin five hour limited fast. Take receipt of personal urinal to carry around for the fasting duration (basically a large brown plastic container) and report for blood extraction followed by pulse velocity test.

Dessert – Return to university after five hours with portable friend and begin one-hour performance time trial.

You pretty much know the routine which surrounds the "starter" but with regards to the "Main" there are a few interesting bits. Firstly, the sugar solution is like drinking nothing I've ever tasted before, it's sickly sweet but has a really light consistency at the same time. The hardest piece of the test, in all honesty, is not having any coffee!

You can only drink water and only during hours three to five, but at least you can have a light meal at this time and as coffee is also considered to be a performance stimulant I can't really have any until after the performance time trial. That's annoyance number one.

Annoyance number two is that I have deep veins… this means a lot of prodding and poking to find them but I have to say Dr. Roberts, despite the swearing did a sterling job as usual.

To be honest I think in his head it's a bit like Russian roulette, fortunately throughout the year he has hit the red line every time and with very little bruising. This comes as a surprise to me as the build up is "not sure I'm going to hit it", "let's tighten the tourniquet a bit more", "can you pump and clench your fist for a bit longer". To be honest, if he tightened the tourniquet and I pumped and clenched my fist any harder I reckon my arm would bloody detach itself!

Annoyance number three, the pulse-velocity test... right this is great, strip down to your underpants and let a male student probe your groin and neck with a "pen-like" device looking to take a reading from the femoral and carotid points. Completely painless, but completely embarrassing, especially when friends insist in taking photos for "research" purposes when you absolutely CANNOT move!

Finally, after a morning of extracting blood and other bodily fluids, being probed and prodded and the obligatory five hours of pissing into a plastic pot, I return to the university. Now I get to chase a digital bitch on a computer screen for an hour while hooked up to various elements of testing equipment checking my heart rate, VO_{2max}, power output and speed. Needless to say I never catch the bitch, I used to get a bloke to chase, but I requested the woman this time... it didn't make any difference at all, she still whipped my ass – funny enough not that different from the real race a week later!

Equipment Fail – six days to go

(Note: if you are squeamish you really, really, really need to consider skipping today's entry!)

Oh God I don't even know where to start and I don't know why I agreed to write this chapter… if this book gets published I may well have to stay at home permanently!

So you know how much I like Mondays right? Well this one may well take the cake!

It's the last day of testing and that means two key things, firstly last of faecal tests but three, or was it four, separate containers today? Four I think. Secondly it's time to gather all the bio-hazardous material lurking around the house and get it down to the post office for Special Delivery, yes it has a shelf life.

Normal procedure, get up before everyone else, lock the bathroom door, lay out all the equipment including the cardboard origami tray. A lack of instructions means I'm still not sure whether it's mean to be "shiny side" up or down, my logic is that it's easier to "scoop" with it shiny side up. Logically, that makes sense, right?

On the plus side of all of this I'm pretty regular, so before long I'm good to go; I assume the position hovering over the toilet bowl with my right hand supporting the cardboard tray beneath the "drop-zone" but in line with the centre of the toilet. It's all good, no different than the previous two days, or was it?

Well how do I describe this? Ever been to the Pizza Hut Ice Cream Factory, or anywhere else were you serve yourself ice cream? Now imagine the valve gets stuck WIDE open and the "tray" is getting full, all you can do is let it overflow into the drain below. If you move you risk spilling "ice cream" everywhere and having a small biological disaster zone on your hands, as there is no guarantee that the "ice cream" will run out anytime soon.

Eventually it stops, and I now have to use my other hand begin clean up operations to the extent of allowing the collection of the sample to continue – I think I puked in my own mouth more than four times during the process. Fortunately the collateral damage was minimal, clean up wasn't too bad, the sample was secured but the acrid stench had burnt the inside of my nostrils, all nasal hair had been singed and no length of time in the shower was making me feel clean.

Thank God that's over… Next stop the post office.

Have you ever been to the post office with three packets container three days of bodily fluids? It's not the most comfortable of situations. I arrive at the counter and I say confidently "three packages special delivery". Would I like them insured? "No thank you" I reply, "what are they?" the attendant enquires. "It's biological and pathological samples" I say hoping that will be the end of it. "Can you say that again, but louder please? I didn't quite understand you". I repeat, but louder this time, it's quite clear that I'm now loud enough to peak the interest of the lunchtime queue. "I'm sorry" she says again "but I don't understand what that means".

"It's SHIT, PISS and SPIT and I need it to get to the lab by tomorrow before it goes off and NO I don't want any BLOODY INSURANCE!"

Yep it was one of those days…

Club Class Baby – five days to go

Today we leave for Barcelona, we're driving and the wife and I are both really looking to the road trip. We have to work most of the day but at 3pm we're out the door and I have just one audio conference to join while in transit (which the boss was happy to agree to) which finishes just as we enter the port of Dover. We're on time for the 17:25 sailing and after a bit of traditional British queuing we're loaded onto the *Pride of Kent.*

I bought us tickets to travel in the club lounge and to be honest we didn't know what to expect BUT simply put it was stunning, in comparison to the state of the rest of the ship, just amazing. It was like being in a posh hotel bar, waiter service, food, magazines and papers. All in all a great way to spend ninety minutes in pure luxury, and a lovely way to start a holiday.

Once on the other side of channel and on the motorway we can hear a sound emulating from the bottom of the car, a whipping noise… Am I imagining it? I drive another twenty miles, traffic continues to flow, the noise disappears, I relax. Another hour passes, the noise returns, paranoia sets in and I have to stop the car at the next services. Assuming I'm simply paranoid, you can't imagine my surprise when I see a wire hanging from the bottom of the car. My mind races, I immediately start thinking about vehicle recovery as I begin to trace the wire to its origin, it's, it's coming from inside my car! I open the passenger side door and realise that the wife has knocked my headphones halfway out the car and they've been bouncing along the road at 130kph for about 200 miles – phew what a relief. The headphones are trashed but the car is fine. I now realise that all the trucks, which have been flashing all night, haven't been flashing due to my inability to correctly fit headlamp diffusers, but rather the fact that my headphones have been generating sparks.

Great roads, friendly truckers and a great crossing I think I might really enjoy this – not included in the written description of today's antics:

- The bastard British truckers who sat blocking the car lanes at Dover preventing our priority boarding and nearly causing us to miss the ferry;
- 3hrs of country and western music, more fun than a hoe

down in the deep south with momma's brother who is also my daddy; and

- ShatNav the only way to travel to the middle of nowhere in France and then discover the farmland you've been directed to is not the hotel you're staying at, you don't speak French and it's one in the morning.

140.6 Miles to Calella – four days to go

Another early start today we drive from Orleans in France to Calella in Spain, not too bad unless you look at the ShatNav and it reliably informs you that despite leaving before 9am you won't be there until after 5pm. I'd love to write a long witty paragraph or page on the car journey, but that's it, it's a car journey and it's not very exciting… The wife did suggest on a number of occasions while driving through the Pyrenees that she was feeling short of breath and perhaps I could have warned her that altitude training would have been beneficial… what a drama queen ;-)

I can tell you, if I haven't already, that the French toll roads are amazing, the Pyrenees are amazing, the Millau Bridge (formally known as le Viaduc de Millau), the tallest vehicular bridge in the world, is amazing and the size of the sex toy supermarket not long after you enter Spain is pretty sensational. I promised the wife we could go back there another time but I was just too focused on getting to Calella.

I can't remember why it happened but I did happen to look at the screen and it said 141 miles to go… it's a scary thought when you're in a car driving through Spain at 130 kph and you think… in four days' time I'll be covering this distance under my own steam – humbling and frightening in equal measure, my friends!

The long walk to T1… swim it? F★★k off! – three days to go

Bizarre…

I've swum the distance in the pool every week since January, I've been swimming the distance in the lake since June, but yet today when I walk along the beach following the swim course, I am totally freaked out! You see when you swim it in a lake, it's generally loops, when you swim it in the pool, it's laps, here it's one continuous straight line… well almost.

Upon leaving the beach, swim 100m to the first buoy, turn right, swim 900m towards the lighthouse, and turn left. Swim 100m to the next buoy, turn left… swim another 2600 f★★king metres against the waves and bloody current, passing buoys every 100–200m AND when you think your arms will fall off… choke on some sea water and repeat until you see a really big buoy, some red carpet and a large tent on the beach. Now turn left and swim 100m to shore. When you reach shore all the blood will have drained from your legs, you stand up, immediately feel drunk and fall back into the sea and repeat.

Eventually I arrive at T1, (by foot of course, above I'm just describing what it was like on race day) the swim exit and place to get out the wetsuit and onto the bike, and off the bike and onto the "run" – it's taken what feels like a good 45min to walk, but of course it wasn't it's just the sheer enormity of the undertaking and dawning realization.

I spend five minutes mentally telling myself to MTFU (Man The F★★k Up) and normality returns

… For now.

#Mediawhore – two days to go

It wasn't the first time I was called this and it certainly won't be the last. You see ever since volunteering for Harrison's Fund

I have tweeted, posted, blagged and literally talked my way into every possible media opportunity available, so when presented with the opportunity to be interviewed by M1TV about the race, my participation in the study and Harrison's Fund I jumped at the chance. Unfortunately someone decided to let Justin come along who tasked us with a pseudo buzzword bingo opportunity – you know the one, you have a random set of words to include in your section.

Justin clearly underestimated my ability to speak nonsense; my designated words were "*Top Gun*" and "University of Hertfordshire" and "Harrison's Fund". The latter two weren't really a challenge as I've been boring anyone with a pulse about these for about eleven months now, and it didn't take long to find a way to weave it into an analogy…

After all, in the past year Alex and I have become firm friends, an inseparable force, driving forward our ideas, taking some risk and putting Harrison's racing on the map (ok it's a really, really small map!) BUT I have been happy to be the Goose to his Maverick, I am his wingman and together we're just like *Top Gun*.

P.S. Spare a thought for Charles who got the word "Nutmeg" and waxed lyrical about the "Nutmeg Diet".

P.P.S. Research shows that ground nutmeg is high in fibre, which can help you feel more full when cutting calories; it is low in sodium and low in cholesterol. Nutmeg is an excellent source of the mineral manganese, which is a catalyst for breaking down fats and cholesterol, an important process in losing weight.

Rack, Pack and Sack – one day to go

Well today is the day, in 24hrs I will be embarking on the longest day of my life, so if you're me that means only one thing, extreme preparation!

I must be the world's worst triathlete, why wear one outfit throughout the race when you could wear three? Well not really, however I was a boy scout once, which means you should be prepared, or in my case over-prepared. This means everything gets carefully laid out for packing for each stage of the race, plus spare watch batteries, spare goggles, spare tyres, tubes, bolts, tools, cable ties, electrical tape, medical supplies, enough food to feed five ironman triathletes etc, etc. Everything gets checked and re-checked and I'm always convinced that I have left something behind.

Next pre-race ritual, hair removal, no I don't have time for it, but I'm nearly twice as fast in water after doing it…

Naturally that's bullshit, it makes no difference whatsoever, but as explained previously I hate body hair, so despite being waxed less than a fortnight ago, I drag the wife into town to find hair removal cream (yes I do wonder why she married me). Great, I'm now in a foreign country looking for Veet, unusually it is not sold in a pharmacy in Spain, but a quick trip to the supermarket and we're back in business – less than ninety minutes later I have less hair than the newborns at the local hospital.

Finally the moment comes, and we're off to rack the bikes and hand in our transition bags which contains everything we need for each stage of the race – if it's not in the bag now, its too late… it's somewhat of a scary moment! This is only made more real when you enter the bike transition and see over 1000 bikes racked in one place and know that by 6pm there will be 300 more.

Nervous much? I'm having a "poo" moment! *[re-read six days to go if you have managed to forget what this is!]*

Death Eater Sky – Race Day!

Amazingly after just one beer the night before, and a final, final pre-check of everything for the morning I managed to actually sleep amazingly well.

The alarm goes off and I wake to have my ProNutro and MyoFusion bowl of super food, basically a fine extremely carb dense cereal from South Africa and a couple of scoops of protein powder mixed with mineral water. It tastes a bit like flavoured chalk and cardboard, but on race or heavy-training days it does the job perfectly with very little impact on the stomach, but just to be sure I wash down two Imodium with some sports drink (over preparation).

Casualwear on, Alex, Jamie and I meet downstairs to walk back to transition to add our nutrition to the bikes, pump up our tyres, hang our helmets and make any last-minute adjustments. Strangely we get approached by a young man in his early twenties in mid town, asking if we are doing the "Challenge" we all think he is a little off his head, but assume he's young and been out all night… Next he asks us if we want to "f**k". I couldn't quite believe my ears, Alex and I aren't exactly small athletes, at six foot and athletically built Jamie isn't small either – we bid our new friend farewell, declining his offer and wondering what his fate might be trying that approach with less than mild-mannered individuals such as ourselves. I do hope he finds some help!

Transition looms and the event could have been British, there is a queue! It's 6:45am, we need to be changed and at the swim start at 8:15am and there's a queue. The minutes pass, 7am comes and goes and we wait… the crowd is getting restless and it's almost ten past before they open the gates. Much grumbling ensues but eventually everyone, remembers why we're here and race calm falls gently over the AstroTurf and spot-lit arena where 1300 athletes gather in ritual of the final preparation. Little did we know how terrible the weather would be later in the same day and that approximately 30-35% of the field wouldn't finish the race.

Back at the hotel, I pack my "street wear" bag (clothes to change into after the race and leave at the finishing tent) and I get into my wetsuit, grab, my goggles and my swim hat.

We line up on the beach in age-group order, bid our farewells to family and friends and enter the zone waiting our turn to "hit" the water on the sound of the horn. The water looks calm, but there is a breeze adding some chop to the water, not a lot but enough to be slightly distracting. I've already described the swim earlier, but I can tell you that I wasn't prepared for the current, people say the swim was long, i.e. more than the specified distances with some Garmin's reporting as much as an extra 600m, but in reality I was slow, very slow. After 1hr 52 I exit the water, shaking my head in disbelief having swum the distance regularly in around 1hr 10, oh well onto the bike!

The bike was going well, but on the second 75km lap, probably around 130km into the ride, I saw the sky in distance had turned black, the Death Eater sky could only mean one thing… a tropical storm. When the storm struck, hail bounced off my visor and I was thankful for my very sophisticated aero helmet and the protection it offered. The rain was relentless, creating areas of standing water up and over the pedals. On the final lap, I cycled through more flooded road and narrowly missed a landslide, which covered the bike and me in debris. Only the front wheel took a bit of a knock and now wobbled, I released the front brake mechanism to allow for more clearance on the rim and rode for "home". I was lucky; some of my colleagues were not allowed to finish the bike leg due to the adverse conditions and ended up being technically disqualified.

The tough conditions, and cycling with flooded shoes, meant that my feet had rapidly turned into two giant blisters and I recall sitting in transition, butt naked, shivering and looking at my watch. 9hrs on the clock, wrecked feet and "marafun" to go, I was in little doubt about the sorry state of

Glad to be finished after the toughest swim of his life

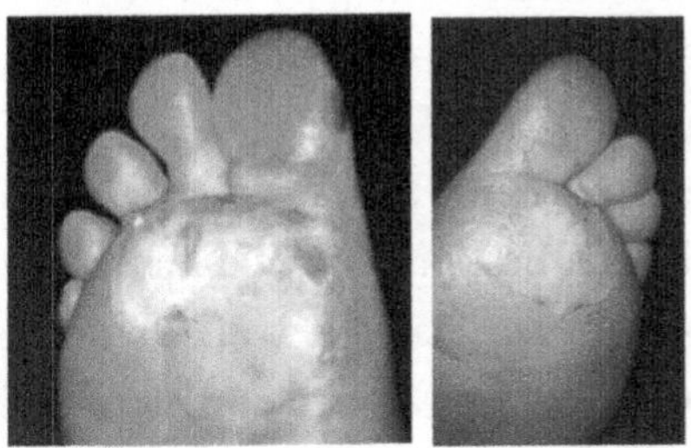

Fancy running a marathon on these feet?
Could you finish? Have you got what it takes?

Always smiling and pushing his own limits:
Gary IRONMAN Smith

affairs, but I wasn't going home without a medal and I didn't come on the journey to go home a quitter – this is where being a good boy scout makes a difference, I changed into a completely fresh set of run clothes, took two Nurofen Express and knowing I was unable to run… I walked the marathon.

I ended up being the last official finisher at a little under 16hrs (official time 15h46'32"). I was escorted by the Triathlon officials the whole of my last lap, people ran with me along the promenade on the final straight, and when I ran into the stadium for the final time, *'Eye of the Tiger'* was being blasted through the speakers, I felt like a pro.

All the time I was being filmed by the M1TV crew, who had filmed me earlier in the week – they'd stayed out all day in rain and cheered me on every lap and were there to see me finish. My friends, my fellow lab rats and complete strangers stood in the rain and gave me a guard of honour to run through.

All the while I was supported by my amazing and wonderful wife, Martha who somehow seemed to be there the whole day and always offering support and encouragement.

A once in a lifetime experience
140.6 miles… Done

The Message: WINNERS NEVER QUIT AND QUITTERS NEVER WIN – FACT.

And as I count down to next year, I would like to leave you with this adaption of a wartime poem in honor of the British man, friend and fellow triathlete who died at Barcelona on the 6th October:

MISSING MAN

We went with tales of strength into the day,… we were young
Mentally focused, wide of eyes, steady and aglow.
We were ready to fight against the odds uncounted,
We knew not, that one would fall with their face to the foe.

He shall not grow old, as we are left to grow old:
Age shall not weary him, nor the years condemn.
At the rising of the sun in the morning, and in the sea
We will remember him.

He will not share the banter of his laughing comrades again;
He will sit no more at tables of his family and friends
He will have no part in the labour of our training or family
  schedules;
He will sleep beyond the boundary that is the final firework
  and transition clock

We will never forget the impact he had on us
We will miss his camaraderie, companionship and knowing smile
He will leave a void for those who knew him, be it months or decades
He was loved and will be loved

On the beach we stood shoulder to shoulder and wondered...

I will always wonder, but I will never forget

In memory of our friend and fellow triathlete, and all those who have lost their lives in the pursuit of "living" and following dreams. It's easy to forget that we all die, we are dying from the moment we are born, the choice is whether or not you choose to live. *Everybody dies, but not everyone lives.*

SECTION 4

The Wisdom Within

CHAPTER 27

"Wisdom" *By Justin Roberts*

The Wisdom of Mr Miyagi: *"To be complete, you have to be as good enough without ironman as you are with it".*

It's late summer 2013, and for some strange reason I've been asked to write about the Wisdom of Ironman. Maybe it's because I am the research co-ordinator for this project, or maybe it's because I'm the only one in the cohort to have completed several ironman triathlons. But right now wisdom for me is taking a different route, having injured my knee right at the peak of training (with the potential risk of not taking part in my next race now); the mind and the body are in conflict. This, I guess, is where wisdom does come into play. But we will get to that...

Before you ask I am not Mr Miyagi, and nor am I going to ask you to wax on and wax off to learn some special triathlon swimming technique (unless you want to of course). For me the metaphor of Mr Miyagi takes on the appearance of all the teachers who have helped me along the way. The true WISE ONES. And when it comes to ironman, wisdom within is a key requirement that many of us lack (at first). Newbies are always so keen to bomb off in training only to realise that the distance was further than they thought. I remember one of my first sessions building up for ironman, the programme read long steady run in heart rate zone one – that's barely breathing, what's the point I thought. But I persevered; man was it a boring session that day. But the point being that in training it's all about slow adaptations. Six months later I was able to 'race' but with the same lower heart rates – that's the point, I had become more efficient. Ah, time to stroke the beard! So what has been learnt from all these races, competitions and challenges? What has the IRONMAN taught me, and how could it help you?

Let's start with two words that resonate both in training and in the event – PERSERVERANCE and DETERMINATION. Yeah ok – cheesy I know – but true. July 2007, some 60km into the cycle course at the Austrian Ironman – legs a little on fire, had I gone off too hard? Then I turned a corner and saw what can only be described as Mount Everest in front of me. Actually it was the Rupertberg, one of the big climbs on this particular ironman course. I could hear the subwoofer bass resonating from the summit, it sounded like I was cycling into a Spanish discotheque from the 1980s.

My first thought: *"holy shit"*

My second thought: *"what the f**k?"*

My real thought: *"can I actually make this?"*

I was out the saddle after a few metres and simply weaving all over the road to move forward. There was a small group of people around me, everyone staring at the ground, gritting their teeth, sweat pouring. We had been told it would be mid-twenty degrees, it was over thirty. It was like cycling up a vertical hill in an oven.

People were literally screaming at you, as if their chants would will you forward and upwards. Some three-quarters of the way up, the subwoofer music changed to a cross between disco-disco and the Prodigy. To be fair – it was quite good. Don't worry, I was wearing a less 'snug-looking' vest compared to my first ever triathlon. Then the DJ came into view – he was a short Austrian man wearing black shades and sporting a moustache that seventies porn stars would have been proud of.

The girl cycling next to me was breathing hard (*nothing to do with the DJ I can assure you*), and unknown to me she was one of the elite girls.

The DJ went nuts. "And here comes an IRON-lady" he screamed.

The cowbell he held was going ten to the dozen. The crowd lining the road cheered, clapped and screamed. Stopping wasn't an option, perseverance was the path laid out for us. And believe me if someone tells you one day that "pain is just weakness leaving the body" – go flip their ass with a wet towel. My muscles were burning; my lungs were at maximum capacity. But (AND MOST IMPORTANTLY) my mind was focused... Focused on reaching the summit – partly out of self-defiance, and partly because the water station was perched nicely up there, and I was gasping.

So now, when the training is hard, the going is tough, I remember Mr Miyagi number one – the Austrian porn-star DJ, who somehow provided the motivation to drive on, to push as hard as I've pushed – but gave me the perseverance and determination to succeed. Bless you Mr DJ.

***

This lesson of keep moving forward came into play in 2009 at the Ironman European Championships in Frankfurt. I was swimming next to a German guy (only because of the flag on his swim cap) who insisted in swimming into me every few yards – he kept bumping my arm out of the water, and after 1km we were effectively brawling. This was one of those moments when the wisdom of focus needed to be played out. I should've focused on the long day ahead and not get sucked into a long-distance swim battle with *ze Germans*. On that occasion I ignored that wisdom, and we fought to get the best line in the swim – and on another day that would've meant a race PB. Instead, I found my back muscles pulling to try and maintain some form of swimming. At around 2km my back spasmed, something went crunch. I felt fear. I felt pain. NOooooo – an injury in the swim. This can't be happening to me. I've trained so hard for this one. NO! NO! My pace went out of the window as I tried to swim on one side. My thoughts turned to panic – then to self-questioning. Should I stop, should I pull out of the race?

I reached the beach and struggled to get out of the water. I was in pain for sure. I looked at my hands – you see before each race I typically write some meaningful nonsense on my hand for motivation. On my left hand was the word NO; on the right hand was PAIN. **Why?** – well the **PAIN** stood for 'PAIN is temporary, quitting lasts forever'. CHOICE number one – I wasn't going to quit. **NO** on the left hand – well that was what I imagined my brother would be saying to me – 'NO YOU CANNOT STOP!' Choice number two: keep moving. So I did. This could be classed as insanity I suppose. I mean if I had injured something pretty bad then I could be doing more damage. But for now I was still moving. If it gets too bad then I will stop. DETERMINATION.

I remember coming into transition two – I wish I had put a kilo of cocodamine in my kit bag. Leaving that zone onto the marathon route, I was a mixture of pain, emotion and fear. I remember seeing my folks who (bless them so much) come to most of my events and are my biggest source of inspiration. I remember thinking, "Don't cry! You wuss!". But as I left my mum and dad behind me, I struggled to hold back the tears. This was painful, very painful, and I had twenty-four miles to go. Ok – new strategy – survive – break it down – what do I need to do for the next ten minutes. Drink – right – get to a feed-station. DRINK! Next: make it to the next bridge – right get moving. By twenty miles I was feeling disorientated and dehydrated. One lap to go. Everyone around me seemed to speak only German. But then I heard a lady speaking English as she ran alongside (I presume) her husband. He looked in bits so I decided to go and talk to him. "How you going?" I asked. "Yeah not bad" came this cool Amercian accent. "Where you from?" I asked. "Hawaii" he said. Job done – that was the next 10km of conversation. Certainly took my mind off the pain.

Thank you Mr Miyagi number two from Hawaii – you're a cool dude and a true ironman – and I am thankful for your wisdom – COMPANIONSHIP. It's so much easier to push yourself when your mind is distracted (and not focusing on the discomfort), and it's always easier with other people around you, especially good friends. I crossed the line, yes in pain, yes dehydrated, but I finished. I earned that medal that day for sure. The wisdom: ask yourself why you are there. If you have options use them, but most importantly never give up. I spent forty-five minutes on a drip in medical and needed a fair bit of treatment later, but that was M-DOT number two completed. Was it worth it? ABSOLUTELY – that's for life, the experiences and emotions are mine – something no one can take away – time to stroke that beard again.

***

March 2011 – I had arrived in Ouarzazate in Morocco. After months of building up, I was here ready to take on the legendary Marathon Des Sables – simply dubbed the *Toughest Footrace on Earth* – a multi-day, ultra-marathon event, requiring competitors to complete the 240km (151 mile) course over six stages. Whilst the first three days are broadly equivalent to a marathon, day four is the often-feared double marathon stage demanding athletes to traverse an 84km (52 mile) day and night stage – with some competitors taking the full thirty-four hours to complete the stage. Whilst day six is yet another marathon, day seven reflects the completion of the course, being a short 17km 'sprint' to the finish line.

Whilst the sheer distance of the event often intimidates competitors, what makes this the 'toughest' footrace is that the environmental demands are of the extreme with daily temperatures easily exceeding 40°C, and whilst I was there the hottest temperature recorded was 56°C on day six – just when you didn't need it. Oh, and I forgot – all competitors have to carry everything they need (food, clothes, medical supplies, emergency equipment, sleeping mats and bag) on their backs. If you then add the rugged terrain, rocky slopes interspersed with towering dunes and salt flats, not to mention the local inhabitants, namely scorpions and sand snakes – it's no wonder you have to be REALLY brave (*I mean motivated*) to even attempt this course.

There was a guy in my tent who has earned the right to be called Mr Miyagi number three. This was his final time taking on the MDS. He had not finished the previous attempt. It was

"Battling the dunes" – The 26th Marathon Des Sables

day two, and we were fast approaching the renowned Heartbreak Hill – in fact it should have been called Mount Ironballs, because you needed some to get up it. I mean here you are in the middle of the Sahara desert. It's hot, **real hot**. You have just enough water to get you to the next checkpoint, but it's hot and there's not enough to avoid dehydration. And to add comedy value to the programme, here was this giant rocky mountain climb to navigate over as part of that day's marathon stage. I was about halfway up when I saw my colleague sitting in the shade of a boulder.

"You ok?" I asked as I approached him.

"Yep" was the reply "just taking a moment".

"Everything ok?" I asked again.

"Yep" he said, "it was at this point last year that I had a heart attack".

What the f**k. A heart attack – was he kidding? Not at all. This was his proverbial Everest. What insanity, what courage, what dedication. I made sure he was ok then continued on.

Later that day, my feet were talking to me. *It was the sound of pain.* Not just any pain but a sharp, exquisite, you're going to die pain. I had 8km to go. I was limping, but moving. My head was pounding, I was dehydrated. "Anything else this bloody desert wants to throw at me?" I thought. I dazed my way into my tent, my home for the week, my salvation. I sat down thinking, why didn't I just stop back at the last checkpoint and call it a day. My feet were clearly buggered, so why didn't I just stop. I remember thinking about Mr Miyagi number three – as he sat on Heartbreak Hill. He didn't quit, and neither was I going to. The wisdom: *the mind gives up way before the body, so keep the mind positive and focused on success* (in this case finishing that stage).

That evening, I was (quite literally) lifted into the medical tent and greeted by the senior French nurse. She looked at my feet...

"Oh lalala" she said.

"Not good?" I questioned.

"Not good" was the reply.

She then proceeded to tell me that I had a blister under a blister and she would have to cut me to help me!!!!. I felt the blood drain from me at that point. I put my arms over my face to cover my terrified look. Was my Saharan adventure over? The guy next to me was worse – he had a blood blister under his toenail and the medics were drilling through his nail to release the pressure – he was in bits and the TV cameras loved it. Two hours later I hobbled for twenty minutes to cover the 300m back to my tent. My feet were fully strapped up in a concoction of iodine, bandage and taping. I was given a pill called a painkiller – wonderful things. I wasn't on the planet for a little while that evening. I felt like I was heading into the rabbit hole – the desert took on all manner of shapes under those glistening stars. I dared not moved, and drifted into an uncomfortable sleep.

I awoke at 1am. The camp was silent. My tent mates were still. And then the pain kicked in. Feckin' hell – what on earth was that. My feet were throbbing and swollen. I needed to take a look. I cut away at the bandages with my pocketknife to reveal a giant mass of skin missing from underneath my right foot. I could feel the other blisters as well.

Choice 1: *SCREAM.*

Choice 2: burst this blister with a needle and then *SCREAM.* Hmmmm…

I'd rather have a chocolate milkshake with 10000000mg of ibuprofen, but let's go with choice two. I got out my lighter and flame grilled the only needle in my pack. My head torch put a single spotlight on my foot. "You can do this, 3-2-1 and then GO". The pain swelled in my foot. I closed my eyes… A new swear word was invented in that one moment – and it wasn't *Bananarama* – bloody hell that hurt.

Sahara day four: Suffering the effects of dehydration, sleep deprivation and PAIN

It was 6am – the sun had broken the horizon and the Saharan racers from across the globe started to stir. Three hours to the start of stage four. I could barely move, let alone stand up. If I didn't move it didn't hurt.

"How on earth am I going to get to the start line, let alone run fifty-two miles today?" I thought.

My game plan: start now – eat something, tart up my feet as best as possible, take *ALL* my painkillers I had left and get to the start line.

Some 2.5 hours later I was at the start line looking like I had been smoking some Jamaican ditchweed for the whole of the previous day. I didn't look wise, I looked stoned. My friend Nick 'the Thriller' Tiller was a bundle of joy. He looked like he meant business that day – he was that proverbial red guitar on fire! He approached me and looked me straight in the eyes and screamed:

"Whatever you do today, FINISH. I don't care if you're bleeding from the eyes, just FINISH". Good advice mon amigo, and he

proceeded to scream at other people who found themselves in his vicinity. All he needed was his own version of the haka and he was good to go.

The gun went off, I could barely walk, but with a slightly lighter pack today I moved forward. As it had taken me so long to reach the start line I was busting for a pee. Choice: stop! Move out of the way of the mass pack and pee. The thing about the Marathon Des Sables though is that they have a major rule – if the guy with the camel goes past you, you're out. I looked across the desert to the quivering horizon. Ah, it felt good to pee. Then I heard a growling sound, I looked to my right. Oh no the camel.

Ahhhhh… move, pee, move, pee, don't pee on yourself.

The words of my friend echoed, "Whatever you do FINISH" – this was the proverbial rod up the arse moment. Albeit a camel!

The sun was belting that day, and I remember setting myself a game plan – get to checkpoint four (of six) by nightfall. The sun had just gone down as I reached checkpoint four – how was I doing this. By rights I shouldn't be walking. FOOD I thought – get some food in. I sat down away from the rest of the weary runners, and didn't feel well. I didn't feel like eating. Had my stomach shut down? What do I do? Ok – can't eat, can you drink? YES – I reached into my rucksack and immediately found a single sachet of Galaxy hot chocolate. Universe you are wonderful – thank you, best hot chocolate I've ever had. Ok – what's next – as Bear Grylls would say – 'move, keep moving'. We had been told by the race organiser to never be on your own in the desert especially at night. It was night; I was on my own – Homer Simpson big **DOH** moment.

A couple left the checkpoint venturing out into the darkness. I tagged onto them. My head was down but I could see their glow sticks on the back of their packs, and they were only 20ft in front of me. I looked down again thinking about the long road ahead, and then I looked up. They were gone. Either kidnapped by the local sandmen, or simply faster than me. Ok don't panic Justin, who's behind you. I turned around. NOTHING. NO ONE – ZIP. I could see a line of headlamps on the horizon. Ok worst fear come true. You see, being an English guy, as far as I was concerned anything on the floor was a deadly scorpion or lethal snake. I froze with fear. Then the words of Mr Miyagi number four (Nick the Thriller) came to mind – "whatever you do, FINISH". Thank you O wise one, a salmon skin roll moment for sure.

★★★

I've been asked countless times – what motivates you in moments like these – fear?? A little (alright a lot!). But in all honesty, I stood there for a moment alone in the desert, cold. I reached into my backpack and pulled out my only spare top to help keep me warm. I remember thinking, "this morning I was in my nice cosy tent and a crack team of highly trained local Sherpas moved my tent fifty-two miles away".

Choice: stop and sleep in the sand (with all those nasty scorpions and camel spiders – *look 'em up if you don't believe me*).

Choice 2: get to my nice warm cosy tent now less than twenty miles away.

Bear Grylls style – keep moving, move, move. The finish line appeared on the horizon later that night as a laser beam above my head guided me home. I was dazed, almost delirious. I couldn't think straight; I wasn't even sure who I was anymore. But I had only given myself a single choice no matter what – FINISH.

The next day I was lying in my tent – the time deadline for stage four was thirty-four hours and some people were still on the course. My resolve had meant that I effectively had the day to recover having completed the long stage by 3am (around eighteen hours). Everyday we received email messages hand delivered by Postman Pat to our tent. Unbeknown to us, many of our supporters were watching the event via tiny webcams at each checkpoint. My brother had been at work that day, the other side of the world in Australia. Somewhere along the line he had missed me going through checkpoint three and feared the worst had happened. Little did he know, and little did I know.

I opened the list of messages given to me by Postman Pat. My feet were elevated, I was nicely relaxed. The first message – "go on Justin keep going". ***Nice – thank you***. Then the next – from my brother and it simply started with "YOU F#@KING LEGEND, YOU F#@KING LEGEND" and it went on along those lines some more. I remember reading that one message over and over. I felt proud. I never gave up, despite the odds. And now I had to finish the whole race, as I knew my brother was watching. That would make him Mr Miyagi number five – we all need inspiration, and often it comes when you least expect it, from the people who matter most.

One of the big lessons learned from Sahara – was simplicity. You see, when you are stripped from the entire daily grind, the endless emails, the untimely bills, admin you just don't need, whatever it is, in this place none of that mattered. All that mattered was to sleep, eat, hydrate, look after feet and run in the blistering heat. That's enough, trust me! When you are stripped of all the 'non-essentials' you are simply left with REAL LIFE, with **being**. One of my emails read: '*take a moment and look around, enjoy the view*'. Day six – on top of a dune I remember doing exactly that. I felt alive. The same as Ironman. The same that some of my explorer friends state when they are 'out there'. This is the core of WHY. The moment of indifference away from 'normal' living to experience that primitive part of you that needs to feel alive every now and then.

***

He doesn't have a white wispy beard or a Japanese look. In fact Mr Miyagi number six is a muscle bound, professional triathlete who goes by the name of Jason Shortis. I've read a few of Mr Shortis's articles about Ironman – but none have touched me as much as the one simply entitled *Reflection*. In this article Jason talks about the importance of stepping back from the training, and reflecting on what 'makes an ironman' – it can't be done alone. It requires others, support from people around you, training partners, coaches, nutritionists, and loved ones. It requires patience from all sides, focus and most importantly balance.

As Mr Shortis alludes to so well, you can't be your best without these people. So one thing that's really important to do, is to look inside and ask "who has helped you", "who do you care about the most", "who has supported you along this path, this journey", and most importantly "what have YOU done to show your gratitude". There is a time for ironman, and then there is a time for other aspects of your life – balance. It isn't easy. But get it right and you will feel more fulfilled irrespective of the time on the clock. For those reading this and thinking of taking on a challenge like Ironman I cannot begin to tell you that having those people at the finish makes the emotion and experience so much greater. They are part of the essence of the ironman spirit – you will know what I mean when YOU cross that line.

***

My dad isn't Pat Morita (the original Mr Miyagi), nor does he have a wispy white beard, or a piercing stare. But in reflection of Jason Shortis's words there have been many times when I have needed advice when things haven't gone right. Dad (for me) would have to be the quintessential Mr Miyagi, and I'm sure you have the equivalent around you. I am currently faced with the single hardest choice for an ironman in training – rest or train. Going back to the beginning of this chapter I hinted that I was injured. Last weekend was our biggest training session for the whole programme – 160km cycling with a two-hour steady run off the bike. I was going fine until 20km into the bike, my gears were all over the place and as a result I had to put the bike into one of the harder gears, which I wasn't used to. After 140km my legs were straining, my knees were killing me. I made it to the car park and thankfully got off my bike. The sun was out, and here I was in familiar territory – but I knew this was potentially serious. My left knee had locked, I struggled to walk let alone run. 100m into the run I stopped and tried to stretch my leg (like that made any difference). I had to finish the session – CHOICE: go slow, stay in a comfort zone. Ok – let's go.

So I finished, but my head is now burdened with thoughts of should I stop, should I pull out of my next race in Barcelona. This is where Mr Miyagi number seven comes in. I wanted to train, I wanted to continue, but my heart was telling me to completely rest. I rang my dad, what would he say. I knew what the answer would be; I just needed to hear it.

"You need to rest it, son" he said – "take a few days off and see where you are from there". This was going to be a battle between the head and the heart, between the body and spirit. As I sit here writing this I am reminded of the quote at the beginning of this chapter – "*you have to be good enough without ironman as you are with it*" – yes ironman is important, but it's not the be all and end all. It's very difficult as you have a training programme to stick to – but this is where wisdom comes into play – being able to know what the training programme is doing, ease off the gas when you need to, step on it when you have to. Now is a time to let the body heal. With hands in prayer position, I bow. Thank you Mr Miyagi. Today's lesson is over… Rest… Be positive, stay focused.

The Message: Listen to the guides around you, they are plenty, they are wise, they are a part of the Ironman Journey.

CHAPTER 28

"Tenacity" *By Kimberley Mangleshot*

What drives me on? "I want to see fireworks at the end for the right reason."

I was never a sportsperson, or athlete, as a child. You would find me tearing about on a bike, on and off road, getting dirty, nursing a grazed knee! You would also see me having a go at the Five Star Athletics scheme, aiming to emulate my heroes of track and field, and trying my hardest to be a good primary school netball player to win a spot in the team and represent my school. But I certainly wasn't an athlete. Summer holidays were spent at the local leisure centre pool, larking around, being silly, but I couldn't swim and never really learnt until I was an adult.

I'm forty-two, having been born in the seventies into a fairly typical working-class family. Mum and Dad both worked as we grew up and I have one younger brother who was a pain in the arse when I was growing up (whom I love dearly now I hasten to add!). My mum had been poorly all through our childhood and I took on a lot of caring responsibilities from an early age. Back in the eighties it wasn't called that; it was simply pulling together, or getting on with it. Along with breast cancer when she was forty-two and I was just coming up to thirteen, she also had something else, which slowed her mobility, and ultimately we found out in 1994 that she had Multiple Sclerosis. We think it stemmed from a procedure in the seventies involving an injection of blue dye to her spine, but we'll never know for certain.

A certain irony also surrounds this as my only brother, Jeff, was diagnosed at age twenty-four with Multiple Sclerosis. Mum passed away in 2000 due to pneumonia associated with the MS. She'd worked as long as she could as an auxiliary nurse and when I was eighteen and had moved out, Mum and Dad moved to Norfolk where life slowed a bit for them. Throughout my teen years they taught me that hard work and energy reaped benefits. Whilst I had sticky times with them as many teenage girls do, on the whole my experiences of growing up and my Mum's poor health made me more determined than ever to be the best person I could possibly be.

"IRON-MUM" Kimberley

One Sunday in January 2013, whilst out running with my friend Sue (and marathon training partner) I was telling her about my thirty-eight week challenge of training for and completing the Challenge Barcelona Iron-Distance Triathlon and the Herts University Research Triathlete Study (HURTS). She was interested and asked me why? It was such a HUGE goal. Three sporting events: back to back on the same day, and under 15.5 hours. Each event alone: a 3.8km sea swim, a 180km road bike ride and a full 42km marathon would be more than enough for the average recreational athlete to train for. What occurred next was no way short of a revelation! Hallelujah! Relaxed and chatty I went on to recount a story that I had completely buried…

It was summer, the mid 1980s, a weekend away with two of my school girlfriends and one of the parents. They owned a small boat, one with berths to sleep in and an engine that powered it up and down the river. It lived on the Thames, somewhere near to Windsor. Happily playing on the boat one teatime, moored up for the night, I somehow ended up in the water. As I hit the water a sense of fear and impending doom engulfed me. I could not swim. I sunk deeper and deeper; arms flailing around, eyes closed, fighting furiously to get back to the surface as my lungs began to burst under the pressure. I found the bottom, but there was no bottom, it was mud, and trying as hard as I could, I could not push off the bottom. I'm not sure how, but I hit the surface and as I gasped in air to refill my lungs, I could see my friends looking over the edge of the boat. I was probably submerged for seconds, but it felt like hours; they could not help me out, and by this time I was shaking and shattered. I found a second wind and 'doggy paddled' pathetically to the bank, looking for a sensible spot to get out at with relative ease. There wasn't one and the only way that I could get out was to drag myself out of the Thames, through stinging nettles, getting stung from little toe to the top of my head in the process.

Back in 2013 I was shell shocked that I had recalled this memory, which had been locked and hidden for twenty years and in that moment knew why I had been attracted to participate in the most gruelling personal challenge that I could ask of myself. Until that run I knew that I wanted to conquer a seemingly irrational fear of swimming and not being able to touch the bottom of a stretch of water, but it suddenly wasn't irrational and in a moment I knew that my thirty-eight-week journey to Challenge Barcelona Ironman would be achievable. All I had to do was maintain my positive outlook on the training programme, do it, and succeed. There was a second reason that I wanted to do it as I had fallen off my bike in 2011 and broken my wrist the very first time I had tried to use those 'silly clip-in pedals' and knew I could beat the cleats! Although I was still completely and utterly terrified of the prospect of this part of the challenge as well – I mean come on, cycling 112 miles clipped to a pair of pedals…

I can run – that's what I've done for the last fifteen years. Larry, my hubby, had taught me to run back in 1996, running through Trent Park in Cockfosters, and since then I have completed a few marathons and entered in a number of races and am a member of our local running club. The key thing with running was, and is, the personal space it brings you when you are out there, just doing it. One foot after the other; on or off road, whatever season, there was always time for me. I'm not a fast runner, but had managed with lots of focus, determination and training to break the elusive four-hour barrier at Chester Marathon in October 2012. I'd even tried two sprint triathlons. Really short affairs a 300m swim, 20km cycle and 5km run, so I knew what the concept of a triathlon was, although I hadn't found them easy.

One of the things that Larry and I did in 2004 was to re-train as personal trainers and establish our own business. We had the opportunity after Larry had taken early retirement from the Bank of England, at forty, part of their ever-decreasing bank structure. We thought why not! His competitive sports background and my 'Joe average' fitness would give us a great balance and enable us to motivate people from a diverse background. Being a personal trainer didn't suddenly make me super fit, but my interest in fitness and wellbeing was being well used. I firmly believe in prevention rather than cure and encouraging people to take personal responsibility for their wellbeing, as you have no idea what is around the next corner. The business is still thriving, but in March 2013 I took on a new challenge, entrusting our business to Larry to keep it prospering. In amongst all the madness of training for an ironman I took on a full-time job!

My life has always been busy – I juggle, we juggle. When you have a family that all like to be active, then you have to be aware of everyone's needs and try to make sure everything fits in. Getting the job just meant that I had to do my training before and after a full working day, before coming home to put mummy hat on, then also do the really big stuff at weekends. "That'll be fine and doable" I thought, if not a bit of a challenge. Factoring in the new full-time role meant more juggling required. I was suddenly becoming an expert.

You'll have read about the process of how we got in and our part of the deal, apart from going out and doing the training, was to give back our time to attend a variety of testing appointments. Justin, the lead of the project, would collate evidence to prove the science behind the study. We've attended lots of amazing sessions up at the Lab and are affectionately referred to as the Lab Rats. We have had blood taken; we've run fast; had VO_{2max} tests on bike; jumped; had angles measured; had heart rates checked (my resting heart rate was thirty-six beats per minute at the last testing in July – not bad for a forty-two-year-old woman eh!). As the project continued we were asked to provide, well, let's just say 'bodily fluid samples' that were sent for assessing. It's utterly amazing what you can find out about yourself from 'wee, poo and spit'. Without giving too much away, I am on a sub study that surrounds nutrition and full supplementation, which meant I got precise feedback on the tests.

Very early into the study something special began to happen. We all started to support each other. Whatever our background and fitness level didn't really matter as we were all on the same journey. At that time, Justin set us four-weekly training programmes, with between seven and eleven sessions in (some of them became brick sessions – two elements together, so some weeks we had thirteen sessions to fit in). The sessions were the same for everyone, so had to be suitable for a broad range of ability, so we were all going through the same, but finding different bits tougher.

As well as weekly update emails from Justin with training, guidance, support and an open door of help, Justin also set up a Facebook group and from that one space a lot of us communicate. There are over 140 members on the page. Considering we are a group of seventy-two participants this is a pretty cool figure. The lab support staff, friends, family, and supporters have joined the group. We certainly have some 'lurkers' who just watch, but when we meet up for events as part of our training it's clear that they are reading the extensive array of posts of the page and getting something from the support we all offer each other. This is where we arrange training rides, runs and swims. Occasionally some of us bump into each other at the Herts Sport Village, where Justin had arranged a discounted membership for us to be able to train.

The pool there is clean and the staff very supportive. They are used to seeing many top-level athletes training, so when we turn up with our bag of fins, paddles, pool buoys, whilst we felt frauds at the beginning they always encouraged us to use them. Not many public pools allow that.

Being part of this unique study, meeting Justin and seventy-odd other people who are aiming to achieve the same goal is pretty special. Reflecting from day one at the first 'cohort' meeting, it was evident that there was a huge range of abilities and personalities, from near and far involved. I felt privileged to be selected and had decided from the start to do exactly what was asked of me. This would be truly life changing. I am proud now, nine months on to be part of such an amazing and inspirational bunch of people and know that I have made new friends for life. Week one of thirty-eight-weeks training commenced in the middle of January 2013.

Sadly, at about the same time in January, my only brother Jeff, who has secondary progressive Multiple Sclerosis was hospitalised with aspiration pneumonia, in Kent, an eighty-mile plus round trip. He was not in a good way and spent several weeks on the ITU ward where it was touch and go and his inner resolve meant he pulled around. However he was in hospital for about nine weeks as each time they tried to discharge him, the pneumonia just came back stronger. I had to find the capacity to whizz up and down to Kent to support him and as his voice does not work very well, even when he is well, basically had to fight his corner. Whilst he has spent some time at home since this bout, he has been hospitalised again and we are trying to get his care package sorted to support him more. He is another reason for me training for and aiming to complete the Challenge Barcelona iron-distance triathlon.

Every day Jeff opens his eyes and takes the world on headfirst. He currently lives alone, supported by a team of fantastic carers who help him to live to the best possible way he can. I know he lives through some of the silly things that we do as a family. Signing up for, and showing him what can be achieved, makes him proud and feel part of everything we do. His strength has strengthened me to find the energy on the days I doubted that I could fit in one session, let alone some of the days when I had to do two training sessions.

Quite early into the training I stumbled across this statement, which I typed up. I stuck it on Facebook, it's on the kitchen wall, and it's in the studio. In fact several of the wannabe iron peeps have it printed too! It's what I have read every day to remind myself about my journey to become an Ironman (Lady!). Quite ironic that our acronym for the group is HURTS...

It will HURT!
It will take time
It will require dedication
It will require willpower
You will need to make healthy decisions
It requires sacrifice
You will need to push your body to its max
There will be temptation
But I promise you when you reach your goal, it's worth it.

I was honest enough from the start to know that this wasn't going to be easy, and to achieve I would need to find more courage, strength and ability than I knew was possible. I would also need Larry to be there for me – this love and support was unquestionable.

Larry has been behind me every step of the way. He has been a competitive track athlete for twenty years and was delighted to see me so fired up and focused on the goal that was being set. He's encouraged and supported me to embrace every element of the training, the study and the transformation that it is bringing to my personal-belief mechanism. He's spent hours with our daughter and dog at weekends, keeping them entertained. Sometimes it's a bit like tag rugby in our house. I walk in, quick catch up then out he goes on his bike or chucks on his trainers (having taken gorgeous daughter to swimming or out on her bike or sat supervising homework). Our gorgeous daughter, who is eleven, and several inches taller than me already – I'm 162cm, think that's 5 ft. 3 in old money, is pretty laid back about it all. I'm not sure if she thinks I'm a) barking mad b) utterly bonkers or c) pretty cool doing this. What I do know is that "hell yes, I plan to be on the beach", is her comment to me riding 180km on my bike. The noisy plastic hand clappers to wave on the event arrived this week and she is going to make a banner, but even that's "yeah yeah". Eleven-year-olds eh…

Larry knew how scared I was of falling off my bike and doing something stupid and he was the first person I turned to, to try to help me get on it and conquer the fear. I'd done all my long cycle rides on the upright spin bike at the studio from January to end March and it was time to get outside on my beautiful pink bike (*Editor note: another ironlady-in-training-fashion-statement*). Four hours on a spin bike makes you realise that you have willpower. 'She', who must be obeyed, my beautiful pink road bike was purchased from a friend, Sarah. She had never really ridden it so wanted it to be ridden with love. I adore my pink bike now, but it wasn't an easy start. I'd ridden bikes since being knee high to a grasshopper and as an adult have a fabulous specialized hybrid, but I simply cycled on that, not clipped in, absolutely no pressure about energy or time.

Anyway, the day that Larry and I tried to get me on 'She', sadly wasn't a good day as even before I got on the bike, outside our house I was fretting and tearful. It was overcast and a little cold. But I was completely irrational! I am a confident able woman and this bike was making me act like a child. Inevitably I did fall off, but only bruised my ego. I came home and put the bike away and Larry gave me a hug. Soon after my friend Kate phoned and suggested we went out for a pootle together. That morning the skies were clear and Kate's empathy to just simply, try a little bit more, meant we cycled for about an hour. On the road! I was clipped in, in cleats! She kept saying, just try to unclip again. Which I did, and then I clipped back in. We chatted all the way up through the villages as if we were out for a walk and by the time we got home I HAD IT CRACKED! Thank you Kate! From that day on, there was no stopping me. Since that day in early April I have ridden in excess of 1500 miles, of which six or seven of the rides have been over one hundred miles and an 'easy recovery ride' is now fifty miles.

There has been one incident where I fell off 'She'. About a dozen of us, from the study, were doing a sixty-mile ride in Hertfordshire and I had mapped the route and was leading it. We were heading for a fellow Lab Rat's house, Chris Petrie, on the promise of tea and cake at halfway. As we went from a main road to his side road I over-turned the corner and hit the kerb. I remember not being scared, but knowing that I was going to go flying. As elegantly as I could and in slow motion I flew over my front handlebars as the bike hit the kerb, kind of like a superman flight. I hit my knee and elbow and rolled onto my back. As the others came round the corner they found me on my back, walloping the ground angrily and calling out "is my bike ok?" One chap was checking my collarbone, another was checking wrist and ankles and I was more worried about the bike. 'She' was fine and I didn't cry. A few seconds later Chris appeared as we had turned into his road and we wondered where we were; we were two minutes away from tea and cake. AWESOME tea and homemade Victoria sponge! As I sat outside his house with my HURTS Lab Rat buddies, supping tea, eating cake, with Justin cleaning and dressing my knee, Jamie Payne, a fellow Lab Rat, sidled up to me and said "I'm coming to you for my MTFU training Kimbo", I had no idea what he meant at the time, but just smiled. We then cycled back another thirty miles and when I got home I realised MTFU, means "Man the F**K up!" I was an Irongirl!

The toughest bike ride that I have done during training was an event called 'Flat out in the Fens' – a full 112-mile road sportive – you would think it would be nice and flat and fast, which is what it was promoted as. It would be the same distance as the Challenge on a similar terrain. That ride involved a drive to Peterborough to meet team HURTS (Lab Rats!). I think about a dozen of us targeted it, including some of the girls. Incidentally, in the study we represent about 25% of the total. If you can imagine a triangular circular route, we headed out as a group of about eight. It was a really fast start… too fast really and several of us spent the first three miles trying to catch Justin and some others; we couldn't, so settled into our own pace.

We were doing really well and had a stop after sixty-six miles. It was flat, open and really pretty in places. By this point it was me, and two Lab Rats, Gary and Mark alone. We were delighted to be averaging 18mph pace, the pace we all need to aim for on the 6th October to give us a fighting chance of completing everything. Then I spotted a map and realised the last forty-six miles were heading West and into the wind. It turned out to be a 25mph head wind. I said this out loud and a younger rider, nothing to do with us said, "oh, what does that mean". Another chap replied "it means its effing hard work". The next forty-six miles were like cycling through mud. I do remember whimpering at times, and cursing why doesn't Cambridgeshire have hedges. We 'lost' Mark as he stumbled across his son who had originally gone off with Justin, but had experienced two falls, and when we saw him, was changing a flat tyre. When Gary and I crossed the finish I let out a huge tearless wail and he gave me a hug. We had done it.

Oh and eating food on the bike! Our training rides are also about trialling the nutritional strategies to sustain us over a 15.5-hour period. I tried a peanut butter and banana sarnie – well that was wet and sweet and not a lot got in my mouth… and I have now reverted to protein and carb based snacks and gels. Man I know how to fine dine on a Sunday! It's made me wonder what my ideal meal post race in Barcelona will be? I fully expect to not want to eat, but a nice bowl of soup, freshly made would be most welcome. However, that may be tough to find on the shores of Calella almost close to midnight. Paella may be the order or perhaps a visit to the beer festival on the beach at the same time! I know by that time I won't want to eat anything sweet.

Swimming… Ok, in 2011 I agreed, with three weeks' notice to swim a mile for my local Hospice. I did it in a pool and raised a few quid. I did it badly, doing poor breaststroke and spitting water and every now and then stuck my face in the water to have a go at front crawl. But I did it and it was the furthest I had ever swum.

In January this year I started the twice-weekly sessions on our programme, and did exactly what Justin said. But it was bad. I had no style, or finesse and I kept sinking. After a month, one of the group supporters, Roland, gave me a 121-swimming lesson. It revolutionised my swim. I no longer sank and things started to improve. I went from being able to do about two-hundred metres of front crawl and then needing to stop for quite a while and now can knock out 4000 metres (over two and a half miles) in just over one and a half hours. Certainly not fast, but steady, even-paced and good breathing. The technique won't win me Olympic Gold, but it will help me get my Challenge Barcelona medal. Swimming in the pool was fine. I can touch the bottom, push off. No real fear associated with that now. But a lake, or worse the sea, what would I do? Justin told us, if we had never swum in a lake, not to go into a lake until they warmed up, but by early July we had to be in it.

That first July Saturday, we met ready to start, at 7am at Denham Lake. Having left my home at 5:30am with my Irongirl chum Jodie to go together, this was the first time I had ever entered a lake or worn a wetsuit to swim in. Having squeezed myself and my anxiety into the neoprene stretchy shell, we met other Lab Rat friends, Mark J and Katherine, at the edge of the lake. It looked beautiful. Serene, calm, and strangely welcoming as the sun rose above the trees. It is a gorgeous venue and one I subsequently did all my open-water lake swims at, bar one.

We'd arranged to meet Roland again as he was going to do a group orientation session for us as none of us were particularly confident and we all had our own demons to deal with. He told us how to get in the lake, down the ladder, slowly and then went through various drills with us. At one point Jodie said to me, "You are fine Kim, don't worry", this was in response to me verbalising over again quietly (muttering like a woman possessed perhaps) – "you're fine, you're not going to sink". I hadn't realised I was talking out loud. I have a device to measure time and distance in the water – a godsend to not having to count lengths in the pool. The gadget clocked me swimming a mere 250metres in that session, but as we got out, having got quite cold, but having swum properly, I felt like I had just swum the full iron-distance. I was exhausted. Strangely the others felt the same! But another big tick, open water swimming done (just had to keep going every weekend, which I did, and get better!).

The last of my swimming fears to face would be swimming

in the sea. Early on I had decided that I wasn't going to try swimming in the sea alone and that this joy would have to wait until I got to Calella, Barcelona. But I had a niggling doubt that if I got there and swam a couple of days before and it screwed my head then I would endanger my whole event. An opportunity arose as Hazel, my friend (and sports massage therapist who has helped keep me injury free), showed me an organised sea swim off Boscombe beach in Bournemouth on the August Bank Holiday Sunday. I shared it on the Facebook group page and before I knew it we had a 'Road trip'. About fourteen of Team HURTS made the 'ungodly hour' very long journey to Bournemouth.

I left home at 4:30am to go to Eva's and she drove four of us there. Eva, one of my fellow Irongirls, is the shark, an awesomely good swimmer! She kept me sane and laughing as the sea event started. The event, or rather, race, ahem we certainly weren't racing, started and a mass of people ran into the sea. Some of us Lab Rats looked at each other shrugged our shoulders and walked in. Eva, big smile on face, did the sugar plum fairy dance into the sea, calling at us all, and I laughed and relaxed. I saw her swan dive and she was gone. Then I started to swim. I had entered to do the full 3.8km event, three full laps, but had a head cold, so had decided that the event was about letting go of water demons and just doing as best I could and time or distance wouldn't matter. It was the hardest thing that I have done during the training. You swam in a rectangle and one side was easy and the other three sides were like either being stuck in mud, or swimming in a zigzag against the current. Oh my... after the first lap I checked my watch and it was slow, very slow, but hey, that didn't matter, my head voice talked myself into a second lap. That was slow too. At times I thought I was the last in the sea as you really cannot get a sense of perspective, remember this basically is the English Channel right!

Towards the end of the second lap as the swell felt bigger

and the sea felt deeper, I looked up to sight the position of the exit buoy and I was, yet again way off course. At that precise moment a support boat sped near me. I was conscious they thought that I was struggling, and I shouted out "I'm not swimming in a straight line", having created a half Christmas tree shape in the sea. They agreed and responded with "are you on your last leg?" and I am sure they do not realise the hilarity in that question as I replied, "I certainly am". I finished the second lap and got out, mustering a run to the finish line, pretending I was running to T1 transition on Race day with a big smile across my face and was cheered over the line by fellow Lab Rat Mark J's wife, Anna – thank you!

Once we all had finished we took our post mortem to a beach-side café and over hot chocolate, we all congratulated and reassured each other, and agreed it was seriously hard, even the seasoned swimmers amongst us agreed the tide was ferocious. The focus for open water and sea swimming for an ironman is to use as little leg power as possible as the cycle and run need them. It's about upper body strength and being consistent. There is a recommendation to kick hard in the last 'bit' so that blood is in your legs as you get out of the sea to run to your transition, it had been great to practice that. I was delighted I had swum in the sea – yay! Even though I had only swum 2.85km in the same time I swim 4km in a lake. I wasn't overly concerned for me that swim was about telling the sea who was boss. The Mediterranean will be kinder and adrenaline can do amazing things to your arm speed.

Throughout my training, which along with swimming, running and cycling has also included twice-weekly weights sessions I have never had any doubt that I would achieve the training and get to Barcelona. I have a mantra at low times on bike or during the longer runs:

"I know I can, Yes I can, because I am".

I say it in my head and sometimes out loud. It sounds very 'Dorothy' from *The Wizard of Oz*, but as I utterly adore musical theatre it's good to have a sing songy mantra to keep me going! Justin set us a task to achieve a minimum of 80% of the training sessions and at each testing session he would check we were on track for this. I am proud of my training and honestly think I have done over 90% of the recommended training. Each time we went to testing we had to hand in training, nutrition and 'illness' diaries. We also had to do online psychology questionnaires. The last of these was very recent, just after our peak training weekend on the 31st August. He wanted to capture our mind set after the toughest week of training.

The Windsor Big Weekend was designed by Justin to be a marker of where we are with our fitness and see how ready we are for the Challenge. It was the best weekend ever and for so many reasons. Justin had arranged that we would swim the full 3.8km swim on the Saturday at Bray Lake, around forty-five of us rose to the challenge. The sense of positivity was balanced with anxiety as we put our wetsuits on at 6:15am. The skies were clear and blue and the sun was starting to rise. We all started together at 6:45am and swam our own 'race'. Some were finished within fifty-five minutes and I was out there for one hour thirty minutes, another solid consistent swim. The lake was gorgeous, but an odd shape so sighting the buoys was interesting especially as the sun was just rising and was in my eyes wherever I looked.

Larry came that weekend to support and participate in the cycling, so after breakfast, Larry, Team HURTS boys, and me Mark and Glenn jumped into Justin's car. I'd printed and laminated arrows to mark out the bike course that we would all be doing on the Sunday. I have received a lot of thanks for this, but if I am truly honest it was entirely selfish as I didn't want to get lost, but forty-odd of my other Iron friends benefited too, a huge win/win. The plan was a 40km loop, four times (one hundred miles) and then off the bike and a two-hour run. Our biggest brick as the ride would take six hours, with the run making over eight hours of exercise. Sunday would be the ideal opportunity to fine tune eating and drinking and working out where we were at. The five of us went round the course, at each turn or roundabout Larry, Glenn or Mark jumped out of the car and tied the arrows on with cable ties, before and after each point. We laughed lots and got the course marked up for the expected forty to fifty riders.

Then we tried to do the same with the run course that Justin had planned, but it wasn't quite so straightforward. We had ended up on 'private property' in Justin's car. Not simply private property, but Crown private property and there was a 'mahoosive' hill, would we really want to run that after one hundred miles on a bike? The combination of the two made us all question the run route. We had a rethink and decided to re-site the start to a car park on the edge of the Windsor Great Park. It was perfect, as it would create our own transition area, however we had to be sure that this was communicated to everyone due to join us. It was around 4pm Saturday by then, and we were meeting at 6:45am Sunday. Facebook was updated, and between us we sent a text to any other Lab Rat we had and asked them to cascade the message to who they knew. We took the view better to get the message more than once than not at all. It worked, well nearly, as everyone arrived at our private 'transition field' on Sunday. Everyone bar Warren had seen the message. Sorry Warren. But the silver lining was that he was randomly asked at a set of traffic lights that had one of our arrows on if he was a HURTS Lab Rat, so he did get to cycle with some of the cohort.

The Sunday ride was brilliant. We could see other riders from our study at different times on the course and gave each other a shout or wave, it was inspiring. I was cycling in my own peloton with Larry, Perry, Jodie, James and Luke. We got separated from

Jodie after a couple of laps as we had to have a pit stop – Perry had a slow puncture and he changed it after fifty miles. Larry pulled away on the fourth lap, which left four of us. We had one quick garage stop for water/fizz on lap four and pushed on. We did the ride in six hours and were delighted; we all took turns leading and encouraging, real teamwork. The day was warm and glorious and at one point a 'proper' road bike race of about sixty riders whizzed passed us all, the noise they made was exhilarating and we all squealed with joy to have been part of what we called the 'Tour de Windsor'.

We got back to our field, put bikes away and run trainers on and headed off into the midday sun to run around Windsor Great Park for two hours. Luke ran with one of his uni friends who was also doing it, so that left me with Perry and James, and Larry pootling around on the bike. I settled into my own pace, which turned out to be a bit slower than the guys, and I encouraged them to leave me. We were passing our other trainee iron people too. The best bit of that run was running past the Polo Club and seeing the water canons on to water the lawn, I ran through it twice, one on the way out and on the way back; it was exactly what was needed as it was really very hot by then. Larry would appear periodically with my water bottle so that I could have a drink and with about fifteen minutes to go I bumped back into Perry and James who insisted that we all stick together and finish the run together, so they ran at my pace (they said they were a bit shattered by then). The three of us and Larry came down to the car park and the smiles beamed from ear to ear. Us Lab Rats are ready. Barcelona here we come.

It's now all about keeping fighting fit. All the hard training work has been done. The foundations are laid. A week after the big Windsor weekend and with four weeks to go I have had a bit of a wobble as I have ended up in hospital on an IV fluid drip to restore fluids as I have severe gastroenteritis, which seems to be a food-poisoning incident. A week on I am sitting in bed having had a week off work, doing nothing apart from rest, so my taper started a little earlier than planned. A few people have expressed concern for me and the Challenge, but I am not worried, as I know that I will get to the start line. I need to focus on getting well and then the rest will be very beneficial. I don't doubt the day will be difficult, but it is simply three distances that I have done several times, just on the same day with no rest. My mind will not be broken.

With three weeks to the event what else will they hold for me? I remember, Saturday night TV when I was growing up, the familiar, "Tonight Matthew I'm going to be…" *Stars in Their Eyes* opening phrase. Turn it on its head… "Tonight (and for the next three weeks) Matthew I will mostly be practising how to change an inner tube". This is the ironman (lady's) greatest fear, well for a novice like me. Mechanical breakdown on the day could be a real game breaker. I am very lucky to have not experienced a flat on any of my rides, but equally do not know how to change a tyre quickly. My last three weeks will find me spending spare time taking wheels on and off in the hope that if I practice enough, then I won't need to put the skill into action! Two weeks out I need to add a little bit more carbohydrate into my eating and make sure that I sleep and do just enough training in amongst normal life. Then I fly to Barcelona on the 2nd October to prepare mentally. Larry and our daughter and two of our friends fly out to support on the Saturday.

At the time of writing I don't know what my journey on Sunday 6th October will be like. I have no doubt that it will be mentally and physically the most challenging day of my life. Seventy-two of us are due to be at the start line (amongst 1000 others), all going off to the swim in 'waves', small groups (opposed to white water rolling too ferociously) at different times. We all have different strengths, weaknesses, paces but we share a common bond – nine months of training and growing. We are all there to complete our own race, our own Challenge. We will give each other a "well done", or "keep going", even the occasional "whoop whoop" on the course when we see each other and energy level permits. Larry, our daughter, and two of my friends from home, Jo and Diana, will have HURTS blue t-shirts on; as will hopefully the majority of the seventy-two Lab Rats' friends and families – so we will have support every step of the way. I will have possibly 300 personal supporters on the course because of this alone, and all the random noisy strangers.

One thing is certain. I will finish it. I will smile as much as possible. My tenacity to complete nine months of training will come together that day and whatever the journey, I plan to embrace the day and aim to remember as much as possible! The cut off may be midnight, which is when they set the fireworks off. My plan is to be behind the finish by then, and see fireworks for the right reason!

Post-event

Hmm, well 6th Sept to 6th October didn't quite turn out to be the month that I thought at the time of writing above. 'Things' happen for a reason and long story short my 'food poisoning' was in fact Coliocystitis, inflammation of the gall bladder. I ended up with a gall stone lodged in my common bile duct ten days before Challenge Barcelona and in hospital for a week with IV antibiotics, pain relief and nil by mouth. One week before with the diagnosis on the table I had to accept that I was not able to participate in the iron-distance triathlon on the 6th October.

I was devastated. I posted to the group Facebook page in my hour of distress and reconciliation to only being able to attend as a supporter. I was overwhelmed by the comments from Team

HURTS and as the news spread my non-iron trainee friends and family. I haven't cried so much – friends, who should have been preparing for their Challenge visited me and gave me the most amazing hugs and virtual hugs. Every time I thought I'd cried all my tears, but it was very cathartic and once I had surgery to remove the stone on the Wednesday before the event I was in a much happier place. I was ok'd to fly at 3pm on Friday as we flew at 10am Saturday. I arrived in Calella with my family and was staying in an Aparthotel with many Team HURTS friends; hugs all round on arrival and far fewer tears.

I was stronger, and was there as the 'Mummy', a role apparently that I had self-coined, but one that gave me the tenacity to dig in and support the seventy other people who had trained so hard for a year. Did I get to see those fireworks for the right reason? Yes, but a different right reason. I was honoured to be given a pass to the finish where I met, along with Justin, nearly every single Team HURTS competitor. To be there and give them a hug and put a medal over their heads made my journey to Challenge Barcelona complete. Thank you all for sharing your finish with me.

Ten days on I have entered the Nottingham Outlaw Iron-distance triathlon in July 2014. My turn to pull all the training together will be in 2014. A damned good excuse to keep meeting up with my ironman friends!

The Message: The journey is as important as the end result; believing every step of the way means you can overcome all adversity.

Editors' Message: True conviction and courage comes from within, it reflects the real YOU, the iron-spirit you have. Kimberley, for the journey you have undertaken, we are proud of you, we salute you too x

CHAPTER 29

"Hindsight" *By Bradley Fleming*

October 2012: Final year of university is about to start; unlike the previous two years I actually had to put in a little bit of effort. Hard work for the next eight months, no time for partying, no time for drinking, it is all about getting a first class degree! Sitting in the first lecture of the year, fully focused on work and Justin stands at the front of the class and says with a cheeky smile "who wants to do an ironman next year?" Obviously I laughed this off but the seed was planted! Two weeks down the line, walking back to the library from lunch, my friend John turns to me with the straightest face and says "shall we do this ironman?". The challenge had been set and I miraculously suddenly found the time I would need. It was time to learn how to swim.

My journey really started three months out from Barcelona!! Having not been in the pool for three months due to a shoulder injury I thought the best thing would be to throw myself in at the shit end. You may have thought I mistook 'shit' for the word 'deep' but this is not a typo! I took the clever idea of going to do not only my first sea swim, but also my first swim of any kind for twelve weeks in the battering slightly over-salty waters of Southend-on-Sea. Getting out of the car the wind smashed into me instantaneously making ALL of my extremities decide they didn't want to be so manly! As I made my way down the steps, down on to the coarse sand the smell of the sea overwhelming. I nipped behind the nearest wall, pulled on the wetsuit, fitted the goggles and dawdled towards the sea. The coldness of the water was my main fear, until I realised that my friend and motivational training partner was about to jump in the murky abyss in just swimming trunks. That meant I had to man up and my attention turned to the waves that I would have to battle my way through. First step into the water and the chill resonated up to the tip of my head. Second step and a soft material brushes against my ankle. Jellyfish? I wish! THERE WAS A CONDOM RUBBING AGAINST MY FOOT! I couldn't cope; I had a little panic attack on the spot. No man wants another man's rubber anywhere near them, let alone actually on their skin. This battle was going to be twice as hard knowing, that not only have I got to battle waves, but also Johnny was going to be swimming alongside me!

Once composed I was able to battle my way through the waves to be twenty metres out. As I started to swim the waves engulfed me! I was planning to try and swim at least 1000m, but I soon realised that I was not going to make that. Firstly, I struggled against the tide and I couldn't make it to the next groin. Having turned around to swim with the tide didn't help much more. I fought as hard as I could but after ten minutes my spirit had gone. What started out as a bit of a funny situation actually turned into one of the most mentally tough experiences of this whole process. I was hoping it would be my last knock leading up to the race, but how wrong I was!

There was one weekend a month out from the race which would identify whether we were ready for race day. THE LONG WEEKEND! Training in the weeks leading up to this moment had been excellent. Confidence was on the rise, swimming had been going well and the sun was out on the long swim morning. Well I hoped it would be, but at 04:30am only the light of the moon was smiling in the sky. A 07:30am start in Windsor was not my cup of tea but then I wanted to test myself against the other guinea pigs, as I knew swimming was my weakness. There was a need for me to know that I wasn't last in the group. As we all jumped into the water there was a thirty second acclimatisation period to get use to the chill. We were off and it seemed like everyone had propellers on their feet as they powered away and flew past me! This was quite unnerving but I managed to get into my own world and plod along by myself. Two laps later I could not believe how comfortable I was. I approached the exit of the lake with my aunt waiting to help me out of the water. As I gazed up at her, waiting for my blood flow to recognise I was standing vertical again, she had a huge smile radiating across her face as she looks and says 1.36 1.36 1.36 (*one hour 36mins*). That couldn't be right, that's twenty minutes faster than I had ever gone before. Her smile jumped across to my face as I realised I had achieved and overcome my biggest hurdle in an astonishing time for me. This was the highlight of the entire programme for me.

I was on top of the world!

Day two and once again it's an early rise form the Fleming household. My aunt awakens me at 4:30am with the moon glistening overhead. This was the long brick session. Despite the excellent result from the previous day there were some nerves ahead of the session. Bike unpacked and on the road, three laps followed by a two-hour run. The first lap and 4/5 had been fantastic and I had felt comfortable throughout averaging a slightly faster pace than normal. Coming in to the end of the second lap I felt a sharp pain in my stomach. Not sure what it was I carried on to the best of my ability but it had affected me mentally and physically. I couldn't continue the pace. I slowed down, disconnecting from the group I was with and continued doing smaller loops closer to the base just in case something went horribly wrong. Back at the cars I stayed put for a bit longer than normal trying to let the pain subside. After twenty-five minutes I felt that I would be able to get the legs moving without too much discomfort. To my amazement I was able to run without any pain and my legs were not fatigued as I expected. 10km down and the legs were still turning smoothly. Despite the F1 'shit stop' everything was looking up. Unfortunately these thoughts came in too soon. Half way around the next loop of the run an excruciating pain stopped me in my tracks. This time I realised that it wasn't my stomach where the pain was emanating from.

It was my nuts!

Four weeks out from the race with the inability to train. Although the taper had begun, I knew I needed to continue keeping my body ticking over. The hope was that the pain would relieve itself and I could train again soon. Unfortunately the hope was misplaced, as I was not able to train again until touching down in Barcelona. Six trips to the doctors' surgery over the four weeks and a four-week course of antibiotics had yet to get rid of the discomfort. I even let the doctor put something down my John Thomas and up my backdoor to try and figure out what was going on but there was no luck (*further details cannot be supplied due to the suppression techniques I am using to never have to think about these two incidents EVER again!!!!*). A week out I made a decision to change the saddle I was going to use on the day to hopefully allow me to not cause too much discomfort to the twins. I jumped on the Facebook group and pleaded to see if anyone had an Adamo saddle that they could lend me for the day! Changing a saddle on the day of a race to one never used before is not the recommended thing to do, but arse pain is better than ball pain… *FACT!*

The four weeks being unable to train had surprisingly left me feeling quite calm about the whole event. I arrived in Barcelona to the glorious thunderstorm's rallying call to the seas to be as choppy as possible. I arrived on the Thursday morning and the state of the sea had the nerves rushing back in to me. A quick unpack and it was time for Sarah and John and I to make our way down to see the battle that we may face on race day. The waves were tough but I had battled Southend and nothing could be worse than that! After a twenty-minute swim I knew that it was going to be tough, but I hoped and prayed that the current would be flowing in the right direction to make it that little bit easier for us all.

The morning of the race arrived with my nerves all over the place. As I made my way into the breakfast room I had to turn around sharpish as my stomach was turning over. Straight to the bathroom I jogged to get the morning nerves out of my gut. Making our way down to transition the excitement was starting to take hold but the nerves were still lurking in the background! Once the bags were completed and tyres were pumped it was time for the slow methodical walk back up to the start line. After lathering our necks in nappy rash cream the time was finally here. As our wave was called into the starting point, I stayed well out the way towards the back of the group to ensure I wasn't engulfed in the stampede. The hooter sounded and I jogged into the sea. The battle had begun! To my surprise it was reasonably easy until turning the buoy to make the long trip back down parallel to the beach. The tide was against us and my shoulder had started to twinge!

I'd made it!!!! I was out the water, the hard part was over. Unfortunately what was going through my head was not what my body was doing. I knew I wasn't feeling fantastic exiting the water but having seen video footage of myself I now realise that I was in a bad way. Being supported on both sides by two helpers I could not support my own body weight fully. As I staggered towards the transition tent, Laura (my girlfriend) ran out from the crowd as she thought I was going to pass out. In my head I was nowhere near as bad as I looked and could only think "don't touch her!" I specifically remembered in race briefing that competitors were not allowed to have any support from supporters. I did not want to be disqualified!! Seeing her gave me that little push I needed and I regained my balance and managed to jog up to the end swim timing gate where I was halted in my tracks.

'You are out of time' the marshal stated. I gazed up to the clock, which said 2:14:42. I knew that I had 2h 15min to finish the swim and I was not going to be cut off under the allotted time. As I went to go past he put his arm in front of me, which I politely moved out of the way with a kind remark telling him to "F#@k Off". No one was going to stop me. I had overcome my biggest hurdle and I was not going to have someone ruin this for me. I knew the rules and I jogged into transition!

As I entered the tent there were helpers on me straight away. They yanked me out of my wetsuit and opened up my bike bag. Being in a much more vulnerable state than I realised I consumed two caffeine gels, a chocolate bar and some jelly babies in the course of two or three minutes. Once I was in my cycling attire I made my way out of the tent to find my bike. I could hear the support from my friends and family cheering me on. They knew that I had overcome the tough bit for me and as long as I could stay pain free the rest shouldn't be too bad. As I hopped onto the bike I realised that I had another participant riding alongside me. This was brilliant, I was out on the bike and I had company. As we were so far back I was pretty sure the officials would not be too worried about drafting. The main task was over, if the twins played along, it should be a smooth ride and jog to the finish line.

Half an hour into the bike I felt quite fresh. I was still cycling with my partner, but now adhering to the strict '7m no drafting rule', when I started to feel slightly unwell. I told her to continue as I was going to slow down to make sure I was okay. Suddenly I felt pain grip every inch of my leg simultaneously. It was as if I had cramp in every muscle at once. I stopped on the side of the road and got off the bike instantly. I bent down to stretch my right… *(lights out).*

Slap to the face followed by another slap to the face and another. I don't understand random Spanish words being shouted at me and it made me more and more confused. All I wanted to do was sleep. As I went to dose off again more slaps repeatedly hit me. Several minutes later I heard sirens making their way up the hill. This was when I realised something had gone horribly wrong. There was a big fuss around me as they tried to work out what had happened. Quite a lot of time passed before they hoisted me onto a bed and into an ambulance. Whilst inside, pins were being stuck into my fingers and arms, but all I wanted to do was sleep! Shouting… sleep… shouting… sleep… shouting!

It seemed like an age before I was back in the recovery tent. After several hours I was pretty much fully recovered. I looked over at the drip in my arm and assumed that I was severely dehydrated. As the doctor came over to check on me I asked him what happened. He looked at me smiling and whispered "you were lucky. Your blood glucose dropped to 28(mg/dL)." I didn't quite know what it meant at the time, but I knew it was bad! (I *subsequently learnt between 70-100mg/dL was normal!)* Moments later my bag was bought into the tent and I rang my mum telling her I was in the recovery tent. After a small nap, the cavalry came calling. My mum was the first person to be let in. As she approached I immediately became overwhelmed and completely broke down. I hadn't finished the race; everything that I had worked for had gone!

Three hours after the initial incident I was allowed to leave. By this time the negative feeling had diminished somewhat and all I wanted to do was get out and support every one of the other guinea pigs across the line. Over the course of the study I had got to know a lot of the "lab rats" really well, and I knew that each one had overcome personal hurdles in order to reach the start line. My job for the day was to support each and every one of Team HURTS to reach the finish line, especially my aunt. I spent the rest of the day out on the marathon course cheering until my voice was lost. My aunt was still out on the course and I was waiting for her to get close. The time was 10:00pm and I knew she couldn't be far away. I made my way down the course away from the finish line until I saw her trotting towards me. She had done it! She was 2km out! We trotted the final part of the journey together and entered the red carpet. Waiting for her were my three cousins and nephew. They crossed the finish line together with me slightly behind smiling from ear to ear. It was a moment I knew she had been waiting for all year. I was so proud to see her crossing the finish line and that was a picture that has stuck with me ever since! As I walked across the finish line I took a moment to get a good perspective of my emotions.

I had to complete this!

Since my return home the question I have been asked more than any other is if I would do it all again after everything that I had been through. One person told me that in hindsight I should not have completed the challenge. The word hindsight stuck with me. It is a word that is most commonly used when looking back on a situation and thinking how one would do things differently! The definition of hindsight is *"understanding of a situation or event only after it has happened or developed"*. I do now have a greater understanding of the event and what it is going to take for me to complete it in 2014, but there is no way I would do anything differently. The experience was emotional from start to finish, and without going through what I did on the day I

Thumbs up:
Brad (left), John and Tony at the swim start Barcelona 2013

wouldn't have had the post-race thought process that I went through. My disappointment from not completing the race was eradicated within a day, but I soon realised how bad things could have been when I worked out that my blood glucose was so low that I could have slipped into a coma and that was the real reason I could not stay awake. With all the happenings of the day I came to appreciate how lucky I was to still be in good health as my situation could have been awfully worse!

In hindsight would I change anything about the day or the ten months leading up to it? No! In hindsight would I say I was lucky? Yes!

The Message: "Don't let disappointment stop you from achieving your goal! There will always be a finish line to cross!!!"

CHAPTER 30:

"No Rush, Get Around"
By Jon Townley

Hi my name is Jon (Hi Jon), and I'm a triaholic.

Before I start there are a couple of things about me that I should bring to light straight away:

1. I have a tendency to do stupid things
2. I (think, or so I've been told) have an addictive personality

So let me give some examples of the above. Stupidity… this ranges from causing myself injuries by thinking I can jump over a cricket stump… that ended up with me in hospital, having some stitches in a "new" hole… through to finding a Second World War hand grenade on the way home from school, and playing catch for a couple of miles… then forgetting I had left it by the sofa, and showing my dad what I had found… I've never seen dad turn white so quick… it was promptly sent to the bottom of the garden and the bomb disposal team turned up the next day…

I don't seem to think things through… and their consequences…

An example of addictive personality is when I had to be physically removed, by a couple of mates, from the fruit machine in the pub on nights out, to go and talk to my girlfriend (who is now my wife… so I can't have been that bad!).

So what is the point of this garbled intro, I hear you ask? Well this study ties in with both… Another stupid idea that I didn't think through, and another opportunity for the addictive personality to take all over…

Let me go right back to the beginning, I was bullied into Triathlon in the early days, by a mate who likes to run. All I liked to do was drink and play football, so never really got involved with any of the disciplines. Our first one was a super sprint, which I borrowed a bike for, and changed with a towel around me, trying to protect supporters' eyes from the potentially scarring vision of me changing from a wet pair of shorts into a dry pair. The borrowed bike's chain came off, but I managed to get around the 17km and 5km trail run. That was that… or so I thought… since then, I have competed in several distances including Padstow with a sea swim, and the flat Eton Dorney triathlon, where I managed the 10km run in under fifty-three minutes… never repeated!!

So this is kind of, where the midlife crisis kicks in. We had already decided that we were going to be stepping up the distances, sprint to Olympic to 70.3 to full distance. Aiming to complete the longer distance as the main challenge for that year, whilst competing in the previous years' distances as events throughout the year. We had decided that 2013 was going to be the year of the half ironman, until I was perusing twitter one day, and saw the request for guinea pigs for a university study into triathlon.

So let me bring you up to about a year ago…

I see the tweet on twitter asking for volunteers to take part in a study. I follow the link and apply after reading some bumf.

Cue the return email stating to be considered you must have a clean bill of health (cough… cough). I know the immediate family history isn't exactly the healthiest bunch; dad has diabetes and has had recent heart conditions.

"If you still want to be considered, you will need to come to pre-qualification test," says Dr J.

So I visit the local GP to get my letter signed (it's true what they say, doctors are getting younger), the doctor makes some comment about an ankle injury from the football days and wanted to look into my history more… fair enough… but I could get hit by a bus tomorrow!! He will let me know if and when the letter is ready to be collected… "the letter is in Reception for collection Mr Townley" £40 later… £40!! I'm in the wrong business… all it says is I should be ok, but I had an ankle injury when I was younger!

So I travel to the University first thing on a Saturday morning, a two-hour round trip… *now this is another show of stupidity*… if going for a "fitness test" don't go out on the piss the night before. I turned up stressed because I couldn't find the building… it's huge!! I'm a little hungover, I talk to Dr J and we start to get the ball rolling; quick chat around the programme… "let me just take your blood pressure"… mmmmm it seems mine may be a little high… Well, when I say a little high… It's sky high! Dr J asks Dr M to have a look and run the ECG… the look says it all… not a chance in hell… I get sent home without any fitness work… Dr J asks me to come back next week… I'm off the booze, off the coffee, bought a Blood Pressure machine, the works… I need to get it down. I'm not sure it was the best thing to do, the added pressure, daily monitoring of my blood pressure readings, I managed to get it down to 140ish over something…

So take two… BP still high, but down enough to be monitored throughout – being sober helped – comments of it went well and hopefully will get on…

WE ARE GO!!!

Meetings pass… training plans are received… in addition to the previous tests also need to visit a heart specialist to have a test and scan… all ok… so we are all set to rock and roll…

Testing continues, as does the training... training is interesting, as I have been training at speed for the smaller distances. Dr J wants us going slower, but not just slower, what seems ridiculously slow. People comment on the speed I'm running at, is it training or quick walking!! Throughout the whole process things (I'm told) are moving in the right direction... just keep it up. Now I used to go to the pub after the smaller triathlons, but now it was getting to a stage of doing up to three hours training before work, and I was in a new job. I'm sure questions were being asked... why?

So there are two things I want to talk about now. First of all, the event itself... but before we go there... there is one part of the study I was called into that will leave a mental scarring... the "diagnostic tests". Now the free supplements and monitoring food intake isn't an issue, as long as you don't feel guilty for writing takeaway curry and nine pints; could have got away without telling them as well!! It's the shovelling of shit. For three days taking "samples" of your number two's is possibly the most disgusting thing I have ever had to do... and I've got two kids! Having to store it and sending it off in the post... it was bad enough doing it... I would hate to be on the other end!

The Event

I travel out to Barcelona on the Thursday before the race with my mate Rich for acclimatisation reasons obviously. Carrying the bike boxes is an interesting dilemma, large and bulky and not easy to control, sounds like me! We fly out of Heathrow. Jimmy White and Laurence Llewelyn-Bowen on celebrity watch and an eccentric Irish man who had carried a double mattress across London to get to the airport! UK end no issues. Nice and relaxed. Land at Barcelona, suitcases out like a shot, stood around for over thirty minutes waiting on the bikes to come out. Start to see others going to the event still in control of everything.

We are told to meet someone to get the transfer to the hotel. Twenty minutes and no show. We eventually see someone and chase them. They tell us we have to travel to Terminal Two to get the bus, so we lift the suitcases and boxes onto a bus to the other terminal, and then drag them over to the transfer bus. Get to the bus for the transfer, the look of disgust from the bus driver on another two boxes, he shouts and I'm sure swears in Spanish, no good to me, can't speak a word!

Told it will be forty minutes before he leaves. Ok, beer and sandwich time! We get back on the bus. We set off. All of a sudden we are back at terminal one picking up someone else. Wasted ninety minutes faffing about.

Hotel is ok at best!

Friday: I spend two hours walking up and down the beach. Find T-zone and the start line, but no registration point. I had convinced myself it was there, but a quick look on Facebook and realise it's somewhere at the top of town. I walk up, find the place, get the documents etc. and am happy as…

Now at this point I would say I was calm about the event, no real worries. I've trained, I can swim the distance, and I can ride the distance. However, my running was always going to be an issue, but I can walk… so I've convinced myself… and I am lovely and calm… until at dinner a certain Dr J walks past. All of a sudden realisation kicks in. Quick conversation with him, and I swear I'm a gibbering wreck, shaking like a leaf, don't know why, nothing was really said!

Cohort meeting later that day. Information passed to us: *"YOU ARE READY"* is the message. Not for the torrential rain that is bouncing off the ceilings! Nor the lightning that is flashing over the sea.

Friday Eve: The family are coming out. They are due to get in at 11ish, so a couple of beers and a relaxing night. Nope... flight is delayed, transfer is messed up, and so we tell them get a cab. I've never known me to be so generous, must be the beers! So they turn up several hours late (and several more vodkas than I wanted). Oh well, we have to deal with what is thrown at us.

Saturday: not a lot really happened. Managed to get Mike "The Flying Dutchman" to tweak the bike. My parents turn up to the resort from central Barcelona. Pizza and pasta for dinner. Torrential rain, thunder and lightning again, then home to bed, but not before.

Night before the race, I slept ok, not too badly...

So *THE BIG DAY* was here. Nearly a year in waiting, and I'm up early in the dark to walk down to T-zone with bags in hand ready to get going. Down to the beach, I wander around for a bit and stare out to sea, looking and trying to stay calm. Wetsuit on. Family photos before going down to the water for ten minutes splash/warm up. Get to see the pros start whilst I'm in the water. This shit is now real. Out of the water and try to get in similar crowd by hat colour. Lots of people running around with whistles to try and coordinate, and not a lot of room to manoeuvre.

So my wave is called. I'm standing on the beach ready to go. My mantra is *"no rush, get around"*. The horn is blown. Everyone runs into the sea... all except for me. I slowly walk in, as if testing the temperature! So swim is started... *no rush, get around*... the first couple of hundred metres out and over, then the first turn. A fair bit of congestion at the buoy, but then out in clear water. During the swim a couple of things stick out. Firstly, the amount of people punching and grabbing feet. Do they not realise it will only take a second to go around me... I'm not that fat! But grabbing my feet... I was nearly 500m out from the coast...

So I come out of the water and look at my watch 1 hr 24 mins, a good fifteen minutes slower than I was anticipating, but the current was strong. Going by the look on my face from the official photos I don't look that happy!

I see the family… and into T1.

Now I take my watch off to get my wetsuit off, as I don't want to rip it. I keep it in my hand with goggles and hat. I get changed. Bottle of coke and a snickers bar, then out to the bike with end of snickers in mouth!

I hear the family, and I'm off on the bike…

After 10m I realise I've left my watch in my bag back in T-zone. I'm told to keep going, so think I'm alright. So back-up plans come into my mind – "send someone in to get it or something"… "maybe borrow the wife's as I pass on the loop to lap two or something"… out from the slow zone.

I hear Dr J… And we are off onto the main course. Someone told me that the course was flat, not getting in and out of Calella it wasn't!! Not what I wanted to see as I've just swum nearly 4km. So head down and go. It's after fifteen minutes, I realise that without my watch, I've got no concept of time or speed, which will throw everything up in the air… nutrition… cut off times… energy… *no rush, get around*. I decided on using the turn points as the good basis of time for nutrition, about an hour I reckoned… but as a rough guide it could work. What felt like hundreds of people passed me… but no panic… *no rush, get around*.

On the bike, a couple of things I noticed. The sponsor's drink was very strong, but when it's lemon it can dry your mouth out!! Also a man sat in a tunnel playing the bagpipes… *(what's that all about?)*. I also noticed on the start of the second lap, no family, so still no concept of time. Start of the third lap, no family, where could they be? Next thing I notice is the big black cloud coming over the hills. I point it out to a steward.

He looks, and shrugs his shoulders at me with a smile! Then the heavens open. The water is flowing. I'm sure I remember thunder and lightning, also cycling through flowing puddles, and puddles that are splashing up over my pedals. I'm absolutely soaked to the point I'm keeping my sunglasses on to protect my eyes. They could just do with wipers…

I'm coming into the end of the third lap. I pass one of the other cohort cycling. "All ok?" I ask. Nope, he has had a wipeout. No back brakes and holding his ribs but still going, bearing in mind there are some up and down hills in the pouring rain!! "You ok to carry on?" I ask. "Too right" (or words to the effect) is the reply. Something Dr J has instilled in us all. I was struggling in the wet with a full bike never mind without any back brakes, but the determination was there to be seen

I pull into the end of the ride, to finally hear the cheers from the family, and some wise spark has given my eldest an air horn!! It seems that they perched themselves in a place that they could see the laps from, but it was the wrong place, but it did sell Mojitos so there was a plus side. Into T2, get changed, then run around to try and find an English-speaking steward to explain about my watch, as it is now "missing".

I start the run, and immediately stop to think "shit this is a marathon, and I've just done the swim and bike". Nearly there… *no rush, get around…* so start the run. Hear the family shout. I shout back about the watch. Lovely photo taken by the wife. So lap one is constant and at a decent pace (1 hr 04 mins I'm told), but then the rain and the knee starts to ache. I've had an issue throughout the summer with my knee, not sure what it is, but it has been constant. So this is where the mantra comes really in… *no rush, get around…* I see Dr J, and nearly pull my hamstring!!

Lap two is a little slower, and a lot more painful. As I pass though the finish zone, I hear Dr J shouting to keep going. He got the answer that my knee hurts, but to be honest it could have been put in a stronger tone!! Lap three… it's dark and wet, and starting to get a little lonely. They have started packing things up. I'm walking due to the knee and start talking to people as we go around, who are suffering from their own issues. At the end my eldest runs with me for a little bit. Lap four… it's very dark and very wet. At the turning point the subway is six inches deep in water. I don't care anymore. The tables at the aid stations are now down to one and choice limited. Starting to feel a little pissed off now. I then start to pick up as I realise the larger numbers are coming to 40km. As I come to the finish, I pass the family for the last time. Both kids run with me to the line. I run past the sign for "Laps – left, Finish – right".

Man that was a good feeling running into the finish zone, timed to perfection as the fireworks are banging and Freddie Mercury 'Barcelona' playing in the background. Anyone would think it was a set up. Over the line.

I'VE FINISHED – Dr J hands over the medal… nice touch!

First words out of my mouth. I will do another one. See how I can get around without the issues. I came in with 14hrs 05mins on the clock. My first look is of disappointment as I was hoping to get 13 hrs something with all the issues. But with it being the overall clock I can take fifteen minutes off. So it is 13 hrs something… high but still thirteen-something!! I walk into the recovery tent. Finishers T-shirt, massive medal, pizza, beeeeeer!! I picked up a cheese and ham sandwich and a beer. I don't like cheese, and didn't drink the beer. I walked out to the family feeling happy, but still critiquing the performance. Family are proud and happy. Kids wearing "Iron Daddy" t-shirts and hand me my own. Next is to walk to the T-zone to pick up all the kit. That is a long way.

End up with me, missus, eldest and my dad all carrying bits and pieces back to the hotel.

A night of non-sleep due to knee and chaffing pains, couldn't get comfortable. But I'm AN IRONMAN… nay IRON-DADDY.

Monday: breakfast with the family and find out that the missus has been updating all my friends at home via Facebook. Emails, texts and messages on the phone… slowly work through them… nice comments.

I'm sat writing this two weeks after the event. I'm still talking about doing another one in a couple of years, but I also think that the realisation of what has happened and the achievement hasn't quite sunk in yet. I'm talking to people and the looks on their faces sums it up, as does their comments around my mental state. I'm sure everyone will say the same, but I couldn't have completed this without the help of Dr J and the team at the Uni. I appreciate it was an "ambition" to complete one anyway, but the time and effort put in by them made it easier for me.

My family's support over the ten months as I had to disappear for eight-hour training sessions only really started to dwindle towards the end! I really appreciate that support from my wife and kids; it wouldn't have been possible without their understanding and commitment to the event as well. Which is why I have been told I need to wait at least a year for the next one. I was sixteen stone when I started Triathlons. I have lost weight, my body shape has changed. I've had comments from friends and family about how different I look. I was tired, struggled, and towards the end really struggled for motivation in the training, but if I can do it, *anyone can…*

Although saying that, the only thing that really hurts is my knee and ankle… so maybe that Dr had a point!!

Jon 'IRONMAN' Townley – got around just fine!

The Message: Triathlon is a journey about you… *no rush, get around.*

CHAPTER 31

"Fun, Commitment and Determination"
By Eva Fleming

In a few words I describe myself as a loyal wife and mother of three young children, full-time working parent; 1000% committed; fun-loving and optimistic individual, driven to achieve and willing to go that extra mile, ready for any challenge. Also known as world's worst cook, non-alcoholic but chocoholic, the journey below explains that strange things do happen…

My childhood was full of *fun, commitment and determination* and with a twenty-year gap I am now even more determined to bring it back!

Being a fun-loving, hyperactive individual determined to accomplish any goals whether good or bad, there was no other way but finish something once started. I don't know how to explain why, and I possibly will never understand it myself, but small tasks never completed me. Give me some special, unusual and really hard challenge and I will show you I am made of iron.

These characteristics could be evident by my actions at the age of five; climbing lorries and trespassing and not being able to be caught by security. That was something! Being able to come out from cornfields without any rubber bullets in my backside was a mission accomplished! As my family was not really sport orientated, this became my curiosity. I learnt all sports from watching Olympic Games on TV.

Starting primary school meant more activities, I would leave home at 7am each morning just to be part of the athletic team before school started, then happily carried on my sport participation in the afternoon gymnastics or ball games until I came home for dinner and went straight to bed. I was that kind of independent committed and highly-determined child already then looking to live my dreams of becoming a successful athlete just like I saw on TV during the Olympic Games.

I loved every challenge, and every time I won a medal it sort of pushed me further. At the age of nine, I successfully passed all the tests to become a member of a very successful swimming club. Once again I was shining and this is purely due to hard work I was willing to give to succeed. After all I wanted was to be just like those athletes I saw on TV during the Olympic Games. It was a very busy schedule with twice-a-day training and competitions every weekend, but I loved hard work and hard work loved me back. I was in love with swimming, in love with hard work, so committed and determined to succeed. My hard work was evident by winning at both National and International championships. I was on top of the world, until having some unexpected injuries and a change of coach. All of a sudden my ideal world was shattered to pieces; new coach dropping me out of the most important championships of my life. "Hate" is a strong word but I couldn't help myself; I was tearful on a daily basis begging for him to see my "COMMITMENT AND HARD WORK". It didn't help, sadly "he just destroyed yet another talent" I thought. My mum was the only encouraging figure in my life to keep my sports dream alive. She would always remind me:

"FOR EVERY PROBLEM THERE IS A SOLUTION". I can still hear her echoing in my ears. This would often help me to bounce back from negative thoughts.

I dropped out of the swimming club, and years passed by

before I joined my local triathlon club. Being the only woman in this tri-club was tough. I had to keep pace whether running or cycling with all the males; there was literally "NO MERCY". No one would show consideration… I then participated in some sprint or Olympic distance triathlons until I joined university.

With the second year into university I decided to visit the UK for language experience. "I will be back in one year to continue my studies!" I promised my mum and dad. "So here I came", unable to speak a word of English let alone to make any kind of conversation, all alone in some strange country. I quickly accustomed myself to English ways of life and, of course, the language.

I'VE ARRIVED…

Many years, a happy marriage and three children later, I always found some excuses for not taking part in any sporting activities. I would often say I needed forty-eight-hour long days to fit in all my daily tasks. It was just about my children, ensuring they did their best in both academia and sport. Full time job and household duties including cooking, looking after children on a daily basis meant "NO TIME FOR MYSELF". "Did I mind it?" "NO!" The worst part of all was doing everything else and for everyone else but "FORGETTING MYSELF". I was longing for a change but "HOW AND WHEN?"…

October 25th 2012 marked my son's birthday and our family gathering was well underway when my nephew spoke of a university study being undertaken with the climax being to take part in what some would only call the mother of all gruelling sports events. The one-day Barcelona Challenge would involve a 2.4-mile swim followed by 112-mile bike and closing with a 26-mile run to the finish. Ok, so what are we studying? How insane some women and men are, or how relentlessly committed one can be? Either way it seemed so far-fetched for me to happily volunteer to be part of the study. I will never forget my husband's face when I announced I would like to be part of it. We spent the best part of the evening watching the footage of the ironman circuit in Barcelona, and a particular video from 1997 where two professional female athletes struggle to finish the race. Again, another look of my other half's face I will never forget and returning one of mine "promising" he doesn't have to worry about me… I knew I was capable of the whole process, after all sport was always my number one, and I did some short triathlon distance events during my teenage years, "some twenty years ago", ha-ha. But fifteen years out of sport my athletic body had changed into that of an elephant's, and I had to change my way of living. Great! God heard me out and I promised to keep him sweet.

Well, my nephew arranged for the initial test to take in less than three weeks. "S#IT" I thought, weighing 93 kg I had only around ten swimming sessions to improve my fitness and shed some of the excess weight. "EVERYTHING IS POSSIBLE IF ONE WANTS", I kept reminding myself. D-day arrived, 20th November, work in the morning finishing early then headed directly to the University of Hertfordshire. I was so nervous thinking I was the only elephant to be screened and fitness tested.

Upon my arrival, my nephew and then some lovely students helping with testing and two senior lecturers leading the whole study greeted me. The most embarrassing moment was the ECG and "I promise it can happen to you all dear ladies if you have been out of sport for such a long time". Wearing a sports bra didn't even cross my mind (*Editors' note: despite lots of instructions!*), so I wore a normal bra only, laughing to myself trying to keep my face straight and definitely not to go red with the embarrassment. "Wow", by now two researchers sticking electrodes around my boobs to determine my heart's status. Then came the silence as I thought to myself "I hope I entertained you both enough today", just sarcastic me, right?

Done!

Congratulating myself quietly for being brave next was to pass a VO_{2max} test, the easier part of the test (in my eyes). "What does VO_2 mean in translation to my language of origin"? At this point, only God and those two lecturers knew what that meant... I quickly learnt it was to cycle as hard as possible in a short space of time until my muscles were unable to move any more. And yet I found the test relatively ok-ish.

"All done", I was told.

Coming out the changing room I was asked to speak to the research lead, my future "boss" to find out my results. Just the thought of seeing the same researcher who earlier did the ECG, I had flashing images of those embarrassing moments earlier on, I just wanted to hide under a table. "Be brave", I kept reminding myself; "you can do it", "keep your face straight and don't go red"!!!!

Done and dusted, I passed and I was in the game!

With one foot in, and by applying fun, commitment and determination I will make my dream of crossing the finish line happen and sod the embarrassing moment!

Definitions of *fun, commitment and determination* in my own words:

FUN: you will succeed only if you enjoy what you do;

COMMITMENT: there is only one option, what you start you have to finish – "don't you ever look back, you only roll forward";

DETERMINATION: keep working hard and watch miracles happening.

I felt like I was given the second chance to live my life, the whole world looked so bright once again. I quickly had to share my exciting news with my loving husband. Next on my mind was "how on earth will I manage everything?" Well, strange things happen, please keep on reading to find out…

As the person I am where money doesn't dictate my life, obstacles kept coming my way. Just bought the house, paying the mortgage, paying the bills and maintaining three kids isn't easy, and my other half warned me and kept reminding me of the cost I was about to throw away just for the challenge. The thought of purchasing my ticket to partake in this event, all the equipment for triathlon, and flight and hotel booking for my family wasn't going to come from the "Pound shop". He was right and I respected his opinions. However, ALL THE TIME MY DETERMINATION AND DESIRE TO CHANGE OUR LIVES grew stronger. "Not everything is about the money," I kept saying to him, silently crying for him to hear me out. "This is our chance to go back to the people we once used to be", "this is our chance to show our children what life is about", to give people around us some inspiration in life. Few odd arguments kept me in check but EVERY NEGATIVE COMMENT PUSHED ME TO PURSUE MY GOALS FURTHER. After all I kept saying what should be will be, our love is stronger than anything so as for some stupid arguments, you better get used to it; we will get through this and ten months later we will be celebrating a "NEW BEGINNING".

TRANSFORMATION process…

…21st January wasn't only my birthday but also the very first day of the next 250 days of gruelling training. It was the day I was looking forward to the most, not because I was twenty-one years old again, but because I couldn't wait for the hard work to begin. Training was the only little fraction of what was expected of me and my fellow participants on the study led by Mr "BOSS". Along with other fellow participants, I was asked to travel to the University of Hertfordshire for several tests every two months. Testing would last around four to five hours each time, so there was plenty of time getting to know both students helping out to keep the process as smooth as possible, and my future ironman colleagues. All I could remember was the friendliness of each individual, the jokes and laughs making the testing so much more interesting. I could already see we were forming one big family. And this big family was HAVING FUN, SO COMMITTED AND DETERMINED to succeed. We all were chasing the same dream, Barcelona Challenge 2013.

With such a demanding training schedule, and its volume still increasing, I was "DETERMINED" to keep up with it. By adding intense training to my already absolutely busy schedule in my parental life such as working full-time and being a mum to three children with one still in nursery, my children's weekend football activities and group-training sessions wasn't always easy for me to join. It was a bit sad especially due to my nature being a very social individual, outdoors inclined more than indoors. I purchased a treadmill and stationary bike, dumbbells, a Swiss ball and aerobics stepper to at least train every evening upon putting my children to bed. I set myself up a routine in line with the research-training programme I followed.

As the training schedule progressed and with my commitment I loved the fact I was getting fitter and thinner. My weight was dropping and so my dress size. Work colleagues were often puzzled as to what I was doing. I was transforming into someone else, a much nicer looking and confident one. Being "OBESE", losing weight was my priority, as I knew that with less weight I could perform better. Shedding the extra weight was difficult as opposed to gaining it, which, for my cravings, was easy. I focused on healthy weight loss around ½ kg a week and this pursued me to make a "PERMANENT" change in what I ate and when. The study was also requiring participants to keep up a diary of what we ate. This was very helpful because each time I had to fill it in I rather kept my food intake simple avoiding writing essays on my (over)eating habits. I thought "less eating, less writing". Miracles do happen, weaning myself off chocolate and keeping my food as natural as possible was a bonus to further weight loss, and further financial burden, he-he. I needed clothes to fit the "NEW ME".

I had now lost around 15kg; I felt fantastic, I felt fresh, younger and energized. Day in day out I would discover what foods made me ill and what foods were boosting my energy levels. I was literally trying new flavors, combining them carefully. I would carry out deep research into different food values and how they would directly impact on both my performance and health. I then found out about protein shakes which I incorporated into my eating habits. From a crap cook I would become that healthy, interesting one getting admiration from my husband and, mainly, children. This new transformation kept me motivated to go that step further and I loved every minute of the programme. I BECAME ADDICTED to the whole study, new beginning and transformation INSPIRING OTHERS around me.

On the "drinking front" it was much bleaker. From non-alcoholic person I became one almost overnight. I clearly remember the Bank Holiday Monday; it must have been in May. Sun was shining, temperature reaching nearly thirty degrees. I was into my fourth hour cycling using my stationary bike (still didn't have the road bike) as per schedule. Suddenly; my other half stepped in offering a super chilled "STELLA" beer to kill off my thirst. Well, first of all I wasn't a drinker secondly I thought "let me taste it then, I am so hot anyway and anything so cold will help" I said. "WOW!!!" it tasted beautiful. I was promised I could finish the bottle after my training session. I think it's good to have some incentives to keep you going, isn't it? From then onwards I must have drank a bottle each day, my husband teasing me, testing my commitment. Once again, the diary kept me in check and forced me to avoid touching "STELLA". "SHE" was in the fridge all the time ready for me, but I was stronger, determined to not touch. "Guess how many times I opened and closed the fridge?" I don't dare answering this question…

"Meet at 4:30am", my both work colleague and study participant agreed. We thought it would be much safer to begin our three to four hour bike session early to avoid dangerous motorists on the road. We also thought that once we accomplished the sessions so early we could have the whole day ahead of us enjoying our hobbies or spend time with our own friends and families. It was really crazy getting up at 4am and the only thought that someone will be waiting for me at the meeting point, thinking of not disappointing, pushed me out of my warm bed. We had nightmares and we had fun, especially when we got lost and mobiles ran out of battery life. There was NO OTHER OPTION, BUT ROLL FORWARD, and we did. I can't be more grateful for his company and seeing how determined he was kept me motivated so much.

One beautiful morning I met up with other fellow participants for a bike group session due to last between four and six hours. Being confident in the morning was just a nice word soon to become a worst nightmare. Only one hour into the cycle I soon discovered I was too slow and possibly the worst cyclist in the group. I really didn't know what was happening to me, and I hit rock bottom questioning my abilities, blaming everything else for not performing. Such things as: heavy training from previous day; food intake; possible dehydration; being overweight; and shitty bike including knowledge of changing gears when and how, kept crossing my mind endlessly. Not knowing how long still to go, and where we were, was another blow in the head. I felt like a hamster going in circles. I felt unable and embarrassed. I even lost all my food because my bike pouch was left open.

But my "NEW FAMILY" was there to rescue me. There was this lovely chap cycling along with me, motivating me and at the same time advising when and how to change the bike gears, and to use my aero bars; another chap offering his food and a few more of them cycling, adapting to my slow cycling. I couldn't be more grateful for what they did for me that day (they know who they are), BECAUSE IF IT WASN'T FOR THEM I WOULD HAVE GIVEN UP right there, right then. After the session, and to my lovely surprise some offered to sit in the pub with me, with "STELLA" on table. Reflecting from that day still unable to come to terms with the fact that I was such a "BURDEN" to everyone, my motivation slipped away and I was ready to crumble.

The following weekend was scheduled for yet another group bike session. On this occasion it was meant to have less

I didn't quit, and 'SHE' was waiting for me

inclines than previously conducted. "Why would I go and embarrass myself again" I thought. It was not worth it; I would rather go and cycle with my training partner instead whom I knew very well and nothing felt embarrassing around him. Soon my nephew rang suggesting we both go to the group bike session. "Did he ever realize how much this phone call meant to me"? He would come round the evening before, and as we were preparing the bikes, he was the volunteer pumping up my tyres frantically laughing at my expense.

EMPTY TYRES????

That moment I realized, "F**k, it was actually my tyres slowing me down last weekend!!!" As I stood there, I could feel such an influx of consolation that the last weekends' issues were not down to my fitness, but mainly due to half empty tyres. I promise you I was so much better and faster the following day, however my food strategy needed more tweaking and attention. It was a great day and a successful one. Thank you my nephew for MOTIVATING ME to be part of the session.

The two big days in Windsor just a month away from the Iron Challenge in Barcelona meant a big test to find out if we were ready. "The strategy you select in Windsor you should aim to stick with in Barcelona" I was told. The very first day was a swimming test, swimming after all, for me especially is very therapeutic and when I saw the lake I was already in my comfort zone. Unfortunately in the evening I felt awful, temperature rising, I felt my head pounding. The following day, trip number two back to Windsor, illness on the way, I hated it, but I FOUGHT MY DEMONS. FUN, COMMITMENT AND DETERMINATION was the only option. Below is tiny extract from my day I posted on Facebook in September:

... It wasn't lack of energy but the "FEAR" of some inconsiderate drivers especially at the roundabouts, I was so scared and this resulted in me being lost so many times, one second I had my cycling partner in front of me, and the next it was just "me, myself, alone" again, got lost... Seeing a crash and police cars everywhere didn't help either thinking of ALL of you hoping you were safe (... and you were). The final call was cycling at great speed down a hill when two coaches were overtaking me creating rear wind that almost had me thrown in a ditch. Picturing my kid's faces I thought enough was enough I am not risking my life, I didn't attempt doing the last lap at all, thinking in Barcelona the roads will be shut off to cars and no danger at all. Highlights of my day, laughing to myself:

1) I learnt to swear so much it became difficult to control my language later that day;
2) Every time I hit the hill I thought I had flat tyres. Checking them carefully, then realising it was me being "crap" at hills, ha-ha;
3) I realised I have to re-consider my food strategy as it was awful; constantly pretending how much I loved gels and isotonic drinks, it ended in nightmare searching for the nearest bush.

On a positive side, what made both days so beautiful were the smiles and jokes of each individual I met, the friendliness and care for each other. I had fun and I will continue having fun in Barcelona during the event. So thank you all helping me to cope... bring on 6th Oct!!!

I echo those words – *fun, commitment and determination.*

ON THE ROAD TO VICTORY...

I arrived in Barcelona; hadn't slept for nearly forty hours and managed to take a wrong train to my hotel. Great! Who cares anyway? I love travelling on the train with the superb company of my girlfriends. Not even attempted robbery on my rucksack contents would spoil my day, jokes, pulling heavy luggage and trying to speak Spanish... Whatever!

Being a water person, I could not wait to play on the beach. Being a bit laid back, however, I forgot my priorities; sorting out my bike and registration first I ended up chasing this lastminute.com. Fun, one of my words was the opening door to my biggest event. Not even huge tides stopped me from entertaining myself, I loved the sea and the sea loved me back, honestly, and how? By washing away the goggles I was looking to use for my event. All gone!!! Couldn't believe the fact I had to purchase yet another pair; luckily I managed to get the same brand. Cohort meeting two days before race was great, meeting everyone and sharing a few jokes. Next morning I was adamant I would get my bike sorted so I waited for our bike mechanic from 8:15am. Actually, he was a genius because he adjusted my bike so well. He also advised me to test it and come back should there be any issues. And did I test my bike? "Hell NO"! I didn't want to stress myself out. I left it to my good friend God, who has helped each time I asked nicely should anything go wrong.

Off I went to register for the race and to meet my fellow participants. There was such a great atmosphere there; everyone's dream was soon to become a reality. As I left all my priorities till the last minute I didn't even have the time to spend with my family, friends and work colleagues. And boy, they had so much fun on the beach! After seeing them on the beach just briefly I went to hotel to prepare all my stuff. I also felt I needed a little time just to myself. Putting the radio on with loud music blasting, dancing around the room I was there so much looking forward to my event. Evening before the event my best friend recorded a little interview with me asking about my preparations and strategy for the day. "I am going to have fun!" I said. "I am going to complete the challenge and I am ever so ready!" I then ended joking for the rest of the evening until bedtime. Just before I jumped in bed I mentioned that my muscles hurt a bit following the beach play from the previous day (no wonder, it was like doing two hours of functional training, jumping on the sea waves…) so I suggested "tiger balm" all over my body. God, IT STUNK!

5am and my alarm went off. My body felt really good, no muscle pain. I put some clothes on and ran to a dining room meeting up with my fellow participant. I was so excited I was unable to make a simple porridge to my liking. He was there just laughing, and I laughed with him. After leaving the dining room I agreed with my fellow participant to meet up in fifteen minutes to do the final preparations around bikes and transition bags. It was a beautiful sunrise walking to transition area; it was such an indescribable feeling, so emotional. Me, with a huge smile on my face, so looking forward to start the race. I had seen people being nervous and I thought I must be "NUTS" to actually be waiting impatiently for sixteen hours of hell to begin. Hard work, I thought… that's the way I like it… The key words were to smile, enjoy and lip whistle to myself should anything go wrong.

"FOR EVERY PROBLEM THERE IS A SOLUTION" was my motto of the day.

I then fully pumped up my tyres, checked my transition bags and ensured that I had my race number pinned to my pouch. I then found my nephew and hugged him tight to assure him that the event will be a huge success. I then promised to see him just before swim; unfortunately, once I put my wetsuit on I was on "CLOUD NINE" and selfishly stood on my own focusing on not missing my start time. I think I was in some kind of ecstatic state, I honestly couldn't see anybody; it was like someone had blindfolded me. I hoped to find my nephew but I wasn't that lucky, I hated myself because I promised him I'd be there. Suddenly I saw familiar faces, our study lead and one other family member, my face just lit up; surely hugging them gave them a message of thanks for their continued support throughout the entire process.

Three minutes to go, the loudspeaker announced. Ten seconds to go. The horn blew. Running to the water I kept to one side to avoid any scramble. I thought I was doing quite well until I swam round the first buoy, I was unable to see where to swim. I had detoured quite a bit until a boatman signposted me to the right buoy. "F★★k" I thought, "here we go, s★★t happens", "just a few extra miles to swim wasn't a problem", I joked… Finally I was on track once again heading hopefully in the right direction. If anyone was to ask what went through my mind during the long swim, there were two things only, "God, be nice to my nephew" and "I can't wait to dance for my supporters" just like I promised.

I kept swimming, singing to myself the same song over and over again. Suddenly I felt a huge hand pushing me down under water, swimming over me; "YOU NASTY PIECE OF S★★T", I thought *(Editors' note: we agree, people like this should be [fill in suitable, yet intensive punishment] – seriously what do you gain!)*. With rage emerging above the seawater I spotted the nasty man in a yellow hat and swore to get my own back! With no hesitation I sprinted over to him and WALLOPED his head *(editors' note: sensational! Woohoo, balance restored!)*. I hopefully sent a strong message to avoid confrontation with me in future. My next plan was to kick my legs as hard as possible to ensure no one does similar stunts to me again. Turning round the last buoy was a bit sad for me, as I knew my preferred part of ironman was soon over. Finally, first steps coming out of the water and hearing all the cheers I couldn't help myself but laugh all the way to the transition zone.

Laughing at myself being unable to unzip my wetsuit, perhaps because I never practised that, but also because I must have looked quite funny reaching for the zip, and the zip was nowhere to be found. I had to ask an official to help me. Then slowly as I could, I changed into my cycling gear. Then I couldn't figure out how to put my helmet on and my race number was a bit scrunched up. "Sod it," I thought, whatever will be, will be… Coming to get my bike and running on red carpet was just for "VIPs" like me, wasn't it just? More euphoria feeling, enjoying the music being played, being cheered by supporters and I danced again with my bike beside me, just like I promised, right?

As I jumped on my bike, there I was ready to endure a hellish 180km. I couldn't wait for sightseeing of the Spanish little villages, just as I planned. Who cares how quickly I manage to complete the bike circuit! Suddenly I turned the corner; "OMG", more support and more screaming! My face never stopped smiling and I loved everything about the event. I kept going over my food strategy, checking my watch to ensure I ate and drank according to my plan. All went okay, more screaming and cheering, at this point I felt very comfortable, singing to myself as more and more cyclists overtook me. Most of them chatted, cheered the athletes on and by now it was better than "Facebook Networking".

"WAIT"!!! "I need to PEE, what shall I do?"

Remembering someone asking that question in one of our university cohort meetings, the only option was "GO AND PEE LIKE A PRO"! I immediately checked for any cyclists behind me and once it was all clear, with my whole determination I pushed and kept pushing. "I DID IT"! Wow, what a feeling, laughing to myself thinking about my nephew's new saddle that he lent me for this event. I swore he must never find out what mischief I was up to. As I continued cycling, there was more fun to come, soon I almost lost my eyes seeing a well-kept naked man on the beach…"gosh, I can do ironman any day to have such a view".

The first lap was almost over when I spotted my training partner cycling, just starting his first lap, that moment he became my hero 'cause I knew he would struggle with the swimming, not that I had doubted him, it's just because it was a hard swim even for me. At this point I knew he would finish his ironman, and I was ever so proud of him I couldn't help but shout to him how much it meant to me. Second lap started, I was DETERMINED to keep my food strategy up to scratch and never at any point did I feel tired. I felt ever so good. I kept looking around for my nephew as I thought that by now he should be catching up with me, although there was a road section where the possibility was we would just miss each other. I couldn't wait to see him and tell him what a beautiful person he was inside out, a real example to my three children.

All of a sudden, on my return for the second lap I saw pitch-black skies and hoped for clouds to break up and disappear. Quite the opposite, it was coming more towards our circuit. "Blimey!" Next I saw the flash across the skies and loud rumbling, water poured all over us. Torrential rain, flooded roads and steamed sunglasses, fear in my eyes and hesitating to touch my aerobars just in case lightning hits me. I actually thought my aerobars were unsafe and the taped handlebars were totally safe. "Who knows and who cares anyway!" I needed to "PEE" again, easier said than done. I knew my "downstairs" was already aggravating me after some six hours on the bike, but I was determined to repeat the peeing process.

"AAAAGH; F★★K, F★★K, F★★K, AGONY; AGONY; AGONY"!!!!

Once I let it out the burning sensation was killing me. At this point I thought "what the s★★t did I sign up myself for?"

And there was more agony to come. Passing through the flooded roads, suddenly my shoes filled with filthy and cold water causing Goosebumps all over my body. "Keep pedalling, faster you pedal warmer you feel," I kept saying to myself. "AAAAGH!" "AAAAGH; F**K, F**K, F**K, AGONY; AGONY; AGONY"!!!!

I have never ever in my life experienced this type of pain, agony that lasted for a good ten minutes when all my toes just kept cramping all at once. DETERMINED to finish my race, I kept reminding myself the reasons why I was doing ironman, and that in a few hours it will be over. I had to keep pedalling, MORE THAN EVER TO PUSH to overcome the agony. Believe me, I have never sworn so much in my life! Once the pain wore off, the same happened to my other foot. I then chuckled to myself pointing a finger at the one above us thanking him for a great test, determined to succeed. Finally the third lap lasting approximately 30km, I couldn't wait to see my supporters. I was so looking forward to their screaming and cheering; I needed a little motivation to carry on. I was right, proud of myself turning the last two corners almost in tears accepting I have just managed to cycle the whole 180km and still had tons of energy to burn. Then, I could hear my supporters, Mr "BOSS" and our Mrs "KIM-MAMA" together with all the Harrison's Fund supporters, it was immense and there was more cheering on my very last turn, my whole family, friends and work colleagues shouting so loud, this time tears rolled down my cheeks I was being overwhelmed with the feeling how much I loved them and how much they all meant to me.

Entering transition area two, I was thinking to change my smelly pants, however, and to my shock, about five children similar to my kid's age scrambled around me offering to help. "How on earth would I dare stripped naked in front of them?" I had no other option but stay in those horribly smelly pants, and after all I had all rights to smell foul. Few minutes later I felt the impact with the ground and memories of how much I hated running kept flashing in front of me. In addition to this, more cramping followed and I was forced to stop. I looked in my pouch reaching for Paracetamol. I took 4x500mg; I don't even know why I took four of them. I think I was in that kind state of euphoria I thought four pills would keep me pain free. And it did. Thirty minutes later I felt like different person. Buzzing, enjoying, committed and determined to finish the race in style.

Immense support kept me going, I danced for my special crowd, just like I promised, showing them my balance skills were still great at the final stage of ironman. I've never run a marathon before, but I was in love with the whole experience, and everywhere the music played I just danced, I danced with DJs and cheered on others. I was hugging almost everyone to show them how much they meant to me and that without them I would never be part of ironman. Our support crowd was the best of all and it was them slowing me right down; suddenly I didn't want the event to end. I was craving that everlasting feeling.

Last lap to go, last 5km to go, now through the tunnel onto the beach area, passing the nasty toilets, along transition zone, last piece of orange and drink, 1km to go… Mixed emotions going through my mind, chatting nonsense to my run-walk partners, last hug and wishing them good luck on their last lap. Few metres to go, my nephew greeting and hugging me, sparing me a few minutes of chat, bike mechanic blasting his megaphone, more hugs and more congratulations, my loving husband and all my children lining up patiently waiting for me, family, friends, work colleagues and Harrison's Fund supporters screaming my name. *Flashdance* 'What a Feeling' being played and me, "the Hollywood actress" ever so proud

This is how it's done – Eva 'IRON-LADY' Fleming

of my latest accomplishment, walking the red carpet, dancing away to cross the finish line… "what a feeling"! Being crowned an Ironwoman was the icing on the cake.

I am currently buzzing unable to digest the facts that by having fun, being committed and having a huge degree of determination, anything is possible. At last I am allowed to taste "Stella", well-deserved "Stella"…

And so can you, all of you can do it. The best recipe is to get your backsides off sofas, stop browsing the internet daydreaming, stop looking for excuses and do something different in your life.

Change will give you motivation, motivation will give you commitment, commitment will give you results, results will give you confidence, and confidence will give you dreams to come true. Smile all the way, cherish every step and celebrate achievements.

Be an inspiration to your children, your family, friends and colleagues.

I just did all the above. My husband and friends are joining me for ironman next year; my children nagging me to find out about kids triathlon, and I am constantly having people approaching me asking me to help them to achieve what I did. I see my future so exciting, bringing more work around promoting sport and health. It will be an exciting future ahead of me and I can't wait to see the change in people's lives, and for them to experience their forthcoming success.

The Message: by applying FUN, COMMITMENT AND DETERMINATION, anything is possible…

CHAPTER 32

"Pain" *By Perry Gear*

As a child I was never sporty, and if I got the opportunity whilst at school to miss a PE lesson you could be sure that I would take it. In fact, I had an ingrowing toenail, which festered and never really cleared up for a number of years, which, for me at the time, was a Godsend. I was known by the PE teachers as "septic" I had absolutely no inclination to exert myself at all until a few years ago. What was the point of running unless you were being chased?

As a result of my lack of physical activity and having given up smoking about twenty years previously, I got bigger and bigger. I knew that I would put on weight after quitting the cigarettes but I took the view that it would be easier to lose weight than deal with cancer. I was slowly becoming an embarrassment to my children. That is not a place any parent wants to be. On holidays I can recall my son saying you aren't going to wear that are you dad!? He was simply ashamed. My children looked at me as someone they didn't want to be associated with in public. I had some serious work to do. I decided to join a slimming club and, as with anything I decide to do, it has to be done properly. I stuck to the eating plan rigidly. I managed to lose four and a half stone in about five months. Having lost the weight and now at ten stone, I was again thin. People would walk past me without recognising me. They were shocked when they realised it was me. Being thin and unfit was not acceptable to me. There had to be a total change.

A friend of mine who is an extremely good runner would chat about his running and I thought maybe I should give that a go. Getting fit was my next big challenge. I joined a local running club having bought all of the kit including a Garmin watch to track my progress. I am a person who needs to see in black and white that painful hard work does pay off. I needed to track improvements. I now had all the gear but no idea. One dark cold and damp Thursday evening in November I turned up at the running club and was directed to an amazing lady called Eleanor who was the group leader. She won't mind me saying that she was in her seventies and her husband Dennis was also running with the club both having in excess of 150 marathons to their names. They were both inspirational and we set off in a group for the first session. I recall it was interval work around a car park and I struggled to keep going for the whole session. Five days later I returned to the club and Eleanor asked me how I had been after the last session. The truth was, I could hardly walk for three days. She then announced that we would be running about five miles around the streets that evening. That session nearly killed me but it gave me determination to keep at it, as it would get easier. That was what everyone was telling me at the time but it was hard to comprehend. Things did get easier and quite quickly.

I entered the Berlin half-marathon as a goal, which seemed, at the time, to be out of my reach. I could not believe that I had it in me to run 13.1 miles in one stretch. It was the first running challenge I had set myself. I simply wanted to take part to prove to myself I could run that far. The time didn't matter, as I was not competitive. Plodding was fine.

Two months later, I was urged to take part in a midweek league race organised by a number of local running clubs. I really couldn't see the point but said I would run on the basis that I would start and finish at the back. One beautiful warm

May evening when summer seemed overdue I was in a pack of about 200 runners. I pushed my way to the back. The starting pistol resonated and ricocheted off the local houses. At that point something amazing happened. I have never felt anything like it before, but instantly I wanted to win and not just stay at the back. I knew that I couldn't win but I had to do my very best. I was, for the first time, experiencing sporting competitiveness. After that I entered every race I could find. I became obsessed with racing although I was not particularly good at it, but I was getting better. I found something I really enjoyed and shocked myself at the same time.

Berlin half-marathon was now behind me and marathons were the next goal. Edinburgh first followed by Milton Keynes, Loch Ness, Barcelona, Berlin and London. I had settled into marathon running and loved it. I had no inclination to do anything greater than marathons. Well, that was what I thought at the time. How wrong can one be?

One sunny day in early autumn I was contacted by a friend from my running club, just before lunch, asking if I had seen the advert in *Runner's World* seeking applicants for an ironman scientific study. "Would you be interested?" he asked. "Well, No I haven't seen it, and No, I would definitely NOT be interested." The thought floated around my mind during lunch in Starbucks. When I returned to my office I had had a complete change of heart. I contacted my mate to say, yes, I have put my name forward by email and not being a person who is generally chosen for anything, I thought I wouldn't have to worry about it again.

I received a standard email saying that I would hear in six weeks. I thought that would be the first and last I would hear. My thoughts started to return to the application process six weeks later and then BANG, an email dropped into the inbox inviting me to pre-screening. Great I thought, at least I will know one person. I contacted my friend to make sure he had received and read the email. Not only had he read it, he had already declined the invite. In a quandary, I seriously thought about withdrawing myself. This was not something I had set out to do and now, if I did accept, I would be doing it alone. The following few days were spent in deep thought wondering whether to accept. My mind was in turmoil and people were telling me that I would never be able to do the distance. I missed the deadline and Dr Justin Roberts, the study leader, contacted me to say he would give me until Friday to say whether I was in or out. I didn't want to commit and then let him down. If I commit to something then I have to give it 100%. I decided to make the call and accept the place on the Challenge.

At the first meeting of the cohort, I recall arriving at the Uni reasonably early and feeling completely out of place. Everyone seemed so much younger than me. Was I making an excuse already? What did I have to lose with just attending the meeting and listening? The horror of the actual distances showing on the big screen and images of people at near exhaustion and collapsing on the course shocked me. Feeling somewhat sick to the stomach I was lifted in spirit by Justin's conviction that everyone in the room could succeed and finish this challenge. It just wasn't going to be easy. That was the deciding factor for me. Somebody had faith that we could all finish.

At the pre-screening test an ECG trace was taken and this was sent to a heart consultant at a local hospital. We were told that if a problem were found with the trace we would receive a call from Justin to let us know. No way would my trace be problematic, I thought, I am a marathon runner who had never had any symptoms of a dodgy ticker and besides; I have regular ECG's to keep my pilots licence valid. Nothing had shown up on those traces in the past except my heart rate was lower than normal but that, I was assured by the Civil Aviation Doctor, was due to my endurance marathon training. I was just fit and that was the end of it.

One winter's evening whilst sitting at home my mobile rang at about 9pm. It was Justin who announced the unthinkable to me. The doctor had selected my trace for further investigation. I didn't hear everything that was being said as countless scenarios were streaming through my mind all at once. What I can recall is the calm way I was being reassured that it is most probably a condition known as athlete's heart. I would need to get a referral to the hospital from my doctor and I would know one way or another very shortly if I could continue on the study. I had set my heart on this study now and some hospital doctor was not going to stop me. Training would start on the 21st January come what may.

My gym training started quietly to begin with until I bumped into Justin one day. Throughout the training programme a number of sessions were undertaken jointly and that certainly focused my mind on making sure no shortcuts were taken. Quite the opposite. "I think we will try this today" or "we will make it a little more challenging by doing this instead" was what I heard. It made the gym work so much more enjoyable to have someone else to train with and reassuring, as the author of the training schedule would certainly know what was right. The programme changed every few weeks and I had no idea what I was supposed to be doing in the beginning of each block.

The sessions on the gym bike were mind-blowingly dull. I endured two-hour sessions at a time in the saddle whist the TV was close enough to see, but not big enough to read the subtitles when I forgot my earphones. I couldn't wait for the better weather to arrive so as to enable me to get out on my road bike in the fresh air and country lanes. By the beginning of February I had had enough. Irrespective of the weather, I was going out on my bike in the real wide outside world. I started off one Saturday to do about two hours in the saddle, which seemed like a massive ride at the time. I made my way from home to Hertford and onwards towards Stansted. Snow showers greeted me every fifteen minutes and I felt and looked like a snowman. My hands and feet were so painful and despite being so cold it felt like hot needles being stuck in my extremities. What was worse the cold and fresh air or the boring gym bikes? I decided to suffer the cold.

The first lab testing came along for month zero. I knew that this would set the benchmark for the rest of the bi-monthly test so for a fleeting moment I thought I could take it a little easier. As tempting as it was I didn't of course take that stand. I had to give it everything I had. I had to start out how I meant to carry on and that was to give everything I had. I can't say that I enjoyed this first session and I left the lab exhausted and dreading the next one, as I now knew what was coming. I detested the VO_{2max} test both on the bike and on the treadmill. It was the fact I couldn't breathe properly and the smell of the rubber mask reminded me of a bad experience I had at the dentist as a child whilst having a tooth out. The bike VO_2 and lactic acid tests pushed me to a limit I had never reached before. This is a good personal experience I kept telling myself and it won't last for too long. The strangest thing I felt during those VO_{2max} sessions was that, in a macabre way, I got some form of boost from the blood being taken every few minutes from my fingertips as that diverted the pain of these sessions. The final sessions were not as bad as I had become accustomed to the tests, environment and smiling faces of the lab assistants; I even found the session to be almost enjoyable. In fact, I was sad when they finished and somewhat alarmed as it meant race day was close to the horizon. The race was always in the far distance up until that point but it was now approaching fast.

At the end of March, with the onset of the warmer weather, group sessions for runs and bike rides started. I began to meet and get to know others on the study and we could relate to the trials and tribulations of the training programme. Until that time these people were, largely, faces in the lecture hall, science lab or commentators on Facebook from time to time. What a great bunch they turned out to be. Full of enthusiasm and ideas and the sessions were never short of laughter and camaraderie. I began to realise that I could complete this challenge with the help of these people. The rides got longer than I had ever experienced and then they were followed immediately by a run. These runs felt unusual to start with as my legs wouldn't work quite as they should immediately after a bike ride. This would have to sort itself out which eventually, with patience, it did

My only triathlon experience in the formal race setting was one sprint in October 2012. That was a disastrous experience as I found I couldn't swim properly and swam most of the 400m using breaststroke with a screw kick. I had been warned that my swim would go to pieces and that is exactly what happened. I managed to complete the bike course with only a couple of problems. I had put sunglasses on to stop my eyes watering but the weather, at 8am was foggy, freezing cold and the heat from the pool swim made the glasses mist over almost immediately. I had no proper kit and consequently had no pockets to put the glasses in. I had to wear them on the very tip of my nose just to be able to see. At the end of the ride I was conscious that I could not cross the line whilst still on the bike. Not knowing where the line was exactly, I had to make an emergency stop and couldn't unclip from the pedals in time. I ended up laying on the floor, bike on top of me, clipped in and the large crowd all oohing and aahing. The marshal then announced to the crowd "that is one way of doing it!" Chain hanging off, pride dented, I had to carry the bike into transition and put my frozen feet into some running shoes. It was only 5km but it took most of that distance to get any feeling in my toes.

Swimming was never my strong point. I joined Tri Force, a triathlon club in about November 2012 with a view to using their excellent swim coaches to improve. The first five or six sessions were spent teaching me some form of basic technique. I managed to progress from a twenty-five metre swim, stopping twice during the twenty-five metre length to swimming a few lengths without stopping. What a great feeling that was! 3.8km still seemed completely impossible for me to achieve as I watched the experienced triathlete swimmers hammering backwards and forwards. By this time I still had ten months to perfect my technique and smash the distance. The coaches were confident that I could do it so that was good enough for me. The pool swims at the gym on my own gradually took over as the training programme intensified to two sessions on a number of days each week, so the Tri Force sessions came to an abrupt end. Distances increased and then along came a wetsuit, which I bought from a friend on the study. This caused its own problems. Never having tried one of these on before I turned up for my first lake swim with some trepidation and had great difficulty getting the wetsuit on. I had been warned that it was difficult to get on and even copious amounts of Bodyglide made no difference. I was then given assistance by others who were probably either feeling sorry for me or had seen enough of my pathetic efforts. Someone soon pointed out that *the bloody thing was inside out.* This caused a fair amount of laughter as I tried to hide my stupidity and embarrassment. I thought I am not going to live that one down. Several months later I pulled the same stunt.

My lake swims were disastrous to start with. I couldn't get my head around the fact that the water I had to submerge my head in was either green or brown. I was used to crystal clear water with a black line to follow. I would stop every few metres convinced I couldn't do this open-water swimming. Eventually my mind accepted the water and I was able to do the 4km swims in Denham Lake without too much difficulty. Another discipline notched up even though the time was about one hour thirty for the distance.

Whilst on holiday in Tenerife in the summer, I used my wetsuit in the sea for the first time. The swell was quite significant and I would disappear down the troughs of the waves so as to be out of sight from the beach. Having never suffered from motion sickness in the past I was a little queasy on this occasion. This soon passed and my mind would turn to more pressing concerns such as watching for jellyfish. At this point after having spent a good few minutes contemplating this, my left hand landed directly in a large white plastic carrier bag floating in the bay. The shock nearly finished me off and in true *Tom and Jerry* style I was almost walking on water for about twenty-five metres, whilst swearing out loud at the top of my voice. After I had calmed down I was just hoping no one else in the water had noticed, although at that time of the morning most people were still, sensibly, in their beds. It was only the mad few who had ventured out to brave the sea.

On this same holiday I bought myself an ex-hire carbon road bike. This seemed to be the most cost effective way to deal with the problem of cycle training whilst on the island. Hiring a bike at the rate of thirty euros per day hire was three times more expensive than hiring a family car.

Not relishing the thought of cycling on my own, I placed a post on the Tenerife forum before I left the UK, asking if

Perry (left) enjoying some light carb-loading

anyone would be interested in accompanying me on a few long cycle rides. I had two replies. One from a lady called Fiona saying that her other half would be delighted to have company, and also from an Aussie girl who had spent the previous year on the island windsurfing. We arranged to meet up in a bar on the first Sunday I arrived just to check each other out. On arriving at the crowded bar the only thing we hadn't discussed was how we would recognise each other. It is very strange that even amongst about seventy-five people sitting outside a promenade bar/café the mad cyclists stood out and I managed to identify them without too much of a problem.

We seemed to get on very well so made arrangements to ride a few days later. I would hire a bike to start with and shove it in the car and drive along the coast to El Medino. This is a resort specialising in windsurfing. Starting from close to the beach, we made our first ride the ascent of Mount Teidi. This is the highest mountain in Spain and when you turn towards the mountain you know (or I do now) that there is about thirty-five miles of unadulterated climb. The early morning temperatures were pleasant but then again it was still almost dark. By the time we had been on the move for about three hours the temperatures were showing on the Garmin to be forty-two degrees in places. That cycle ride was one of the best experiences ever. I recommend it to everyone if you are even on the island of Tenerife. If it had not been for this study I would not have contemplated hiring a bike to ride the mountains. My co-riders, Ric and Nic, were great company and we had a real laugh, until I fell off the bike at the cable car station being the highest point of the ride. Oozing blood yet again, I had got used to falling off, so I wasn't too worried, but I still had to ride back down the mountain. That proved to be exhilarating. I have never ridden so fast on a bike, hitting 43mph at one point with tight hairpin bends to slow into. Ric, who was accustomed to riding this route often shot round the bends like a maniac hardly slowing at all. This is one of the routes on which you can see team Sky with Wiggins and Frome riding during the winter months.

Several more rides followed to different places. The biggest problem was keeping hydrated. It was impossible to carry the amount of water needed and frequent stops were made at little shops and bars to buy iced water, which heated to the point that you could put a tea bag in and make tea, within about twenty minutes. Nutrition was less of a problem as you could stop and eat the figs, which grew on the trees at the side of the road and also the prickly pears if you could get past the spines. That was pure magic.

And so onto the race…

One week before the race, I was a little shocked to find that my age category (very old) has changed from one of the first waves to enter the sea to almost the last. I was relying on that extra time to get me through. I have now reconciled this in my mind and in a way embraced it to make me more determined to try harder to make up some of the time.

On arriving in Calella following an uneventful journey I settled into my hotel trying to stay as relaxed as possible. I couldn't quite believe that I was at the start of this mammoth event. The evening was spent at the study race briefing, which was, in my mind the start of the emotional rollercoaster, which was about to follow over the rest of the weekend. Alex, of Harrison's Fund gave a talk, which was incredibly moving. With TV cameras scanning the group I just thought 'pull yourself together'.

On the morning of the race I entered the restaurant in the hotel at 5:30 along with Eva, one of my co-competitors, and we sat chatting over breakfast. She could tell I was nervous even though I tried not to show it. We gave each other encouragement and eventually it was time to rack the bike and deposit the race bags in transition. Leaving the hotel laden with bulging bags and pushing my bike was now the time the real nerves took hold. Bike parked, bags pegged there was nothing left to do other than to return to the hotel and put on the wetsuit. I left for the start with Eva and followed others from the study. This gave some comforting reassurance just seeing familiar people all in the same situation. However, the enormity of it all was really sinking in and I was getting into a panic about the sea swim. I had swum the iron-distance in the sea during the summer so it should not be a problem. Lined up on the beach in my pink-hatted wave, I tried to relax. I moved myself from the very centre of crowd to the side hoping that I could escape the pandemonium, which was about to ensue.

On the signal to start I made my way into the water and started to swim towards the first buoy. Complete panic really set in, and I was gulping down mouthfuls of salty seawater. I simply could not swim with my head in the water. I tried a bit of breaststroke then like a child, tried front crawl with my head out of the water. I was left with about five stragglers from my wave all having their own similar issues. I kept saying to myself out loud "I can't do this" and how am I supposed to swim another two-and-a-half miles when I can't even get to the first buoy 200 metres out. I know that I should have been saying I CAN do this but I was at the point of despair. I seriously considered putting my arm up at that point and bringing it to an end. I felt devastated that I had come this far and couldn't hack the swim on the day. Not to be beaten, I eventually reached the first buoy where a kayak rested on the water with two occupants. This would have been the opportunity to ask to be taken out.

No I thought, let me try it to the next buoy but I will use backstroke. That is one stroke I had not liked in the training, as the ceiling in the pool always made me feel dizzy. Watching the sky above me it felt good on this occasion and I relaxed a little still telling myself that I must keep moving in a forward direction. I now seriously started to rehash my race strategy as back stoke really did not form part of the master plan. Using backstroke uses a lot more leg power and I was thinking that even if I made it to the end of the swim on my back my legs would be shot for the bike and run. A kayak approached me with what in my mind seemed like a cattle prod telling me to change direction. Without the ability to sight on my back I was now taken up a heading and was on my way to Majorca, swimming ninety degrees to the rest of the swimmers. I can recall apologising and then took up my true course again.

On reaching the buoy where we turned out to sea I decided to try the front crawl again. That now worked for me so I had calmed down enough to swim better. I set myself the next target of reaching the outer buoy without stopping and said to myself if you can reach that then you can do this swim. I succeeded in my personal mini challenge and things were looking up. My goggles filled with water a few times but that was not a major problem. Sighting was a problem and I found myself off track many times. To occupy my mind I gave myself trigonometry calculations to correct the drift just as I would when flying. This passed the time, and eventually I reached the home stretch heading for the beach. That seemed a long way whilst swimming although it looked to be quite close. It was the proverbial oasis in the desert situation.

I was a few feet from the shore and I tried to stand only to find that it was still too deep. I was mindful of having to swim almost onto the beach. Two helpers were there ready to catch me and I stumbled and held up my arms seeking assistance. Before they were able to grab me a wave dragged me forward and I had to quickly put my hands back into the foaming water. Stumbling, the back of my left hand hit the stony shore and above the sound of retreating sea taking pebbles and the foaming water I heard a loud crack. My stomach hit the floor as hard as my hand had. I knew something was now seriously wrong by the cracking sound and I kept pulling and twisting my wrist and telling myself that it didn't hurt so it must be ok.

I glanced at the exit timer and entered T1. I headed for my bags only to find that I couldn't take them off the hook as my left hand did not have the power to do so and wouldn't respond. I felt completely gutted and just stood there wondering how I was going to carry on. An official could see my plight and offered to help. Within a few seconds I had three helpers. I asked where I could see a doctor, and was told something along the lines of "out by a lorry". That is what I remember of the conversation. I asked if there were any close by and said I needed one immediately. Someone rushed off and a few minutes later appeared the saviour of a doctor. She examined my wrist twisting and pushing on it gently. Strangely it didn't hurt too much at that point. I now wonder whether I was just willing it not to be damaged despite my greater suspicion. I asked if she thought it was broken and she said no she didn't think so. She made a first class job of strapping the wrist very tightly and the other helpers put on my socks, shoes and other clothes as it was an impossible task for me at that point. There seemed to be zero strength in the left arm and excruciating pain started with the slightest exertion. I found my limited supply of paracetamol, took two and was walked out to find my bike.

It wasn't too hard to find my bike as there were only about ten bikes left in the racking area. I lifted my bike off the rack and then found that the back wheel wouldn't rotate. I couldn't believe my bad luck at that point. Eventually, I undid the wheel and let it rest into it natural position which cured the problem. I have no idea how the wheel could have become misaligned as it was spinning earlier when I pumped up the tyres. I was now ready to roll. I was hoping to be able to follow others onto the courses. I had no idea where I was supposed to be going as everyone else had left apart from me. I was then pointed in the right direction. My dad and son, Daniel, were waiting for me, which was the first well-needed tonic. I can't express how good it was to see them at that point. Everything had become very black up until then and I thought everything was against me. I mounted the bike at the start line and made out onto the road. That was a very trying part of the course as it was continuous speed humps for about one mile. I had to let go of the handlebars with my left arm on each one.

I reached the roundabout and was greeted with an amazing welcome from Justin shouting support. I recall shouting back that I think I may have broken my wrist. Within a few metres a fantastic crowd of HURTS supporters were cheering me on. It was at that point I decided that whatever happens I am going to finish this race. I settled down on the bike trying to find the position that gave the least pain. There were not many positions I can assure you. I ventured onto the drops and there was no difference in the pain that was generated. It was a different story when I wanted to reverse that and then transfer to the top. I had to stretch my whole arm out to the side and then bring it round gently. I thought if anyone is watching they will think I am mad. The roads being of good quality helped. Problems occurred when I reached the roundabouts with the rumble strips, as I had to cycle one handed at that point. That was fine whilst it was dry, but as the ride went on it became a different story. I chatted to a few from the study when I saw the Harrison's tops and we gave each other encouragement.

On my second lap whilst heading towards Calella, the sky ahead resembled something out of a horror movie. It was completely black, laced with the occasional strand of lightning forking the ground. I knew that it wouldn't be long before I would be entering a huge storm. It started with a few drops of rain, which, within a couple of minutes became torrential. I couldn't see more than a few metres ahead of me. The man-made open drains, which carried the water from the high ground to the sea, were torrents of brown muddy water. The roads were deep with surface water and in places the floods had started to develop. In those places the water was up to pedal level and my feel were dipping into the water on each revolution. You can only get so wet I kept telling myself, and to be honest this episode of the ride relived the pain I was enduring by changing my focus.

At one point I pulled up level with another cyclist from the UK and we chatted for a couple of minutes discussing whether we should stop for safety reasons. I said I hope we are not going to be penalised for drafting, but he was sure that it wouldn't be a problem because of the weather. At that point this old chap named Pedro (yes there were some older than me racing) went scooting past and I thought bloody hell no way am I stopping if he can ride like that. I then managed to overtake Pedro and it was a game of cat and mouse for a good while. At the end Pedro cranked up the game and sped off into the distance and that was the last I saw of him until inside T2. I stopped and we exchanged a few complimentary words. After racking the bike, I made my way into the marque and luckily the same helpers were around again. They immediately came over to assist and within seconds the doctor also appeared as if by magic. She checked my wrist again and seemed quite happy which was a great relief. I was dressed for the next element by the helpers. I was thinking this is not a job I would fancy doing – putting other peoples shoes and socks on them.

I was now entering my own comfort zone part of the race with the running. My legs felt good and I wondered what impact the constant arm movement, back and forward, would have on the wrist. The binding was very tight still and the pain was bearable. After the first lap I thought the strapping was getting too tight. My fingers and thumb now resembled fat sausages. I was a little concerned at this point and asked if there was a doctor on the course only to be told that they are now all at the finish. I decided to continue one lap at a time and make sure that they did not get any larger.

Eventually, I made it to the end of the run and what a great surprise to find Kimberley and Justin giving out the finishers' medals. Elated, I could hardly believe I had completed the whole event. I made straight for the medical tent to have the strapping cut off my wrist and for a fresh looser one to be fitted. The emotional rollercoaster this event has invoked is quite unbelievable. I am not sure where it all stems from, but it may be the disbelief that I could achieve my goal and succeed in finishing or it could be the wonderful support from everyone.

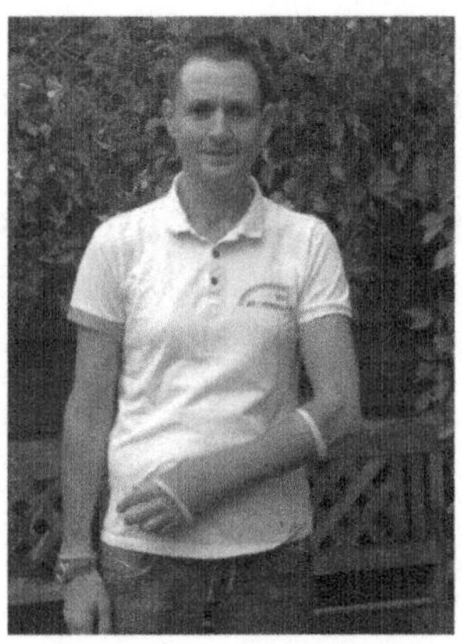

IRON-TOUGH – Perry "the legend" Gear

I suspect a combination of both. This is not how I really imagined it would be like at the end.

Quite incredible.

In the beginning, some friends said, "you won't be able to do an ironman". Well, I just did, with a few twists along the way.

In conclusion do I have any regrets?

Not really apart from the time I allowed the heart question to hang over me.

Would I do anything different?

No, I don't think so.

Would I do it again?

You try to stop me!

There will be ironman number two in 2014 without any doubt at all.

I have met some fantastic people along the way on this study, who I hope will remain good friends. I have learnt so much about myself and also, in a strange way, about those who I know and are not on the study. The experience has been life changing in so many diverse ways. My life has certainly been changed for the better because of it, and for that Dr Roberts, I thank you for allowing me the privilege of taking part.

The Message: If you always do what you always did, then you will always get what you have always gotten. Time to change – follow your dream – you will achieve.

CHAPTER 33

"Expectations – The Hare and the Tortoise" *By Justin Roberts*

"Work it, make it, do it, makes us harder, better, faster, stronger – now that that don't kill me, can only make me stronger. I need you to hurry up now, 'cos I can't wait much longer" – Kanye West.

Roth, Germany – one of the big iron-distance events. One of the oldest I think. It's the one which many triathletes talk about. It was about 120km into the cycle course, when the one and only Chrissie Wellington bombed past me, her face focused and calm, surrounded by four men who simply looked in pain. I was moving, but she was flying. What an athlete. I think I made a comment to the guy next to me (*of course we weren't drafting!!!*) along the lines of "that's Chrissie!" He muttered something back but I didn't get it. "How you going?" I asked. "F**ked" was the reply. *'Nuff said.*

The rain came down around 3pm – I was about five miles into the run course. Then it rained some more, and then the Nile unleashed on us from above. Oh, and then lightning bolts struck the ground all around us. I mean as if the ironman isn't a challenge all by itself, now I've got to dodge friggin' lightning, soaked, getting cold. I'm not superman you know. I'm not Thor either. I saw a lone figure lying at the side of the road – perhaps he's got cramp I thought. As I passed him, it was clear he was sparko. The medics were around him. Oh dear, he didn't look well. He was clearly older than me, perhaps early fifties. I hoped he was ok. I reflect back on the ironman events

I've covered, and at each one there was always someone like Mr Fifty lying at the side of the road. And when I've read about the accidents that have occurred in these ultra events, often it's been stereotypical Mr Corporate who clearly has taken on the challenge but not done the training. That got me thinking...

July 2012, I wonder if I could get some normal folk, normal relatively healthy mortals to take on their first ironman and do some research on them. Hmmm, good idea I thought. Just need an event to compete at, a research idea, and most importantly some willing guinea pigs, ummm lab rats, I mean participants (that's apparently the correct terminology). I had recently written to the organisers of the Barcelona Challenge Triathlon, and put in a request to support me. An email came back within hours – mostly in Spanglish – a cross between Spanish and English, but it looked very promising. Ok, now for the lab rats. The editors of *Triathlete Europe* were kind enough to put a simple advert out to the masses. I figured I would get ten or twenty completely insane people willing to give this a go. I was wrong. I was inundated with applications to *'take part'*. Has the world gone crazy I thought, or have I stumbled upon something? There were applications to take part in our research from all over the world. At one point (around October 2012) I could have really used a PA it was that busy. Then came the need to filter the completely crazy from the possible inclusions.

***

Late October 2012, over 120 'recreationally active' folk arrived at our Performance Testing Laboratory for a number of pre-screening tests. Firstly a health screen and consent form, then a heart check, then a fitness assessment. If they passed, they were effectively in. We had a cohort meeting in early December ahead of the January start date. The aim of the research was to initially investigate multiple parameters to a six-month endurance training programme ranging from cardiovascular changes, biomechanical assessments, immunological adaptations and nutritional assessments. For me, in particular, I was interested to understand nutritional patterns in relation to increased training volume, as well as adaptations to serum Vitamin D, which is often insufficient, and hence should athletes be mindful more of their diet as they prepare for such events.

The cohort met one Monday evening, shyly taking their seats in one of our lecture theatres. The show began with a video – what is ironman like – a 2.4 mile sea swim (*video showed people collapsing at the end LOL*), an 180km bike (*video showed people stopping, cramping, throwing up, falling off*) and then a 42.2km marathon (*the video showed people on drips, people crawling, lots of pain!*). The group fell silent. I think I had done the trick of capturing their attention. But most importantly the video switched to the end, the finish line, and the moment of triumph, realisation, and celebration. Their smiles resumed – *phew!*

I looked around the group; all of them fell within our criteria and were classed as recreationally active. Some of them had done events before, the odd half-marathon, marathon, or a sprint triathlon. Some had done nothing. NONE HAD UNDERTAKEN AN IRONMAN. They all looked a little scared, but yet quietly pleased to be there – ready for the long road ahead, the challenge of taking on their first IRON-distance race in October 2013.

The first testing block started in January, and all participants were given instructions to maintain their normal training over December. So start date, January 2013. A nine-month training programme had been devised, and small chunks were released each three to four weeks to keep them guessing (and to prevent some people getting too far ahead of themselves). The testing involved a multi station approach: cardiovascular screening, blood samples, functional testing, gait analysis, running economy, and lactate threshold testing. Good fun. This required a crew of nearly thirty support testers. Bless you all, all giving up your time for free to make this research come to life.

As the results came in I started to have some doubts, would this person make it? Would that person give up? I decided not to set expectations, but to '*lay it out, for y'all to play it out*'. The problem with classing people into categories is that it doesn't work with triathlon. Some people are swimmers, but can't run well (that would be me). Some are cyclists, but not swimmers. Some are born runners; others are just blessed. But deep down, I was worried that maybe I had created a monster. I mean those people you see at the side of the road, collapsed from exhaustion – was I about to put nearly one hundred people into that arena, of which some twenty might not make it. Stop! There are nine months to go, that's a long time. Let's see how they go.

***

Month four, test block three – the first of the cohort faces appeared at the lab entrance at 8:30am – they smiled. They looked like athletes in the making. Fitness was up, training was well underway, and bodyweight was down. It was looking good amigo. Interestingly, as I sat down with each person to go through their individual training zones, the comments back were mixed – some had REALLY improved, some had only marginally improved. Some had been on holiday and figured they were already the stuff of IRON – but the results showed otherwise. And so began the process of mentally filtering those who fitted into the HARE category, and those in the TORTOISE category.

Most interestingly, not one of them claimed to be able to 'smash it' – everyone had their personal concerns. For some it was the swimming – the worry that perhaps they would be swept out to sea or didn't have enough jet propulsion. Well that could happen, I suppose. For some, it was the distance and the ability to keep the heart rate down. For some it was the 'fear' of being able to run, or how to fuel. Whatever their concerns, they were coming thick and fast. The big observation was one of confidence – for many it wasn't high.

But then again, nor was mine when I first started and even now I have to 'talk myself into' race mode. And so there are several things I would like to say about these extra-ordinary people who have made it to September and have four weeks to the 2013 Barcelona Challenge Iron-distance Triathlon.

Number one – as we approach the end of the training, I am now more confident than ever that most will finish. Yes, some will struggle, but they have come so far, and with the big training sessions, I have watched confidence and self-belief grow. From all my experiences and challenges, this is one of the best things to observe for sure – seeing other people shine, and knowing you were a small part of that.

Number two – it's not a question of IF you finish, it's WHEN. It doesn't matter if you are a HARE or a TORTOISE – you will finish – think back to my colleague Nick 'the Thriller' Tiller in the desert screaming at me "whatever you do – FINISH" – this is pretty much my only advice for race day. Only entertain the idea of the finish line – and each step is one step closer.

Number three – HARES beware – know your pace – and I don't want to see any of you having a Cadburys caramel at the side of the road whilst us TORTOISES pass you by. Race with pace, but know your pace.

Number four – TORTOISES – just believe – focus on your own game plan, your own strategy and enjoy the day as much as you can.

Number five – It's been emotional. Over the past year I've had the privilege of meeting some truly remarkable people, all of whom I am very grateful for your selfless devotion to the study and the race. I am grateful for your time, your dedication, and your relentless patience for yet another nutritional diary. For those who didn't like their blood being taken but braved it out – good on you – part of the mental toughness training required for the race (wink!).

Something I would like everyone to consider – the word TRIATHLON – should be called TRY-ATHLON. It's all about endeavour, trying your best, never giving up, and finishing with pride. Well, the first two parts you have all shown. Now it's down to race day – never giving up, and finishing with pride. And when you cross that line you will know what I mean – **YOU WILL BE AN IRONMAN.**

It's one of the greatest feelings I've experienced – crossing that IRON line. In my head, the tri-top was zipped up, my hands were stretched out above my head, and my faced looked exhilarated. YEAHHHH!… In reality, I had forgotten to take the sponges out from my shoulder straps – DOH! My tri-top was half way undone – DOH! My hands were barely in line with my shoulders – not exactly a victory celebration – DOH. And as for exhilarated – I simply looked exhausted! DOH. So as you approach the finish area – do some checks: zip up tri top, remove sponges, wipe the snot from your face, look strong, and smile. And at the very end don't run past the finish, stop, get those arms in the air and SCREAM. **NOW YOU ARE AN IRONMAN.**

★★★

It was a week later – I'm sitting in the Punch & Judy in Covent Garden, London. My face is still a little weathered from the race, I still look a little dehydrated and tired; but I'm sporting a red KARTEN AUSTRIAN IRONMAN FINISHERS T-shirt. The medal has been wedged to my chest for the past week. I DID IT, I DID IT. My face is beaming; my friends and family are there. Celebration time. First beer in ages – hmmmm – refreshing. Five minutes later I'm pissed! Yeah! Celebration. There is a guy cooking a giant paella right outside the pub, I feel the need to go and stick my face in it (not really). It's a good night. I had vowed never to do an ironman again. Yes it bloody hurt! I can still feel my lungs – or is that the alcohol talking?

Then an arm reaches over me and pulls me in like a giant bear hug. It was my friend "I really wanna do one of those events J-man, but will only do it if you join me!" In a daze, "yeah why not?" – shit what have I said. No backing out, I've said it now. I remember feeling both excited and OMG! What have I done – don't say I have to do it all again. NOooooo. And so began adventure number two – thankfully it was a way off yet.

For those reading this in the study, it's important not to let things go – you are all now very fit. VERY FIT in some cases. This begs the question of what next? Do you go bigger – what's bigger than an ironman? A Decaman (ten ironmans!), an ultra marathon, an expedition? Do you go faster? Well that comes back to the type of person you are. I remember post-Sahara, sitting with my friend Nick the Thriller and a top sports psychologist reflecting on our learning from the Toughest Footrace on Earth. Nick surprised us all when he uttered the words that he wasn't satisfied! Not satisfied? You've completed

151 miles in the absolute blistering heat of the Sahara. What floats your boat *mon amigo*. He said that he wasn't satisfied because he knew he could push harder, he wanted to explore the real limits of his physiology. Man that's bold, that's brave. Fair play, got my respect.

For me, finishing ironman didn't mean trying to go faster next time, and post-Sahara I didn't feel the need to try and do something even more testing or extreme. There are four things that resonate with me:

1) The event needs to be a challenge of some kind;

2) I need to enjoy it at some level;

3) I need to have an experience which brings out the primitive part of me, to feel alive, to feel that I am **BE**-ing; and

4) I need to have a purpose, whether it be inspiring or helping someone else to achieve a goal, or perhaps supporting those people who are not able to do the things we take for granted.

Over the past few months I've heard various expressions from the study group, some think they are failing, some feel like they aren't good enough. This must be disheartening for them, but one thing I would like to reiterate to everyone – there is no such thing as failure if you have at least tried. And try your best. Failure is knowing you want something, but doing nothing about it. Success starts with a TRY, and it doesn't matter if you fall a little, it doesn't matter if you get it wrong, it doesn't matter if you can't swim the full distance from day one.

Small steps equals giant goals.

Giant goals equals IRONMAN.

Ironman equals bragging rights for life.

And for those who tell you, or rather whinge "I can't do that, I'm not good enough, I can't swim, I don't have time, excuse, excuse, excuse" – give them a proverbial slap, remind them that they are alive, what more reason do you need to try something, anything you want to try – give it a GO! *One day, you won't be around*, one day you will wake up and feel like it's all too late, on that day do you want to feel regret. I think the extra-ordinary people on this study have got it right, they've taken a chance and given the training a go. Some haven't made it to the start line, job changes, less commitment, but they gave it a go. The question is what did you all learn along the way, what did you learn about yourselves. And I hope that the answer you come up with is RESPECT.

Respect not just for yourself, but respect for your fellow competitors, respect for the people who have supported you, and respect for anyone brave enough to face their own fears and demons and drive up the courage to conquer them. And so it doesn't matter if you are a HARE or a TORTOISE, what matters is what you feel inside. What drives you, and what drives you to inspire, motivate or help other people in some way. For me, that's the true spirit of IRONMAN. Don't believe me – go and stand at the side of the road at any iron-distance event on the planet – watch the runners go past you – they will have many expressions – focused, calm, tearful, in pain, exhausted. But what you will see if you're lucky is the essence of the event – the camaraderie between the competitors. If someone is struggling you will see other people helping them, or asking if they are ok. Whilst we all have our own race to contend with, deep down we all enjoy seeing people succeed and finish this race. That's what brings us together, as we share our own stories of highs and lows along the course. The spirit of ironman lies in the bars and restaurants the next day, when we all relive our heroic achievements.

I recently presented at a nutrition conference in London, and I put up a slide which read "train like an athlete, eat like a nutritionist, sleep like a baby, win like a champion" – so true.

This group have definitely trained like athletes. Those in study one who have received advice from me should be eating like nutritionists (wink), you have all completed sleep diaries and first observation is that most of you are sleeping like babies – so all to say is WIN LIKE A CHAMPION. What does this last part mean – it means SCREAM, give it hell Rydell, and feel the belief and confidence in you. It also means CELEBRATE – you have achieved the seemingly impossible. You've earned that proverbial beer. It also means share your success with others around you, let them feel like champions too. A champion doesn't need to brag, the medal speaks for itself. The END.

The Message: You are alive, what more reason do you need to give something a go; if not for you, then for those who can't. **This is the essence of Ironman.**

I can.
I will.
End of story.

About Harrison's Fund

The proceeds of this book are being donated to Harrison's Fund, a registered charity founded by Alex Smith, a contributor of this book. Alex gave up his job rebranding businesses in order to focus his time on finding a treatment and cure for Duchenne Muscular Dystrophy. Harrison's Fund is named after Alex's eldest son who in 2011 was diagnosed with the fatal, life-limiting condition.

Duchenne Muscular Dystrophy is a stinker of a disease. It's the most common fatal genetic disorder to affect children around the world. If you've got it, you can't produce dystrophin, a protein you need to build up your muscles. As a result, every muscle in the body deteriorates. At the moment there is no cure.

The facts about Duchenne are inescapable:

Duchenne Muscular Dystrophy is 100% fatal;

Most kids with it die in their late teens, or early twenties;

Most with it are usually in a wheelchair by the age of twelve; and

It leads to respiratory failure, heart failure, and other debilitating orthopaedic complications.

One in 3,500 boys is born with it, and in the UK 2,500 kids have it at the moment. You can have it, no matter where you are or what your ethnic background is. A third of all cases start in the womb, with no warning before the baby is born. Girls can also get Duchenne with around 1% of Duchenne births being female.

Harrison's Fund **has one goal**.

To get as much money as possible into the hands of the world's best researchers, who are working to find a cure for Duchenne.

It sounds like a horrible disease. And it is. Which is why we want to eradicate it.

We're different from many other charities out there because we're focusing on treatment rather than palliative care. And we work Internationally. We invest in research that takes the science out from the lab, and into human clinical trials.

So that, hopefully soon, more of those with Duchenne can grow into the strong men they're meant to be.

For more information visit: harrisonsfund.com